LEISURE MIGRATION
A Sociological Study
on Tourism

TOURISM SOCIAL SCIENCE SERIES

Series Editor: Jafar Jafari
Department of Hospitality and Tourism, University of Wisconsin-Stout,
Menomonie WI 54751, USA.
Tel: (715) 232-2339; Fax: (715) 232-3200; E-mail: jafari@uwstout.edu
Associate Editor (this volume): John Urry
Lancaster University, UK

The books in this Tourism Social Science Series (TSSSeries) are intended to
systematically and cumulatively contribute to the formation, embodiment, and
advancement of knowledge in the field of tourism.

The TSSSeries' multidisciplinary framework and treatment of tourism includes
application of theoretical, methodological, and substantive contributions from
such fields as anthropology, business administration, ecology, economics,
geography, history, hospitality, leisure, planning, political science, psychology,
recreation, religion, sociology, transportation, etc., but it significantly favors state-
of-the-art presentations, works featuring new directions, and especially the
cross-fertilization of perspectives beyond each of these singular fields. While the
development and production of this book series is fashioned after the successful
model of *Annals of Tourism Research,* the TSSSeries further aspires to assure each
theme a comprehensiveness possible only in book-length academic treatment.
Each volume in the series is intended to deal with a particular aspect of this
increasingly important subject, thus to play a definitive role in the enlarging and
strengthening the foundation of knowledge in the field of tourism, and consequently to expand its frontiers into the new research and scholarship horizons
ahead.

New and forthcoming TSSSeries titles:

DENNISON NASH (University of Connecticut, USA)
Anthropology of Tourism

PHILIP L. PEARCE, GIANNA MOSCARDO & GLENN F. ROSS (James
Cook University of North Queensland, Australia)
Tourism Community Relationships

BORIS VUKONIC (University of Zagreb, Croatia)
Tourism and Religion

Related Elsevier Journals
Annals of Tourism Research
Cornell Hotel and Restaurant Administration Quarterly
International Journal of Hospitality Management
International Journal of Intercultural Relations
Tourism Management
World Development

LEISURE MIGRATION
A Sociological Study
on Tourism

József Böröcz

Rutgers University

*Institute for Political Studies of the Hungarian
Academy of Science*

Pergamon

U.K.   Elsevier Science Ltd, The Boulevard, Langford Lane, Kidlington,
          Oxford OX5 1GB, U.K.

U.S.A.   Elsevier Science Inc., 660 White Plains Road, Tarrytown,
          New York 10591-5153, U.S.A.

JAPAN   Elsevier Science Japan, 9–15 Higashi-Azabu 1-chome, Minato-ku,
          Tokyo 106, Japan

First edition 1996

Library of Congress Cataloging in Publication Data
Leisure migration: a sociological study on tourism by József Böröcz.—1st ed.
p.cm.—(Tourism social science series) Includes bibliographical references
and index.
ISBN 0-08-042560-7 (hc)
1. Tourist trade. I. Title. II. Series.
G155.A1B617 1996
338.4'791-dc20   95-43336

British Library Cataloguing in Publication Data
A catalogue record for this book is available from the British Library.

ISBN 0 08 042560 7

Typeset by Gray Publishing, Tunbridge Wells, Kent
Printed and bound in Great Britain by Biddles Ltd, Guildford, Surrey

Szüleimnek

CONTENTS

Preface

This text owes its existence first of all to a combination of Hungarian schooling with the extraordinary accessibility of the North American system of post-tertiary education, particularly to the practice of accepting foreign intellectuals as graduate students *with* financial support. Then there is, of course, the astonishing list of people who lent selfless assistance to my endeavors during the preparation of this text. I am indebted, above all, to Alejandro Portes and Christopher K. Chase-Dunn, for the help, stimulation, and encouragement they gave me during the preparation of this study. Katherine Verdery's and Melvin L. Kohn's enthusiastic support, and shared interest and fascination in my region, was very important to me.

Judit Bodnár has been my first and most involved, tireless reader throughout this project. Marlie Wasserman—then at Rutgers University Press—gave an extraordinarily supportive critical reading of the text for which I am very indebted to her. Lanfranco Blanchetti-Revelli, Erica Bornstein, Eric Kaldor, Niloofar Haeri, and Michelle Madsen Camacho also gave me very useful comments on various chapters.

This work owes, then, much to a research grant provided to me by the Österreichische Fremdenverkehrswerbung (the Austrian Tourist Office), under the directorship of Dr Klaus Lukas. Mrs Anneliese Hora, Head of Marketing Research at the Austrian Tourist Board, was helpful in helping me with the particulars of the grant. I hope they found the final report of the survey portion of my research useful for their interests. I also hope that the economic and political development of Hungary will soon enable a much more significant traditional Hungarian demand for travel in Austria so that the touristic ties of the two countries could become more symmetric and equitable.

Herr Professor Dr Josef Mazanec, Director of the Institute for Tourism and Leisure Economics at the Vienna University of Economics, was extremely helpful in several ways. He urged that such a study should be done, and he suggested some potential sources of funding for it. It was under his directorship that the Institute for Tourism provided institutional affiliation as well as physical room for me as a research fellow during my field research, appointed me as the leader of a project seminar, provided access to an original version of the questionnaire on which *chapter 8* is based, and generously allowed me to use the Institute's impressive computing and library resources. I appreciated very much Mag. Raimund Fuhri's excellent computer expertise and support.

Professor Jafar Jafari, Editor-in-Chief of the world's best tourism research journal, *Annals of Tourism Research*, the Chief Editor of the Tourism Social Science Series in which the work is published, and an unrelenting organizer of scholars interested in tourism worldwide, expressed an early interest in my work in tourism and he was the person who originally suggested to me that I should contact Professor Mazanec in Vienna. I am grateful to all of them for their benign patronage. When the manuscript reached his series editor's desk, his crisp and straightforward advice was very helpful in producing the version that is before the reader. I also warmly welcomed Professor John Urry's special editorial suggestions.

My Hungarian employer at the time, the Budapest-based Hungarian Institute for Public Opinion Research, provided additional funding, and the all-important official legitimation for the gathering of the materials included in *chapter 2*. They also contributed to processing initially the secondary statistical materials presented in *chapter 5*. I am particularly thankful to Tamás Szecskő, Director, Ádám Levendel, Deputy Director, Vera Hárs, Chargée d'Affaires Etrangères, and Enikő Pap, Secretary. Further funding was provided by my subsequent employer in Hungary, the Institute for Political Science of the Hungarian Academy of Sciences, OTKA, the Hungarian National Scientific Research Fund under number T 6739 and Rutgers University.

The Program in Atlantic History and Anthropology and the Program in Comparative International Development of The Johns Hopkins University awarded me with a travel grant that allowed me to visit and indulge in various sociological and tourism research libraries across Europe, including, most prominently, the Centre Internationale de Recherche Touristique at the Université Aix-Marseilles, located in the Vasarely Foundation Building in Aix-en-Provence, under the very helpful directorship of René Baretje. This study is indebted to all of them in Hungary, Austria, the United States, and elsewhere. I am also grateful to the School of Social Sciences at the University of California, Irvine—my employer during the revision of this work—for providing computing and other resources.

It was Professor Michael Grimes at the Louisiana State University in Baton Rouge who introduced me to the sociological potential of macro-comparative analysis. If it were not for him, I would certainly not be here. My modest ability to communicate in German I owe to the "Kaiser-u. Königliche" Central European tradition and to my friend, Silke-Maria

Weineck, who was more than a German teacher at The Johns Hopkins University.

The survey reported in *chapter 8* was executed by Constanze Anton, Martin Bosch, Georg Burkhart, Romana Filipin, Wolfgang Fischer, Sabrina Igalffy, Gerhard Knötzl, Wolfgang Pabinger, Oliver Rath, Sabine Riedel and Ulrike Rosenfellner, advanced students of Tourism Studies at the Vienna University of Economics as participants in a project seminar on survey research in 1989. They took part in the adaptation of the questionnaire, and they did much of the interviewing, coding, and recording of the data. I truly appreciate their work. I am also thankful to Young European Federalists Bettina Mähr and Philippos Agathonos for putting me up in Vienna on such an erratic schedule as mine was during much of 1989.

Architect Jenő Jedlóczki, my long-time friend, drew the beautiful maps presented in *chapters 2* and *3*. I am extremely grateful for his prompt, high-quality, and free assistance. Magda Csizmadia and the late Gyula Pártos helped me out with the difficult problem of comparing GDP/cap levels across sociopolitical systems, both in conceptual terms and by offering some empirical material used in *chapter 5*.

Appendix 1 lists those linguists throughout the continent of Europe who made invaluable contributions by sending me information on the approximate timing of the first written records of the word-equivalents of 'tourist,' 'tourism,' and 'touristic' in their own languages. Often, this involved extracting information from such unpublished sources as the files of records of etymological and language-historical dictionaries, information that would have been extremely difficult to obtain in any other way. Their selfless contribution cannot be properly acknowledged.

I owe special thanks to the librarians–archivists at the Austrian Central Statistical Office and to Ákos Probáld, head of the Tourism Section of the Hungarian Central Statistical Office, for providing access to the criterion variables analyzed in detail in *chapter 5*. That chapter benefited from some extremely useful suggestions by two anonymous reviewers, and Raymond Grew, Editor of *Comparative Studies in Society and History*. Similarly, parts of *chapter 4* improved because of the comments I received from *Theory and Society*, and sections of *chapter 5* profited from advice from reviewers for *Annals of Tourism Research*. My fellow graduate student at The Johns Hopkins University at the time, Timmons Roberts lent very useful assistance to the preparation of the earlier version of *chapter 5* by smoothing my bumpy English writing. The entire text improved because of Amy McConnell's reading as style editor.

Binnie Bailey, Cristiana Camardella, Pat Skalski, Anna Stoll, and Vonnie Wild—all of them in the Department of Sociology at Johns Hopkins—were also very instrumental in helping this study along its way.

Acknowledgments

A version of *chapter 2* has been published in the journal *Comparative Studies in Society and History*. It is reprinted here by kind permission from Cambridge University Press, the journal's publisher.

An earlier version of a part of *chapter 3* was presented at the annual conference of the Social Science History Association in Baltimore, November 1993.

Part of the argument presented in *chapter 4* has been made in a paper first published in the journal *Theory and Society*. It is reproduced here by kind permission from Kluwer Publishers.

Part of *chapter 5* is based on data gathered and initially processed with a research fund provided by the Budapest-based Mass Communication Research Center. An analysis of the Hungarian segment of the data has been published in the journal *Annals of Tourism Research*. Segments of the text of this chapter are reprinted here by kind permission from Elsevier Science Ltd (Pergamon imprint).

Chapter 9 is partly based on research supported by the Austrian Tourist Office and includes excerpts from a study that served as a research report.

List of Figures

List of Maps

List of Tables

Chapter 1

Leisure Migration

Budapest's number 2 is surely among the world's most scenic tram rides. Running in Pest alongside the Danube, it passes by the neo-Gothic building of the nation's Parliament as well as the less glorious former headquarters of the bygone Communist Party, used today as a modest office building of the National Assembly. It zooms by several ministries, museums, churches, and such grand buildings as the Budapest University of Economics, the School of the Humanities (slated to be returned to the Catholic Church as the Budapest "Gymnasium" of the Piarist Order), and the Hungarian Academy of Sciences. The passenger has a long, perfectly undisturbed look across the river at the knoll of the Buda Castle District with the Royal Palace and the predominantly eighteenth- and early-nineteenth-century architectural assembly of the Burghers' Town—featured on UNESCO's list of protected sites designated as "world heritage" since 1987 (Várnegyed 1994:3)—as well as the Gellért Hill with its striking wooded area. Tram number 2 performs an important practical function in the transportation system of the city by running at full speed throughout most of its north–south route—except for an approximately 500-meter stretch. In that section, it decelerates almost to walking speed.

Two possible reasons for the tram's odd behavior compete in Budapest urban folklore. Sporadic official explanations suggest that the waterfront viaduct under the tracks is in such disrepair that it could be destroyed by the tram cars running at their usual speed. Other parts of the same structure appear, however, to be in no better shape and the tram does shoot through those sections without any apparent restraint. What is noticeable about the slow stretch of the tracks is that, between Roosevelt Square and the Square of March 15, three foreign-owned five-star hotels occupy the river bank on the Pest side. The screeching and banging noise of the tram at its usual speed would, no doubt, irk the international visitor crowd staying in those establishments, sitting in the open-air cafés

1

in their front, and strolling on the promenade. Politicians and bureaucrats, students as well as professors, members of the local public at large endure as the car inches ahead in slow motion, covering the span in front of the hotels. Theirs is a practical, quotidian lesson in the comparative sociology of backwardness, along with, should the second explanation merit any credence, a brief exercise in international tourism under semi-colonial conditions.

    This study is a central European contribution to the comparative, historical sociology of international tourism and uneven development. Contrary to the popular view that tourism is "what we do when we are not doing anything," and the often unwitting practice of brushing aside tourism as a bogus phenomenon not worthy of the high-minded social sciences, it sees in tourism an object worthy of critical analytical attention.

"We" do quite a number of things when doing apparently "nothing" under the auspices of international tourism. "We" engage in consumption without any productive activity. Thereby "we" separate spatially two components of the accumulation process, not unlike multinational corporations or a great many migrant families. "Our" spending and other behavioral patterns are shaped in a way that is, by default, different from the way local society structures its consumption and conduct. "We" thus radically separate "ourselves" *qua* tourists from the locals, creating and fixing markers of distinction between "us" and them. "We" then celebrate an abstract sense of the exotic through a sanitized and aestheticized image which reduces the perceived complexity of the other's experience and complicates communication. It is in this sense that the tourist is indeed "a visitor in a hurry who prefers monuments to human beings" (Todorov 1993:344). As individual tourists, "we" are quite transient—"our" presence institutionalized as tourism is, however, quite lasting.

The world has become quite a touristic place indeed. Different parts of it are, however, touristic to a radically different extent and in very different ways. It is obvious that the observer's position in the touristic intercourse makes a serious difference in his perception of the significance of its impact. It is possible to be careless and shrug off issues emerging from the global tourist trade as epiphenomenal—as long as the analyst's mind is set to holding as important the social experiences of such, and only such, populations of the world which participate in the game primarily as tourists. That restriction of focus is, however, difficult to maintain because of the global spread of international tourism. Such thinking is not only long outdated but also smacks, from a post-colonial perspective, as intellectual production "complicit with Western international economic interests" (Spivak 1988:271). Put differently, working in social contexts which are subject to the sundry inflows and insistent presence of foreign tourists makes it extremely difficult to assume away the phenomenon of tourism as something that is simple, straightforward and, thus, unproblematic. Frankly, the image of "us" as "Innocents Abroad" is quite naive.

Significance of international tourism

Tourism is a very serious business. Defined for standardized data collection purposes by the World Tourism Organization as travel for reasons other than obtaining incomes with at least one overnight stay abroad, estimates of the number of global international tourist arrivals ranged between 287 million (WTO 1986:20) and 365 million (Senior 1982:66) person-trips during the early 1980s, creating officially record-ed monetary receipts of US\$94,600 million (WTO 1986:21) to US\$121,500 million (Senior 1982:10). In addition, domestic tourism is estimated to have involved a global total of more than 3000 million trips in 1983 (WTO 1986:28). The addition of transport and other infrastructural investment—which tourism shares with other sectors and does not appear in tourism receipts or expenditures statistics—further increases the relative weight of tourism in world trade. As a result, tourism is said to be the largest industry in the world, having surpassed the oil business during the mid-1980s.

By 1985, estimates of foreign tourist arrivals surged to between 334 million and 385 million arrivals (BarOn 1989:Table 2), implying 2,571,800 to 2,964,500 million tourist nights (BarOn 1989:Table 2). According to conservative estimates by the World Tourism Organization, this generated US\$109,000–111,000 million in international tourism revenues worldwide (BarOn 1989:Table 2). Direct spending on inter-national tourism represented, during the early 1980s, the equivalent of 5% to 6.4% of total world exports (Senior 1982). In 1984, a publication by the World Tourism Organization estimates that international tourism receipts accounted for 5.2% of world exports (WTO 1986:8 and 21).

Tourism has also been an important component of political discourse worldwide. Liberal colloquy hails international travel as a civic liberty and a main gage of any regime's international acceptability: lack of freedom of travel to and from given societies has been a key element in the denunciation of isolationist states, *vide* East Germany, Cuba or North Korea. Socialist discourse emphasizes a universal right to free time as protection against excessive exploitation. Conservative parlance under-scores the importance of such leisure activities which contribute to the person's all-round education, the preservation of cultural heritage through erudition. It is trivial to demonstrate the potential significance of international tourism for all of the above.

Tourism is one of the most powerful components of the secular trends described by sociologists as internationalization (Lanfant et al 1978) or increasing transnationalization (Sklair 1991), presented by culture theorists as globalization (e.g., Robertson and Lechner 1985; Robertson 1990), and analyzed by human geographers as time–space compression (e.g., Harvey 1989). It increases handsomely the importance of the service sector worldwide. Massive contemporary leisure travel is comparable in its significance to other flows of capital, labor, coercion, information, knowledge, and value across societal, cultural, linguistic, regional and state boundaries. Tourism is, clearly, a very appropriate subject matter for systematic social analysis—especially for that of the global, comparative, historical variety.

Tourism comes in diverse forms, and the significance of international tourism is a social fact itself. It fits in, and comes into direct clashes with, the practices of the society in which it appears. The insertion of international tourism into local practices takes place through a great variety of institutional forms, and precise analysis of those patterns is one of the most important tasks of the social sciences of tourism. This book aims in that direction.

Selected Issues in the Social Science of Tourism

Jean Stafford portrays the large field of the science of tourism—or, in his French neologism, *téorologie*—as entirely "preparadigmatic" (Stafford 1985). While that dismissive portrayal may be an exaggeration, many tourism studies do indeed give the impression of somewhat dubious analytical rigor and tenuous theoretical orientation. Eric Cohen's erudite synopsis of the literature cites examples of studies on tourism seen in such diverse perspectives as "commercialized hospitality," "democratized travel," "a modern leisure activity," "a modern variety of the traditional pilgrimage," "an expression of basic cultural themes," "an acculturative process," "a type of ethnic relations," and "a form of neocolonialism" (Cohen 1984:374–6). Reviewing over 150 items in what he terms the field of "touristology" over ten years ago, Cohen's summary reads as a warning signal revealing diffuse and often monologous work on a relatively low level of abstraction: "while field-studies have proliferated, many lack an explicit, theoretical orientation and hence contribute little to theory building" (Cohen 1984:388).

A comprehensive overview of the enormous tourism studies literature is beyond both the scope and ambition of this book. (For further reading, the reader is urged to consult, along with the above quoted work by Stafford 1985 and Cohen 1984, John Urry's useful summary of the theoretical aspects of tourism 1990a:7–15 and Crick 1988.) The overview below addresses, first, some fundamental theoretical issues of tourism: the modern Stranger as a metaphor of modernity, the tourist as a species of the Stranger, and the historical specificity of tourism. (A metaphor is a figure of speech in which a term is transferred from the object it ordinarily designates to an object it may designate only by implicit comparison or analogy. In the present context, it denotes abstraction which is not analytical or whose sphere of interpretation is not appropriately specified. Terms are capitalized when used metaphorically. Lower-case letters signal the more direct meaning.)

This study presents an argument for understanding tourism as leisure migration and proceeds to draw a brief outline of the literature on tourism and uneven development by focusing on the three basic social-institutional aspects of tourism: sending societies, the tourism industry, and receiving societies (see also Jafari 1989 and Przecławski 1994).

Stranger and tourist: metaphorical or historical objects

The tourist ambled into the work of sociology's classics by way of Georg Simmel's brief treatises on The Stranger (1971[1908]) and The Adventurer (1971[1911]) as social types. As Dennison Nash (1981) points out, cosmopolitanism and the "blasé metropolitan attitude" (Simmel 1971[1903]:329; see also 1978[1907]) as social psychological predispositions are quite in harmony with tourism as a cultural pattern of travel. Although Simmel never analyzes explicitly the tourist, "wandering" (Simmel 1971[1908]:143) or, a few pages apart, "mobility" (Simmel 1971[1908]:154), are key components of the definition of the Stranger engaged in the quintessentially modern condition of simultaneous "nearness" and "remoteness" (Simmel 1971[1908]:146).

In Zygmunt Bauman's modernizationist reading (1990), the Stranger represents the breakage of a presupposed "primordial coordination between physical and moral proximity" (1990:24). In a homage to Simmel's classical formula of the Stranger "who comes today and stays tomorrow" (Simmel 1971[1908]:143), Bauman's aliens "appear inside the confines of the life-world and *refuse to go away*" (1990:24): They cease to be aliens but fail to become neighbors. The result is a series of *"mismeetings"* (*Vergegnung*: Bauman's borrowing from Martin Buber's playful modification of the German term *Begegnung* [meeting], Bauman 1990:25). In the process, Strangers and locals pay, through Bauman's (1990:25) borrowing from Goffman (1971:312), *"disattention"* to each other, so that their relationships are *"de-ethicalized"* (1990:25). A pervasive sense of moral indifference (1990:29)—the hallmark of cultural modernity—has thus set in.

The metaphor of Strangeness-as-modernity—expressed in Julia

Kristeva's insistence that "a person of the twentieth century can exist honestly only as a foreigner" (Kristeva 1986:286)—elevates the experience of the futility of genuine contact with the Other to the level of a new ontological condition. An allegorical protagonist in the dissolving cut from *Gemeinschaft* to *Gesellschaft*, the Stranger thus impersonates modern Man. (An allegory is an extended metaphor where an abstract idea is represented by a character.) Consider this quote from the concluding paragraph of Kristeva's Freudian-semiotic analysis articulating Strangeness as internal to a modern "us":

> In the absence of a new community bond—a saving religion that would integrate the bulk of wanderers and different people within a new consensus, other than "more money and goods for everyone"—we are, for the first time in history, confronted with the following situation: we must live with different people while relying on our personal moral codes, without the assistance of a set that would include our particularities while transcending them. A paradoxical community is emerging, made up of foreigners who are reconciled with themselves to the extent that they recognize themselves as foreigners. The multinational society would thus be the consequence of an extreme individualism, but conscious of its discontents and limits, knowing only indomitable people ready-to-help-themselves in their weakness, a weakness whose other name is our radical strangeness (Kristeva 1991:195).

The literature on the Stranger demarcates its hero astutely from neighbors and aliens. Observe the following epistemological portrait of the Stranger as a metaphorical subject by Madan Sarup:

> Strangers are, in principle, undecidables. They are unclassifiable. A stranger is someone who refuses to remain confined to the 'far away' land or go away from our own. S/he is physically close while remaining culturally remote. Strangers often seem to be suspended in the empty space between a tradition which they have already left and the mode of life which stubbornly denies them the right of entry. The stranger blurs a boundary line. The stranger is an anomaly, standing between the inside and the outside, order and chaos, friend and enemy (Sarup 1994:101–2).

This initial conceptualization of the tourist as a species of the stranger is indispensable because of the intuitively as well as analytically consequential historical and culture-sociological ingredient that that approach provides: the disposition of simultaneous remoteness and proximity. The literature on the Stranger, however, does not offer tools to discern any finer distinction among the various types of the Stranger: The tourist, the political refugee, the foreign business consultant, the government advisor, the investor, the reporter, and the economic migrant are all equally fitting references for this image. In order to enrich our understanding of the tourist and the touristic variety of Strangeness further, it is necessary to make a step back to that level of abstraction where the classical understanding of Strangeness began.

Moving back, one of the obvious questions that emerges inevitably is about the social context of the analysis. Reading the literature on the Stranger, it is difficult to escape the impression that its subject matter is thematized from the perspective of the previously not colonized, affluent, white, gentile, "western", bourgeois or "middle class" society in mind which has only recently found itself in the condition of *receiving* the Stranger. Any such tacit restriction ought to be released for the idea of the Stranger to be applicable to a comparative sociology of tourism. Sending and receiving societies, as well as whatever institutions bring them into contact with each other, are equally legitimate subjects of the study of the touristic variety of Strangeness.

Much North American and west European writing implicates as the source of Strangeness such an eclectic assortment of subjects as the immigrant—typically of the less affluent, culturally and ethnically distinct and subordinate variety—the Jew, Alfred Weber's free-floating intellectual thematized by Karl Mannheim (Bauman 1988–89; Mannheim 1936 [1929]), the "Orient" (Said 1978), "the feminine," and/or death (Kristeva 1986: 286 and 1991:185). In these examples, the Stranger's metaphorical character runs increasingly rampant. Meanwhile, the "tangible" tourist goes quietly unacknowledged.

Given its metaphorical, "unclassifiable" nature, the idea of the Stranger in this form is excessively elusive for a sociological analysis of tourism. The subject matter for, and the basic institutional categories of, a sociological analysis of tourism, can only be produced by way of careful further classification. It is necessary, at a minimum, to engage a twofold process of distinction: a separation of tourists from other strangers, and, within the tourist field, a distinction among various kinds of tourists, hosts, and actors on behalf of the tourism industry. That of course also implies a more differentiated mapping of Strangeness.

One of the ways that can be achieved is by focusing on the stranger's presence or absence in the local labor process. The tourist can be demarcated from the other main social types subsumed under the stranger—the rich varieties of the migrant and the expatriate expert— by *not* performing income earning activities while away from home. *The Tourist is the leisure migrant.* Based on this simple political-economic definition, locals include those who derive their livelihood from the local labor market. Most tourists are locals elsewhere most of their time; many locals are also tourists elsewhere, sometimes. Because tourists are consumers and not producers in the local context, the key institutional link between tourists and locals is that furnished by the tourism industry (the provider of the means of consumption to tourists and employment to locals).

One advantage of the leisure migration approach is that it provides the study of tourism with a point of reference—the literature on labor migration and refugee flows. This strong strand of the social sciences has, for its part, conspicuously ignored leisure flows. A comprehensive, comparative-historical sociological analysis of human migrations cannot afford such blind spots and ought to insist on the consideration of all, including short-term and transient, human flows. This study thus challenges both the dominant mode of analysis of international migration and a large part of the "tourism studies" literature by thinking about tourism as a form of migration. For an analysis of tourism as leisure migration, the literature on labor and refugee migration also reads as an enormous exemplar of theory building research and offers a host of parallel conceptualizations readily available for further extension into the realm of leisure flows.

Much research on labor migration has been concerned with the emergence and over-time stability of migrant flows, emerging patterns of migrant incorporation, and the consequences of migration for receiving and emitting regions (see, e.g., Portes and Böröcz 1989). Origins, stability, patterns and consequences are the central issues of a sociology of leisure migration as well. The main dividing line in debates within the labor migration literature is between push–pull theories— which assume that labor flows are automatic consequences of global inequalities and use the individual as the unit of analysis—and the historical-comparative institutional economic sociology approach. This second perspective contends that migrant flows are products of the interplay between external penetration and internal social processes, and that they are sustained and shaped by transborder migrant institutions, both formal and informal. Located in the latter tradition, this study will rephrase many of these themes with respect to leisure, not labor, migration.

On the basis of the definition of tourism as leisure migration, it is possible to proceed to a distantly related, conceptual controversy in the tourism studies literature which addresses tourism as an historical-sociological topic. One group of scholars, best represented perhaps by the erudite argument of anthropologist Dennison Nash (e.g., 1981), holds the concept of tourism to be widely comprehensive. (See also Sigaux 1966. For a popularized echo of this view, see Feifer 1985. Mead (1914[1972]) and Black (1985) use a similarly retroactive terminology when addressing the eighteenth-century British Grand Tour as tourism and its participants as tourists.) This idea requires that the "leisure" included in the concept of tourism not be tied to any socioeconomic formation. On this basis, Nash is able to argue that not only has tourism existed in the "west" ever since the Ancient Rome, but it is also observable among "simplex" societies. The obvious strength of this idea is that it makes the analysis of tourism accessible for a wide variety of historical-comparative approaches. Some historical and anthropological material supports this idea in the sense that observed behavioral patterns can be found, both trans-historically and trans-culturally, to resemble phenomena associated with contemporary tourism quite closely. (See also Urry 1990a:4 and the large literature on the Grand Tour sampled in *chapter 2*.)

Nash has been criticized (e.g., Akeroyd 1981; Cohen 1981; Graburn 1981; Pi-Sunyer 1981) by those who, relying on an idea best outlined perhaps by French sociologist Joffre Dumazedier (e.g., 1968), stress the historical specificity of leisure, tied more closely to the production process. In addition, a narrower concept of tourism is advocated by those who strive for historical concreteness in sociological analysis, thereby connecting the concepts of leisure and tourism, in terms of their emergence in history, to the capitalist mode of production or capitalism as a sociohistorical formation.

Most research on tourism focuses on its consequences. International leisure migration affects social life by exerting influence on those groups of the society which participate in it, by transforming the societies which it penetrates, and by sustaining the tourism industry, the institutional channel of leisure flows.

Leisure migration and sending societies

More than the exclusively "economic" consumption of goods and services obtained abroad, outgoing leisure flows represent "invisible imports" in a broad sense. Experience gained through leisure travel is fed back to social practice, creating links which are often transient for individual participants but produce relatively stable structures of economic, political, and cultural articulation among communities, sectors, societies, and regions. The main effect of outgoing international leisure migration on sending societies lies in this feedback process from travel abroad to the home society. Stay-at-home members of the tourists' society, just like in the case of labor migration, gain knowledge about economic, political, social, etc. conditions and customs in the outside world through their social networks with travelers. Tourist photography, family travel film and video, travel souvenirs, and the consumption of tourist art in general, work as symbolic preservatives of travel experience and a means of communicating the same to nontraveling members of the home society. Mailed-home travel postcards serve clearly the latter purpose. The feedback of experience with the contrast between home and abroad affect concrete definitions of national identity, and create and feed stereotypes of all kinds.

To the extent that they involve the expenditure of domestic incomes abroad, all forms of outgoing international travel represent imports to sending societies. Travel from poorer to wealthier societies may be a channel for serious monetary leakage which is difficult to control by states.

The sending country's position in the international system and the socioeconomic position of outgoing travelers within their respective society jointly set limits on the free time and money available for travel abroad, the scope of potential travel destinations, the preferred types of tourist attractions, and the availability of various travel types. Tourist attractions occupy a wide field ranging from a quintessentially modern fascination with nature, wildlife and "primitive" cultures through an interest in preserved original or artificially manufactured historical sites, prostitution, and various forms of art appreciation, to an apparently equally unsatiable, general interest in the sanitized, nature-less and de-historicized manifestations of metropolitan life in the centers of the industrialized world. Tourist types range between risk-taking, "do-it-yourself" or "explorer" travel understood, after Erik Cohen, as the travel pattern of those who maximize "strangeness" and passive participants of fully commercialized, ready-made, massive package-tours maximizing "familiarity" (Cohen 1972). Cohen's typology of "tourist roles" thus renders the Simmelian theme of "strangeness versus familiarity" in the reverse perspective of the tourist without reference to the broader problems implied in the Stranger's role as a personification of modernity.

This taxonomical variety among types of tourists has defined an important dimension in the tourism literature. Standing between the Frankfurt School's critical work on mass culture and Baudrillard's simulacrum as detached representation, Daniel Boorstin's critical essay on the cultural importance of *The Image* in America (1961) devotes an entire chapter to castigating tourism as the ultimate "pseudo-event" which inhibits instead of fostering cross-cultural communication and understanding. For Boorstin, "[t]he tourist's appetite for strangeness (...) seems best satisfied when the pictures in his own mind are verified in some far country" (Boorstin 1961:109).

In contrast, Dean MacCannell's influential work on *The Tourist* (1976), inspired by Durkheim, Goffmann, and the semiotic turn of the social sciences, suggests that the essence of the touristic experience is a striving for "authenticity" through travel. Adapting Erving Goffmann's "front" versus "back" typology of public spaces, MacCannell portrays tourists as constantly trying to "peek" behind the symbolic "curtains" erected before them by locals who, in turn, attempt to conceal "reality" and thereby to create group solidarity. *The Tourist* represents a clear overture toward the poststructuralist line of scholarship by considering tourism as a ritual performed to the differentiations of society. If signifiers and signifieds are detached from, and replace, each other in tourism (see Culler 1981)—as they do universally according to Baudrillardian poststructuralism—then representation of the other in tourism is problem-atized and the fragmentation and disorientation of touristic experience becomes a marker of the social. For MacCannell, the Tourist is a metaphor of society—this time not of the modern but the postmodern variety.

Boorstin's and MacCannell's adroit theoretical formulations use the same sociological dimension for oversimplification. Their difference is due to the reverse directions of their interest. MacCannell's characteri-zation of "staged authenticity in tourist settings"—whereby locals show tourists images which are constructed to appear as if they were authentic—focuses on those tourists who minimize their use of the tourism industry. Boorstin, on the other hand, overgeneralizes from the package tour experience and neglects the rich variety of other touristic genres. Both works strip the host–tourist relationship of much of its complexity.

John Urry's detailed and insightful monograph on British travel, *The Tourist Gaze* (1990a) portrays the tourist experience through yet a different kind of metaphorical looking-glass. Influenced by a Foucauld-ian, contextual concept of power and a poststructuralist emphasis on the visual—particularly in relation to the celebration of the commodity (e.g., Harvey 1989)—Urry (1990b) observes that "the way in which 'tourism' has been historically separated from other activities, such as shopping, sport, culture, architecture and so on, is dissolving" (Urry 1990b:33). The result is "a universalizing of the tourist gaze" (Urry 1990a). Here, again, tourism stands as a metaphor of society at large: The Gaze is a synec-doche of tourism. (Synecdoche is a figure of speech where a part stands for a whole.) *The Tourist Gaze* thus intimates an extremely streamlined image of the phenomenon of tourism. Its main metaphor—the Gaze—locks the imagery into the "depth-less" dimension of visuality. This clever synecdoche provides an intuitively extremely accessible portrayal of the inherent voyeurism of the tourist experience.

Accessibility, however, comes at a certain price. It is undeniable that the gaze is an unremovable component of consumption, particularly of the consumption of a generalized sense of strangeness as in tourism. Yet, one wonders about the extent to which for instance the prostitution, the environmental destruction, the economic restructuring, or the general commercialization induced by the penetration of tourism, are adequate-ly addressed by looking at the Gaze as the focal moment of the phenomenon. To put the question differently, if we see tourism as being all about the Gaze, we blur the distinction between actual travel in tourism and, say, tourist video. That of course raises the question why, then, we need an analysis of such mundane topics as the changing political economy of the (British) tourism industry—which is one of the topics *The Tourist Gaze* covers. Furthermore, if "[t]he actual purchases in tourism [the hotel bed, the meal, the ticket, etc.] are often incidental to the gaze, which may be no more than a momentary view" (Urry 1990:26), one cannot help but wonder about the utility of containing the subject matter in this narrow and "often incidental" vessel.

Leisure migration—an industry

A singular characteristic of leisure migration among all human flows is that it is mediated by a transnationally organized institutional structure, the tourism industry (United Nations 1982; Sampson 1984). For destination societies, the high concentration of capital in the intricately interwoven hotel, airline, and tour operator branches may create "classic" situations of foreign trade and direct foreign investment dependency. This is especially so in the case of previously colonized Third World destination societies where institutionalized patterns of international penetration already exist, and in situations where a destination country's tourist product lacks uniqueness to such an extent that it can be substituted by the multinational companies for some other country with relative ease. The combination of the two characterizes many "tropical paradise island" destinations: for instance, airline and cruise liner schedule and route modifications which may appear minor or "rational" from the metropolitan centers cause, as a rule, extremely rapid and "irrational" fluctuations of conditions in these small post-colonial societies. The relative power of the tourism industry trans-nationals *vis-à-vis* such destination societies, states, and tourism businesses can be described as oligopsony—a situation where a limited number of buyers are able to restrict the room of maneuver of sellers—due to their access to major tourism markets.

Albeit to a much lesser degree, tourists and sending societies at large are subject to the oligopoly—where a limited number of sellers are able to restrict the room of maneuver for buyers—of transnationals in the tourism industry. The key components of transnational power *vis-à-vis* these societies can be located in their control over international long distance transport—an extremely capital-intensive industry—their exclusive and direct access to the tourism markets of wealthy societies and the upper classes through advertising, and their established presence in metropolitan cities worldwide. Tourism transnationals also tend to monopolize, according to a study commissioned by the inter-national association of travel organizations, "managerial expertise and positions, marketing skills, financial resources, and intra-industry contacts" (Britton 1982:339 quotes IUOTO 1976:36–64, 701, and 778). The organization of the international tourism industry resembles a pyramid, with transnationals at the apex, branch offices and national tourism industries in middle positions, and tourism-related small-scale retail enterprises at the bottom (Britton 1982). As Pearce summarizes, the essence of this hierarchy is the "concentration up, dispersion down" principle (Pearce 1988:14) whereby virtually all tourism is forced through channels controlled from a small number of transnational headquarters.

The tourism industry is a structure of economic institutions which strive for increasing control over space on a global scale, providing flexibility to adjust to seasonal and other variations in such increasingly valuable resources as climate, environmental conditions, and labor costs. This characteristic is not unique to the tourism industry. It manifests a more general tendency of the global organization and constant re-organization of production under late capitalism.

The tourism industry is unique, however, in the sense that the product which it markets is the very geographical, spatial, climatic, and cultural diversity of the global economy itself. Consequently, there is a striking resemblance between the global organization of leisure migration and that of the mass media; travel advertising (Thurot and Thurot 1983) and the organization of commercialized travel experience powerfully exemplify the interpenetration of business and discourse. (*Chapter 2* presents a more elaborate argument on this subject as well as the temporal anchoring of the emergence of tourism.)

Leisure migration and destination societies

Broadly conceived "invisible exports" through international leisure migrations involve the inducement and sustenance of momentous flows not only of people, but also commodities, money, power, and knowledge. Competition for control over (potentially) scarce resources such as space, food, or water between the tourism and other sectors, or mass-produced "tourist art," racial and socioeconomic hierarchies and ethnic stereotypes, are examples of the complex consequences of these flows. The extent and "net balance" of exchanges among hierarchical zones of the international economy, military–political blocs, single societies, nations, states, peoples, regions, communities, and the trans-national and national tourism industries, etc. is the focus of an extended disagreement concerning the developmental effects of tourism in destination areas.

Grandiose national plans for tourism-based development have been built on traditional economic arguments supplying predictions of spectacular business success through surging foreign exchange earnings from incoming tourists, coupled with expectations of increased employ-ment, broader interpersonal ties and a better understanding among

14 *Leisure Migration: A Sociological Study on Tourism*

people of different national background (e.g., Hodgson 1987; Grünthal 1961 quoted by Bachmann 1987:70; Vellas 1985:176; Ouma 1970; Williams and Shaw 1988). The argument for tourism-based national development programs has been summarized by the World Tourism Organization through the example of Spain where:

> tourism could be held to be the stimulus behind a whole economy's expansion and has seemingly enabled the largely farming communities of Spain's Mediterranean seaboard to move, relatively painlessly, from a life lived at near-subsistence level to one enjoying a relatively high prosperity in less than two decades. It is assumed that tourism is capable of similar successes in developing countries all over the world, whatever the nature of their economies or their social structure (WTO 1975 quoted by Cleverdon 1979:4).

The affinity of the "tourism-as-engine-of-growth" rhetoric with neo-classical economics is revealed in its tendency to place the blame for the lack of successful tourism-based development on the state, usually the local state. As a tourism industry publication intimates with respect to strategies for remedying the economic ills of Latin America:

> [a]nother development that could have a significant impact in helping reduce the high unemployment throughout the region is the trend toward increased interest in tourism. Unlike most major nations of the world, the Latin America [*sic*] states, with the exception of Mexico, have paid scant attention to capitalizing on their wide variety of tourist attractions as a means for earning foreign exchange. In 1986, however, there were a number of signs indicating that governments were interested in removing some of the government-imposed barriers to travel and beginning to focus on the need for increased air services with lower international air fares (Waters 1987:74).

No doubt, a small number of cases—indeed, Spain among them—do support the optimistic contention regarding the beneficial economic effects of the resulting fiscal and other linkages. That is the main reason why many—advanced and underdeveloped, capitalist and socialist—states have actively promoted tourism-based development projects over the last several decades. However, a series of critical studies have demonstrated that inference from successful cases is, to say the least, not universally valid (see May-Landgrebe 1987).

The critical literature has shown that the penetration of international tourism produces foreign exchange leakages through direct foreign investment or other forms of foreign control over the national tourism industry (Wood 1979; Bryden 1973). The tourism sector creates mostly low-paid menial jobs—the lowest tier of the tourism industry mainly consists of labor-intensive occupations—thus putting a downward pressure on wage levels in general. It tends to create insulated tourism enclaves which provide exclusive access to the best local resources for tourists and those members of the local elites powerful enough to

associate with tourists (Haug 1982; Britton 1982). Tourist inflows have
been found to contribute to inflation, higher land values, excessive
propensity to import and low rates of return on investment (Mathiesen
and Wall 1982). Tourism is a major perpetrator in environmental
pollution and deterioration (Mäder 1988; Farrell and McLellan 1987),
and it has been portrayed as a crucial cause of the disruption of the social
fabric through commercialization and depersonalization (e.g., Pi-
Sunyer 1977). It encourages the proliferation of petty crime and
prostitution (Cohen 1982; Graburn 1983). Various combinations of the
above ills have also been documented (Wu 1982; Britton 1982). Tourism
has been portrayed as a form of imperialism, cultural and otherwise
(Nash 1977), and a creator of one-dimensional chains of dependency
(Høivik and Heiberg 1980).

The tenor of the critical literature on international tourism in the
context of dependency and underdevelopment is well illustrated by a
quote from Frantz Fanon. Writing in 1961, Fanon prefigured many a
theme of tourism as imperialism as he related:

> The national bourgeoisie will be greatly helped on its way toward decadence
> by the Western bourgeoisies, who come to it as tourists, avid for the exotic,
> for big game hunting and for casinos. The national bourgeoisie organizes
> centers of rest and relaxation and pleasure resorts to meet the wishes of the
> Western bourgeoisie. Such activity is given the name of tourism, and for
> the occasion will be built up as a national industry. If proof is needed of
> the eventual transformation of certain elements of the ex-native
> bourgeoisie into the organizers of parties for their Western opposite num-
> bers, it is worth while having a look at what has happened in Latin America.
> (. . .) [T]he national middle class will have nothing better to do than to take
> on the role of manager for Western enterprise and it will in practice set up
> its country as the brothel of Europe (Fanon 1963[1961]:153–4, partially
> quoted in Crick 1988).

Due to the time sequence and the ideological and political irrec-
oncilability of the two approaches—i.e., the condition that the neo-
classical discourse emerged earlier than critical studies—and despite the
fact that much of the critical literature on "tourism-as-imperialism" is
structured as a reactive rhetoric, meaningful dialogue between the two
approaches has been virtually nil. To the extent that they engage in
debates, the critical approaches are aimed, implicitly, to debunk the
perceived shortcomings of their neo-classical straw-man adversaries, and
representatives of the other side largely ignore such anti-neo-classical
scholarship.

Much of the rhetoric concerning the impact of the penetration of
international tourism reproduces more general themes of the major
debates between modernization ideologies and the critical dependency
literature as well as the principal strengths and weaknesses of those more
general, paradigmatic debates. A major limitation of the argument

advocating "tourism-based national development" is that it regards tourism as an agent of change on the national level. In other words, tourism is assumed to be an undifferentiated independent variable introduced in the extremely simplified context of single "nation-state-society" entities which are—other than through incoming international tourism—perfectly unconnected to the outside world in general and to other "nation-state-societies" in particular. Tourism is thus assumed to be a modern-day economic *deus ex machina*, a benevolent external factor that is completely independent of any global, regional, or subnational structural process or constraint.

The critical literature, on the other hand, is dominated by a perspective which depicts tourism (just like all other links of poor and powerless societies to the outside world) as an instrument serving some kind of "master plan" of underdevelopment, relegating "native" societies to a passive, subordinate and/or comprador role serving metro-politan interests and devoid of agency.

Such simple criticism of the evils of touristic practices is not a monopoly of political-economic analyses. The penetration of tourism from without is portrayed in an equally monocausal fashion in work on sex tourism by exposing a particularly violent aspect of the more general process of the objectification of the other through commercial leisure travel. Sex tourism, a major "invisible" export earner in such countries as Thailand or the Philippines, and certainly very much part of the overall social matrix of tourism, brings together the general tendency of objectifying the other through tourism with the more concrete instance of objectification through sexual oppression. (For critical work on sex tourism in the context of economic misery, see, e.g., Phongpaichit 1982, and Launer and Wilke-Launer 1988). Critical work on tourism is a particularly crucial subject matter for feminist scholarship, post-structuralist and otherwise. Cynthia Enloe (1990) gives a good example of this approach in an informed and angry chapter devoted to sex tourism in her book on *Bananas, Beaches and Bases.* For Enloe's British feminist perspective, "[tourism] is about power, increasingly inter-nationalized power" (Enloe 1990:40) so that:

> travel for pleasure and adventure has been profoundly gendered. Without ideas about masculinity and femininity—and the enforcement of both—in the societies of departure and the societies of destination, it would be impossible to sustain the tourism industry and its political agenda in their current form. It is not simply that ideas about pleasure, travel, escape, bed-making and sexuality have affected women in rich and poor countries. The very structure of international tourism *needs* patriarchy to survive. Men's capacity to control women's sense of their security and self-worth has been central to the evolution of tourism politics (Enloe 1990:40–1).

Michelle Madsen Camacho's study (1994) specifies these considerations by showing how the disciplining and control of gendered service labor is intertwined with modernization ideologies even outside the context of, and quite apart from, prostitution proper.

As a result of the one-dimensionality and one-sidedness ("active-exploiter–passive-exploited") of its master rhetoric regarding the post colonial context, the critical literature is not capable to account for any case where tourism indeed contributes to national socioeconomic development. That is a problem because some evidence is indeed available to that effect.

What both perspectives lack is a more precise specification of the conditions under which tourism contributes to social and national development. That can be achieved by releasing simultaneously the two restrictions common to both sides of this debate: the methodological simplification of single-directional causation, and the theoretical simplification of ignoring or slighting the noneconomic dimensions of tourism. The riddle of the relations between development and tourism can only be solved via a culture-, politics-, and ideology-conscious economic sociology of the complex, two-directional interplay of the two.

Tourism under state socialism

There is very little literature to exploit the theoretical potential offered by the widely observed insertion of international tourism into state socialist contexts. Tourists from socialist states are missing entirely from the tourism studies literature which reads, as a result, as a less poignant rephrasing of the popular joke about the possible slogan for a Soviet equivalent of the American Express Card: "Don't leave home!". . .

Many descriptive studies emphasize the restrictions placed on foreign tourists at such destinations under heavy surveillance by the socialist states and stress the hardly counterintuitive suggestion that more reforms are needed if the socialist societies are to compete in the tourism market. If the literature on the Stranger was of limited utility because of its overly high level of metaphorical abstraction, much of the social science on tourism in central and eastern Europe appears to join a large part of the tourism literature in general in erring on the side of providing too little analytical abstraction.

Such studies often paint a caricature picture of life under state socialism, and tend to reflect the perspective of the Western traveler wandering into such contexts. Market potential studies represent a particularly straightforward genre of the latter type (e.g., Buckley and Witt 1990). Unduly little work has been done on the origins, the specific patterns and characteristics, and the broad sociopolitical, -economic and -cultural effects, of international tourism under state socialism, notwithstanding the fact that some socialist states had actively promoted international tourism and that large segments of most European state socialist societies had been avid tourists until the system's very collapse. Among the few exceptions, we find a good descriptive paper by Derek Hall which provides a succinct summary of certain important geographical and sociopolitical aspects of tourism under the Stalinist, most dogmatic version of state socialism in Albania and North Korea (Hall 1990) and an informative summary by David Harrington on the Bulgarian experience since the collapse of state socialism (Harrington 1993).

Direct comparative work on state socialist and capitalist countries, let alone such work driven by "mid-range" theoretical questions of any kind, attempting to link the tourism-related material to other bodies of work in the social sciences, appears to be missing entirely. This pattern of neglect does not cease with the collapse of state socialism. A recent publication purportedly on *Tourism in Europe* (Pompl and Lavery 1993), for instance, represents its subject largely through the all-too-usual "western" geographical synecdoche: Its discussion is almost exclusively on that part of the continent which has never been state socialist. The first seven substantive chapters talk only about the European Union and its immediate neighbors and the following eleven country-chapters are also all on the same, western part of the continent. The only chapter on the former state-socialist countries (comprising roughly one-half of Europe) is a brief economic-geographical overview entitled "Tourism in Eastern Europe," tacked on to the very end of the collection almost as an afterthought.

This study seeks to redress a series of apparent gaps. It speaks to the problem of the bi-directional relationship between international tourism and the two fundamental structural characteristics of contemporary global capitalism: uneven development and the formation and failure of imperial blocs. Its ambition is to understand some of the complex, manifold, and often contradictory, ways in which international tourism as a phenomenon by its very nature cutting across national boundaries and virtually all realms of social life, has contributed to the reproduction and the transformation of the contemporary world system, and the ways in which big structures of contextual capitalism have made possible, shaped and constrained leisure migration on a scale ranging from global to local. It scrutinizes one of the most tourism-exposed parts of the world where state socialism and corporate welfare-state capitalism met for four decades.

Plan of the Book

This work places international tourism in its global context by focusing on what Charles Tilly (1984) calls the "big structures" of the world: a hierarchical edifice, organizing the globe's societies into groups marked by sharply different levels of incomes, rates and regimes of capital accumulation, living standards and political liberties, and the split interstate system of blocs defined as opposing political–military alliances, whose conflict had dominated the international arena for over four and a half decades following World War II. For this purpose, Austria and Hungary offer an optimal comparative context. Located in the heart of Europe—the continent which sends and receives over three-quarters of all international tourist trips of the world (Senior 1982; WTO 1986)— these two roughly equal-size, landlocked countries with an extended joint history have been for the last few decades the two societies most exposed to incoming international tourism on either side of the "Iron Curtain."

The Austro-Hungarian comparison makes possible the utilization of a "minimum difference" approach. Since the end of World War II, Austria has been a capitalist welfare state under the doctrine of military-strategic neutrality, in many important ways occupying an intermediate situation between the two blocs. During the same period of time, Hungary grew from an example of Stalinist terror into the state socialist society that deviated farthest from the initial Stalinist pattern of state socialism. If their comparison yields meaningful differences, it can be concluded relatively safely that, for other societies, farther towards the extremes on the two sides of the capitalism-state socialism divide, the differences would be at least as noticeable.

This study combines analyses of global- and regional-level observations and data with those pertaining to a comparison of the case of the two countries. It implements an eclectic, recklessly multimethod research strategy, utilizing a mixture of research methods ranging from historical narrative through content analysis, linguistic history, the statistical modelling of secondary data, ethnographic fieldwork material, and a questionnaire survey taken in conjunction with this inquiry.

First, the study examines quantitative historical data to demonstrate an association between the structural patterns of the uneven development of industrial capitalism and flows of international tourism throughout the continent of Europe and in the comparative framework of Austria and Hungary from the time of their joint Dual Monarchy to recent time. Then it outlines and compares the ways in which the structures of the two countries' external linkages had been reconstructed after World War II. On that basis, the work reviews more formal evidence about the importance of "big structures" for leisure migration by testing the statistical effects of such macrostructural inequalities as uneven development and political–military bloc-affiliation on the likelihood of international tourism in Austria and Hungary between 1960 and 1984. It observes important differences in the arrangements of incoming tourism in the two countries.

The book then proceeds to outline the differences between the two countries in terms of the institutional features of incoming international tourism by summarizing ethnographic fieldwork data and other evidence. Using mainly secondary economic statistical and analytical materials, the study then focuses on the ways in which the amalgam of formal and informal economic institutional arrangements distinguish this pair of capitalist and state socialist societies from each other, and examines the extent to which differences in the profitability of the tourism business can be explained by that institutional-level contrast. The analysis presents a brief narrative of the truly momentous touristic events of the years 1988 and 1989, supported by a brief overview of original survey evidence concerning the social composition of the Hungarians who flooded the Austrian capital—mainly shopping for durable household appliances and consumer electronics products—after the lifting of virtually all administrative and customs restrictions on their travel to the "west." It concludes by a summary of the meta-theoretical implications.

The presentation of the material follows the logic of the theoretical questions asked. As Figure 1.1 summarizes, *chapters 2* and *3* demonstrate an associative relationship between uneven development and the origins

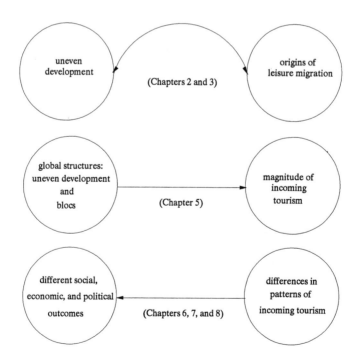

Figure 1.1. Schematic Logic of the Empirical Model

of leisure migration. *Chapter 5* tests a set of causal hypotheses pertaining to the effects of uneven development and political blocs on incoming international tourism. Finally, *chapters 6, 7,* and *8* specify some of the effects of global differences in tourism on local outcomes.

Chapter 2

Travel-Capitalism: The Structure of Europe and the Advent of the Tourist

In one of the twenty lines it allocates to a description of Hungary, the nearly 300-page edition in 1877 of *A Satchel Guide for the Vacation Tourist in Europe* summarizes the architectural and aesthetic worth of the country's capital city for sightseeing American visitors by pronouncing that, in Budapest, "the churches and the public buildings are of no particular interest" (Satchel 1877:194). During the four years that elapsed since the 1873 ceremonial unification of the towns on the two banks of the Danube that formally established Budapest as the official capital city of Hungary, the news had not reached the anonymous author(s) of the guidebook in Cambridge, Massachusetts: They still talk about "Pesth and Buda, or Ofen, as the Germans call it."

Twenty years later, the 1897 edition of that same guidebook takes a more amiable but scarcely enthusiastic pitch, allowing that "some of the new public buildings are elegant in their way" (Satchel 1897:184). Twenty-seven years later—following a world war, two revolutions, and a foreign military occupation resulting in the dismemberment of the Austro-Hungarian Dual Monarchy—the presence of what has remained of Hungary is noted by an increase to eighty-one lines (Satchel 1924). Except for a one-sentence reference to a Danubian steamboat trip downstream from Pressburg (Bratislava, Pozsony), the entire description remains restricted to Budapest. Nearly two generations after the pronouncement of the disparaging opinion above, the 1924 text notices that Budapest's "picture at sunset is one of the most striking in Europe" (Satchel 1924:272) and that "it is not only the most considerable city of Hungary, but is probably to be numbered among the four most beautiful capitals of Europe" (1924:273). (Fifty-one years after the merger of the two cities, the book still spells, incorrectly, the city's name as "Buda-Pest.") The guidebook then proceeds to enumerate some churches and public buildings worth a visit, referring to them by their name in German. (Hungarian had been the official language since 1844, that is, eighty years before this edition of the guidebook was published.) Most of those buildings had been erected before 1877. What had changed?

This chapter considers the emergence of uneven patterns of international tourism as leisure migration within the context of the uneven development of European industrial capitalism. Far from a comprehensive treatise on tourism history, it addresses the nexus of the two processes by bringing together evidence from various sources.

Origins of Leisure Migration

Leisure migration is that type of trade in which the consumer travels to the commodity, resulting in geographical movements of people for the purposes of consumption. The contemporary institutional patterns of leisure migration which cross state borders—international tourism— emerged during the nineteenth century. The process was coterminous with the spatial completion of the modern world economy. Many historians of tourism notice a connection between the spread of leisure migration and some aspect of the sweeping transformation that changed the face of the continent with the advent of industrial capitalism. The observations which dominate the field tend to pick up on particular elements of what appears to be an encompassing relationship but do not make any clear conceptual or empirical connections between the two processes. In the following, I, first, provide a brief overview of two such partial connections and then present some empirical material to discuss the conceptualization of a more general association between industrial capitalism and leisure migration.

Grand tour, tramping and the problem of precursors

Many observers of tourism point to the Grand Tour of the (primarily male) children of the British (for example, Turner and Ash 1976; Graburn 1977; Boyer 1982) aristocracy, which peaked between the late sixteenth and the late eighteenth centuries, as the immediate prototype or precursor of modern tourism. Interpreted as a direct descendant, a popularized version, of the former, this type of travel was putatively educational: It prepared the male children of good birth or fortune in the school of life, mainly for diplomatic service through the pleasurable instruction acquired by visiting foreign lands. As Francis Bacon suggests in his essay, "Of Travel," placed suggestively between his treatises "Of

Superstition" and "Of Empire," "travel, in the young sort, is a part of education, in the elder, a part of experience" (n.d.:71). The itinerary for a typical British Grand Tour involved about three years of a leisurely voyage with the ultimate destination in central Italy, most often Rome. The only variation was whether the Grand Tour traveler crossed or by-passed, either on the eastern or the western side, the Swiss and Austrian Alps on his way from England to Rome and back. Few British travelers missed Paris en route.

Contradicting the aristocratic depiction of the Grand Tour, John Towner (1985) presents evidence that Grand Tour participants were less recruited among the aristocrats or the rentiers (as in Boyer 1982:134) than the gentry and various commoner groups he calls the "professional middle classes" (1985:310). William Mead's assessment implies the predominance of the aristocratic component but allows that travelers from other backgrounds existed, suggesting that "those who traveled abroad belonged, as a rule, (. . .) to a picked class, and with their aristocratic temper, their wealth, and their insular characteristics, they presented, along with marked individual differences, a well-defined tourist type" (Mead 1972[1914]:3). Jeremy Black's circumspect defini-tion of the British Grand Tour—"the classic trip of wealthy, young men to France and Italy for several years"—implicitly allows for the inclusion of wealthy commoners (1985:Preface). For the 151 Grand Tours reconstructed from the period of 1547 through 1840, Towner has found that only 16.6% of the participants were members of the aristocracy or the landed classes proper although these classes represented 2.3–2.5% of the population and controlled 14.1–15.1% of the national income (1985:305–308). The rest—that is, 83.4%—of Grand Tour travelers were classified as gentry, clergy, professionals, merchants or members of the armed forces. These groups comprised 4.4–6.7% of the population and realized 13.1–17.4% of the national income (1985:305). From this, it follows that, although both aristocrats and wealthy commoners were obviously overrepresented among Grand Tour travelers, the latter were more overrepresented, in terms of number and income, than the landed classes. Towner's data also suggest a shift in the class composition of the British Grand Tour over time from the landed classes to commoners (1985:310). This shift implies, in turn, a gradual decline in the impor-tance of the educational element as a purpose of travel and supposedly an increase in the "influence of the general cultural environment on travel motives," manifested, Towner surmises, in generalized interest in the arts and sciences (1985:312).

A source from 1733 offers the following social register of Germans on the road: "guild-member artisans, merchants, certain scholars, soldiers, students on their way to the universities, young people of rank in search of political experience in the world, artists and virtuosi, official travelers and, finally, rulers" (Marperger, 1733 quoted by Martens 1986). (Gáldi [1957:139], containing the first written record of the current Hungarian equivalent word for tourist, *turista* in 1798, suggests a similar connection. Its context is the following: "Katona, Geographus, *Turista* s a' t. Tudosoknak," i.e., "soldiers, geographers, *tourists* and other scholars.")

The readership of German travel literature—a genre proliferating during the late eighteenth century—was, William Stewart points out, the "economically ambitious but politically frustrated" German bourgeoisie of the time (Stewart 1983:32). Lucette Desvignes (1988) offers a strikingly similar tally of travelers in the French region of Burgundy during the eighteenth century. Her list includes:

> messengers, merchants (. . .), men of letters, the clergy, diplomats and military personnel (. . .), students, travelers, the ailing who seek cure at medicinal waters or advice from famous physicians, those in search of adventures, gallant or otherwise, painters (. . .), financiers (. . .), men of the sciences wishing to understand and compare, enthusiasts of nascent industries, widowers and the unemployed (. . .), numerous foreigners (. . .), isolated individuals or entire families complete with chambermaids and servants, (. . .) intendants in charge of dispersed landholdings, and, most rarely, nobles visiting their lands (. . .) (Desvignes 1988:112).

As an important further corrective, Judith Adler (1985) argues that the elite Grand Tour was not necessarily the most important of the many historical precursors of contemporary leisure travel. She cites the tramping tradition—compulsory long-term international travel as part of craftsmen's training, called *tour de France* or *compagnonnage* in France and *Wanderjahr* or *Wanderpflicht* in Germany—as a widespread method of education, market control, and professional network building by guilds and other craftsmen's associations throughout Europe. (To be noted also is the etymology of the English word *journeyman* and the connection between the words travel and *travailler-trabajar* ("to work"). The German verb *trampen* survived and denoted hitch-hiking, a popular mode of youth travel during the 1960s.) This working-class travel system involved, in all likelihood, a greater number of participants and covered a broader geographical area than its elite counterpart (1985:337). Adler echoes claims by early French labor historians in suggesting that this tradition represented "one of the most powerful working class institutions ever developed in France" (1985:340).

Adler's objection reveals a serious shortcoming of a conceptualization exclusively focused on the Grand Tour to explain the emergence of leisure migration. Today's tourism comprises a very diverse set of activities. Virtually all the historical travel types—including the explorer and the pilgrim, the monk, the merchant, the student, the refugee, the missionary, the hermit, the water and mountain cure seeker or on the more sinister side, the smuggler and even the conqueror with his Golden

Hordes—can be shown to correspond, in some way, to various facets of contemporary tourism (Cohen 1972; Turner and Ash 1976). Singling out the (British male) aristocracy as the only source of worldwide cultural patterns regarding contemporary travel appears arbitrary. Retrospective search for cultural-historical prototypes thus loses utility in explaining the origins of tourism because it is too fruitful.

Evidence concerning the social composition of the English Grand Tour, eighteenth-century travel by Germans, travel in Burgundy, and the tradition of tramping, suggests that the one-to-one association of the aristocracy with early tourism—and its corollary, the assumption of a simple, unilinear descending cultural pattern of leisure travel—is empirically untenable. Even these early and rudimentary forms of what can be regarded at least partly touristic social patterns of travel registered an important, even dominant, involvement of various groups of the emerging bourgeoisie and early craft organizations of direct producers— the two fundamental class components of industrial capitalism. This conceptualization of the class background of early travel allows for a more sensitive appraisal of the cultural patterns produced by the Grand Tour.

Technological change

The worldwide spread of contemporary international tourism has often been causally attributed to the industrial revolution, either as a direct effect, by pointing out how industrialization created the transportation-technological preconditions for massive travel, or indirectly, through the emergence of monied middle classes and greater productivity (Ritter 1966; Burkart and Medlik 1974; Graburn 1977; Cohen 1972). The latter brought out paid holidays which, in turn, met an assumed general human propensity to travel (Nash 1977).

The existence of the obvious direct connection between industrialization (especially that of transport) and massive international leisure travel is difficult to deny: In order for travel to take massive proportions, a certain set of technological inventions in transportation had to have been put to use. However, insisting on a simple, direct causal link between the dynamics of technological development and tourism, without considering the wider economic and social embeddedness of both of these as social facts, would be very suspect. Such a perspective could present the industrial revolution as an independent variable whose geographically uneven spread is considered given and unproblematic. This would, in turn, preclude advancing theories of leisure migration in connection with the uneven development of capitalism. Any explanation of leisure migration solely on the basis of technological change would render it

impossible to ask the question why, at commensurate levels of industrialization, the structural conditions and effects of leisure migration are often
so diverse in international and interregional comparison. The industrial
revolution is an explanation, but it is, clearly, only a partial one.
Understanding the emergence of international leisure migration
requires attention to the context within which large-scale technological
change took place.

Industrial capitalism

The emergence of tourism as we know it presupposes, beyond the
spectacular development of transportation technology and increased
technological productivity in general, the transfer of a certain amount
of surplus value to wages spent on such types of nonessential consumption as leisure travel. Beyond the quantitative availability of time not
absorbed by labor activities, or, free time, tourism also presupposes that
free time be regulated and packaged in weekly and annual blocks. The
partial transfer of surplus value for leisure spending beyond the simple
reproduction of labor and the enactment of related legislation was, of
course, far from trivial or automatic: A primary focus of working class
struggles in the mid-nineteenth to early-twentieth centuries was precisely
the issue of the reduction and regulation of labor time, that is, rephrased
from our point of view, struggle for the provision of ample free time to
be expended on leisure activities. The standardization, normalization,
and commercialization of free time is one of the most obvious outcomes
of this struggle. Thus, industrial capitalism is a key factor in the
emergence of the institution of leisure migration.

  The penetration of leisure migration presupposes the availability of
the services and infrastructure used for commercialized travel. That
requires a certain level of surplus in the society at the destination, so that
labor and infrastructural resources can be devoted to the service of
foreigners and the transformation of social structures into ones capable
of and willing to accommodate a primarily commercial flow of
strangers. This change can be rife with tensions similar to those marking
the transition to regulated leisure time in societies generating the outflow
of tourists. The penetration and extended presence of commercial
leisure flows, in turn, reinforces these tendencies of social change and
transforms societies receiving tourists by setting off a cycle of commercialization, standardization, and normalization often described in the
literature on the sociocultural effects of tourism development on local
communities (for example, Pi-Sunyer 1977; Meleghy, Preglau and
Tafertshofer 1985). These considerations point far beyond the question
of technological change *per se*.

As noted earlier, a singular characteristic of leisure migration in all human flows is the existence of a transnational *tourism industry*: a branch of the service economy specialized in creating and satisfying demand for leisure travel. International tourism applies the principle of mobility across state borders to the realm of leisure. Global capitalism is an increasingly densely organized web of complex linkages made up of contacts and flows of commodities, money, capital, information and people; the tourism industry combines all of these in providing leisure services to traveling customers.

Surely, there has been considerable variation in the degree to which various historical or contemporary types of travel have utilized the processed products offered by the tourism industry. (See the discussion of Cohen 1984; Boorstin 1961; and MacCannell 1976 in *chapter 1*.) However, due to the highly capital-intensive nature of transportation, it has been clearly impossible to elude completely the services of the tourism industry. Every instance of the tourist experience is composed through the interaction of tourists, hosts and the tourism industry.

What is qualitatively new about leisure migration is its implanted position in the increasingly encompassing social process of capital accumulation that marked the emergence of industrial capitalism. This contextual aspect sets leisure migration apart from various precapitalist types of travel. Although leisure migration is obviously a form of travel (and travel has certainly been observed throughout history), it is a specific form of travel, with international structures and dynamics systematically rooted in, and inextricably intertwined with, those of an increasingly internationalized industrial capitalism.

A corollary of this conceptualization is that emerging patterns of international leisure migration should be related, in some systematic fashion, to those of emerging industrial capitalism. This chapter explores that relationship by examining whether patterns of uneven development can be detected in early international leisure migration. If so, it compares those patterns with the uneven industrial development across the continent of the capitalist world system by contrasting the spread of tourism over social space and time (as reconstructed from discursive representations of leisure migration) with economic and historical material concerning patterns of industrial capitalism in Europe.

Touristic Discourse of (Under)Development

Leisure travel produces a large body of popular discourse applied to comparative and international (under)development. This chapter examines quantitative evidence concerning two forms of popular discourse in tourism. (To be sure, this study of discursive practices related to early leisure migration involves two distinct fields of discourse. The guidebook survey pertains to what is called in Saussurian linguistics *parole*, that is, it observes recorded forms of a set of actual utterances by members of the speech community—while the overview of the dynamics of vocabulary change concerns the field of *langue*, that is, it observes sets of lexical elements and the rules pertaining to their usage. This distinction would have profound consequences in a linguistic study. For this analysis, however, those concerns are of little relevance as both discursive aspects are used here as indicators of social processes.)

From the tourists' point of view, we scrutinize differential representations of foreign lands as tourist attractions in guidebooks conceived as printed schemata of travel destinations and aimed to provide comprehensive pictures of the European continent for outside tourists. (It is important methodologically that the guidebooks be from outside Europe: The main interest of this inquiry is the relative weight attached to various parts of the continent which would be inevitably distorted by the inside European perspective, say, of German or French guidebooks. It would be nearly impossible to control for the magnitude and direction of this bias. As soon as outside origin is made a criterion of inclusion in the study, the focus is immediately on North American guidebooks. The reason for this is the very social composition of nineteenth-century tourism of non-Europeans in Europe, which is reinforced by the difficulties of locating such guidebooks published elsewhere. The North American focus may cause a certain, apparently unavoidable bias in favor of Britain, the only English-speaking country of Europe. An additional methodological requirement for selection is that the guidebooks must claim to describe the entire continent of Europe. This claim makes them directly comparable to each other and allows for controlling them for the size of the various country units included in their description.)

This chapter explores, from the perspective of the host society, the differential dynamics of the emergence and solidification of terms for strangers as commercialized leisure travelers—the conceptual equivalents of the English terms *tourist, tourism* and *touristic*—in the historical vocabularies of the European languages. The lexicohistorical segment of this study aims to provide a temporal map of the transition to standardized, normalized, and commercialized patterns of leisure travel as reflected in the conceptual sets of host societies by tracing the spread over time of the first written records of the appropriate lexical units. Oriol Pi-Sunyer observes that "if tourism commoditicizes culture, natives categorize strangers as a resource or a nuisance rather than as people" (1977:155). This study aims to capture this moment of change by considering the appearance of the conceptual equivalents of 'tourist,' 'tourism,' and 'touristic' as replacements of 'traveler' and 'travel,' to mark this transition. (The following linguistic markings are used: Simple quotation marks (e.g., 'tourist') stand for denotations; italicized characters (e.g., *turista*) symbolize signifiers.)

The date of the first written record of a given word with the appropriate denotation is used to indicate the point in time at which that particular lexical element was fixed in the given language.

This approach assumes that the relationship between spoken and written aspects of speech is constant across various European languages during the period under study. That assumption is of course violated in the case of some languages which developed their scripts during the period spanned by this study. Linguistic-historical information, as perhaps all others in this study, should be taken with a modicum of caution: Lexicographic data are always very approximate, usually late and subject to disputes. The author hopes that potential problems with the reliability of the data will not misorient the conclusions to be drawn from them. To this end, the analysis will concentrate on the relative approximate timing of these records by grouping the time datapoints into three large categories. This methodology does not assume equivalence in terms of the relative openness of the various languages to lexical borrowing. What is investigated is not the loan word equivalents of the English words *tourist*, *tourism*, and *touristic* (which may or may not exist in any other language at all), but the first written record of the semantic equivalent of these concepts—'tourist,' 'tourism,' and 'touristic'—created either through borrowing or any other process of lexical change.

This guidebook survey will reconstruct the mental maps of Europe as a hierarchically structured, complex sociogeographical unit presented to outside tourists as a system of destinations. These representations are assumed to have been composed through a series of comparative editorial decisions assigning differential weights of importance and attractivity for specific regions and localities as components of the whole. The content analysis presented here is aimed to elucidate the systematic patterns, if any, of those decisions. The diachronic overview of lexical reflection on international tourism in Europe utilizes material from the very beginning of the nineteenth century through recent times. The study of guidebooks concentrates on publications dated between 1870 and 1925.

Direct descriptive data on international tourist travel are scarcely available for this early period. International tourist information, accommodation and ticket reservation networks, travel-related banking services, and state-imposed control, surveillance and recording procedures concerning foreigners and their travel documents—the main sources of secondary data on international tourism today—existed, at best, only in very rudimentary forms at the time. Even if they were widely available, focus on early travel agency records would pose serious data reliability problems. Much of early tourist travel took place outside the scope of travel agencies. The evaluation of individual travel agency records would also pose complex problems of national and class bias. Statistical reporting conventions about temporary, leisure-oriented travel was not consolidated until well into the twentieth century even in those states most exposed to incoming flows. It was not, however, until as recently as the early 1960s that basic definitions concerning international tourism statistics, including those of the tourist as opposed to sojourner, and so forth, were established (IUOTO 1963; Leiper 1979). Inquiry into the emergence and solidification of structures of international leisure migration is compelled to rely on one or another form of indirect information.

This analysis will, thus, take a rather complex approach. It will not aim to examine directly the dynamics of early travel. Instead, it seeks to infer about the uneven development of leisure migration by exploring discursive practices in and concerning international tourism. The discursive field of international tourism thus reconstructed is then contrasted with structural features of industrial capitalism's uneven development in the nineteenth and twentieth centuries.

The role of print, especially printed books, in standardizing language and other cultural practices, normalizing intellectual life, and commercializing society in general, is a commonplace observation on the history of capitalism. Elizabeth Eisenstein (1968), for instance, describes the main impact of printing on society as "consolidation" (1968:20), "fixity" (1968:21), and the "amplification" and "reinforcement (. . .) of persistent stereotypes" (1968:27). The inquiry here studies a specific genre of printed books: those written and published with the explicit purpose of standardizing, normalizing and commercializing travel behavior. The guidebook is the printed medium of leisure migration. Aldous Huxley succinctly summarizes this fundamental aspect of the genre by exclaiming about Karl Baedeker, the editor and publisher of the famous German guidebook series:

> Imbecile! But a learned, and, alas, indispensable imbecile. There is no escape; one must travel in his company—at any rate on a first journey (Huxley 1925:44–5).

Mental Maps of Europe, 1870–1925

Guidebooks

Appleton's European Guide Book Illustrated was published simultaneously in New York and in London in 1870. This single portable volume, as outlined in the Preface, was meant as a comprehensive yet impartially selective source of references containing:

all the information necessary to enable the tourist to find his way without difficulty from place to place, and to see the objects best worth seeing, throughout such parts of Europe as are generally visited by American and English travelers. [The author] has endeavoured to give concise and reliable information in relation to all objects which, by common consent, are best worth a visit—giving fewer details in relation to matters of inferior or secondary interest (1870:5).

The text is based largely on the author's *bona-fide* travel experiences, supplemented by a long list of readings in English, French, and German, including such guidebook series as *Black's Guides*, *Baedekers* and *Les Guides Joanne*, along with individual works on Ireland, Britain, the Low Countries, the Alps, Switzerland, Germany, the Rhine, Italy, Spain and Portugal. The material is organized into chapters on each country. There are, however, telling discrepancies: The book includes chapters for Germany and Italy which were not yet established as unified, self-contained states at the time of the book's publication. Meanwhile, it ignores, for instance, the Austro-Hungarian Dual Monarchy as an independent entity, subsuming it under the heading of "Germany." Each such chapter is made up of a short section of general practical information followed by a series of routes. The book as a whole offers 165 such routes in fourteen countries. For each route, it provides the distance in increments of one-quarter-miles and the fares for first- and second-class railway, coach, or boat tickets in British currency.

The imaginary itinerary of the guidebook proceeds from the west towards the east of the continent. It embarks on the British Isles, advances to France, the Low Countries and what it calls Germany, makes a detour to the Latin Mediterranean, then concludes with Russia and a summary chapter on Denmark, Sweden, and Norway. The description of the routes is preceded by a chapter introducing the traveler to such practical aspects of leisure travel in Europe as how to procure American and British passports, estimate expenses, and transfer funds. The guidebook also provides useful information on baggages, customs, couriers (that is, traveling servants), railway traveling, hotels, local guides called "valets de place," and a brief reminder that different languages are to be encountered during the trip.

A Satchel Guide for the Vacation Tourist in Europe (1877, 1889, 1895, 1908, 1912, 1924, and 1925) a very popular guidebook series, was periodically revised. The first volume was published, according to the preface to revised edition of 1889, "seventeen years" earlier in 1872. The use of the term "vacation tourist" indicates a clear touristic orientation. The author of the preface to the first edition defines the vacation tourist as a traveler "who can spend but three or four months abroad" (1889:v). For the benefit of those with even less time at hand, the book includes a brief section with trips of three-to-four weeks duration. The *Satchel Guide* is

34   *Leisure Migration: A Sociological Study on Tourism*

not intended "for those who take a year or more for the tour" (1889:v) but for the "pedestrian" for whom cost may be a consideration. The author claims to have tried "most of the 'tramps' [*sic*] he recommends— as well as some that he advises the reader *not* to attempt" (1889:vi). No written sources are acknowledged.

Like *Appleton's*, the *Satchel Guide*'s routes are organized into chapters by country. Its novelty is that the individual routes connect to each other in a chain-like fashion, offering the impression that the book is the description—or, given the genre, prescription—of a single monumental trip across the old continent. The sections on practical travel advice about preparation and useful tips during the journey are longer than *Appleton's* but cover only ten European countries. Again, short trips to destinations whose countries are judged not to merit individual chapters are often presented as part of chapters for other countries. The itinerary of the series replicates *Appleton's* movement from west to east, except that the *Satchel Guide* does not include Nordic destinations until as late as its 1925 volume and consistently ignores Russia, Serbia, and Romania. Its journey towards the east also stops with Austria–Hungary (called, here, "Austria") and Italy.

Mental maps

The quantitative details of the guidebooks' mental maps which distinguish the countries "best worth a visit" on the European continent are indicated in Table 2.1. (Appendix 2 describes the exact procedure.) *Appleton's* offers the most comprehensive assessment of the continent; the representations in the *Satchel Guide*'s various editions cover a somewhat narrower scope. Its internal proportions remain practically unchanged until after World War I, and the editions appearing from 1889 through 1908 are in fact literally identical. In *Appleton's* (1870), Great Britain (the sum of the percentages for England, Wales, and Scotland) dominate the scores. Between 1877 and World War I, Britain and Italy are equally favored as the most desired destination countries. Each occupies between one-fifth and one-third of the space of representation in the guidebook. By 1924, however, Britain clearly loses out to Italy in terms of importance and attractivity, so that the space received by the latter in the guidebook suddenly increases to more than 150% of Britain's. By this measure, the *Satchel Guides* suggest that countries on the European perimeter, such as Russia, various European parts of the Ottoman Empire, and even Scandinavia, play an explicitly subordinate role in European tourism.

The data in Table 2.1 reflect the absolute weight of the countries of Europe in the eye of the outside beholder. Given the unequal size of the

Table 2.1. Mental Maps of Europe, 1870–1925: Representations in Tourist Guidebooks[a]

Countries	1870 pp[b]	%[c]	1877 pp	%	1889–1908 pp	%	1912 pp	%	1924 pp	%	1925 pp	%
British												
Possessions	175	26.6	85	28.6	72	30.1	78	30.2	101	22.0	98	19.6
Great Britain	148	22.5	75	25.3	65	27.2	70	30.2	93	20.2	90	18.0
Ireland proper	27	4.1	10	3.4	7	2.9	8	3.1	8	1.7	8	1.6
Belgium	15	2.3	8	2.7	6	2.5	7	2.7	23	5.0	23	4.6
Netherlands	11	1.7	4	1.3	4	1.7	4	1.6	12	2.6	12	2.4
Germany	83	12.6	40	13.5	28	11.7	29	11.2	55	12.0	55	11.0
Switzerland	53	8.0	28	9.4	27	11.3	29	11.2	35	7.6	35	7.0
France	115	17.5	28	9.4	23	9.6	24	9.3	62	13.5	62	12.4
Austrian												
Possessions	24	3.6	16	5.6	14	5.9	16	6.2				
Austria proper	12	1.8	14	4.7	12	5.0	14	5.4	17	3.7	17	3.4
Hungary proper	2	0.3	1	0.3	1	0.4	1	0.4	4	0.9	4	0.8
Bohemia proper	10	1.5	1	0.3	1	0.4	1	0.4				
Czechoslovakia									2	0.4	2	0.4
Italy	120	18.2	88	29.6	65	27.2	71	27.5	149	32.4	115	23.0
Sweden	5	0.8									30	6.0
Norway	4	0.6									33	6.6
Denmark	3	0.5									13	2.6
Spain	34	5.2										
Portugal	4	0.6										
Greece												
Serbia												
Russia	12	1.8										
Finland												
Bulgaria												
Poland proper	1	0.2										
Romania												
Total	659		297		239		258		460		499	

[a]Excludes Andorra, Liechtenstein, Iceland, Monaco, San Marino, and the Vatican.
[b]Number of pages.
[c]Percent of total descriptive pages in book.
Sources: Information in the *Appleton's* and *Satchel* guidebooks cited in the bibliography.

destination countries, more precise measures of their relative weight can be obtained by controlling for their size. Table 2.2 contains the same data but controls them for the population size of the respective destination areas. With its overrepresentation between relative weight rated between 8.8 and 14.1 times its actual weight, Switzerland is by far the most steadily appreciated destination of these guidebooks. The British possessions and Italy also occupy very favorable positions with scores between 2.2 and 4.3, even in terms of these controlled measures. Only Austria proper matches Italy's and Great Britain's relative attractivity until World War I. France and Germany loom around the mark of fair representation. The *Satchel Guide*'s 1925 edition appears to have been

Table 2.2. Mental Maps of Europe, 1870–1925: Representations Controlled for Population Size[a]

Countries	Guidebook edition/Population estimate						
	1870[b]/ 1880	1877/ 1880	1889/ 1890	1908[c]/ 1910	1912/ 1910	1924/ 1920	1925/ 1920
British Possessions Great Britain[d] Ireland proper	3.1	3.3	3.5	3.2	3.2	2.4	2.2
Belgium	1.5	1.8	1.6	1.6	1.7	3.1	3.3
Netherlands	1.6	1.2	1.5	1.3	1.2	1.9	1.7
Germany	1.1	1.2	1.0	0.9	0.9	0.9	0.9
Switzerland	10.3	12.1	16.1	14.1	14.0	9.5	8.8
France	1.6	0.9	0.9	1.1	1.0	1.7	1.6
Austrian Possessions	0.3	0.5	0.6	0.5	0.6		
Austria proper	1.3	3.4	3.6	3.3	3.6	2.8	2.6
Hungary proper	0.2	0.2	0.3	0.2	0.2	0.3	0.3
Bohemia proper	1.1	0.2	0.3	0.3	0.3		
Czechoslovakia					0.3	0.3	
Italy	2.2	3.6	3.4	3.4	3.4	4.3	3.0
Sweden	0.6						5.0
Norway	1.2						13.2
Denmark	0.8						3.7
Spain	1.1						
Portugal	0.5						
Greece							
Serbia							
Russia	0.02						
Finland							
Bulgaria							
Poland	0.07						
Romania							

[a]Excludes Andorra, Liechtenstein, Iceland, Monaco, San Marino, and the Vatican.
[b]First date is publication date for guidebook and second date is population estimate.
[c]See Figure 2.4, which provides a visual presentation based on the data for 1908 in this table.
[d]No separate population estimates could be secured.
Sources: Information in the *Appleton's* and *Satchel* guidebooks cited in the bibliography.

upgraded for more attention to the Nordic countries, boosting the overrepresentation of Norway, for instance, above the mark of thirteen times its actual weight.

The lower half of Table 2.2 contains equally important information. It indicates the underrepresentation or complete absence of at least half of the continent's countries and surely more than half of its population— a strong piece of evidence concerning the inherent unevenness of the development of international leisure migration in Europe, important points for our argument. It will be useful to observe this on Maps 2.1 and 2.2 which relay much of the findings of Table 2.2 in a visually more perceptible form.

The master map used for these maps indicates, for easier reference, state boundaries as of 1988. For the maps, the results of Table 2.2 were recoded into the following three categories: first, obviously overrepresented areas in which the controlled representation values assigned were more than twice as much weight as warranted by the size of those areas (i.e., $x > 2$); second, more or less fairly represented areas in which the controlled representation values assigned were between half and twice as much weight as the size of the areas involved (i.e., $.5 \leq x \leq 2$); and, third, obviously underrepresented areas in which the controlled representation values assigned were less than half of their "true" weight ($x < .5$).

Map 2.1 reflects *Appleton's* mental map of Europe. It favors clearly two contiguous destination areas: the British Isles and the block of Switzerland and Italy. The fairly represented area extends to much of the territory between these two along with the Iberian and the Scandinavian peninsulas. The continent is split almost exactly along its north and south line of gravity—the border between today's Sweden and Finland, Germany and Poland, Bohemia and Slovakia, Austria and Hungary and, finally, Italy, and Slovenia. East of that line, a large horizontally lined area denotes those countries either completely missing or represented less than half of their "true" weight. As far as *Appleton's* is concerned, touristic "objects best worth a visit" (1870:v) are found in the western half of the continent, while those of "inferior or secondary interest" (1870:v) are located towards the east.

Map 2.2 extends a similar value judgment by the editors of the *Satchel Guide's* editions between 1877 and 1912. Again, the British Isles, and Switzerland, Italy, and—from this time onwards—Austria proper, are the most valued tourist destinations. In the guide's editions in 1877 through 1912, however, fair representation is restricted roughly to the area connecting the two blocks—that is, France, the Low Countries, and Germany—and the rest of the continent is obviously ignored. The guide suggests that European international tourism is (or, given the genre of guide books, "should be") largely confined to a stripe approximately one

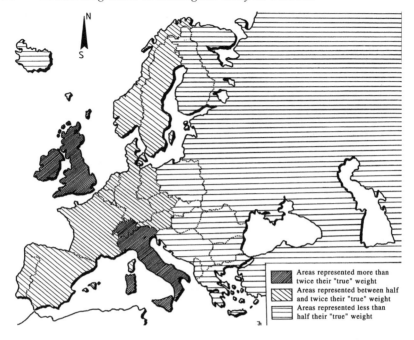

Map 2.1. Mental Map of Europe According to *Appleton* (1870)

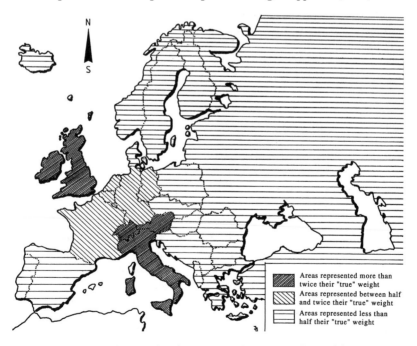

Map 2.2. Mental Map of Europe According to *Satchel* (1877–1912)

thousand miles wide crossing the continent between Britain and Italy from the northwest to the southeast, an area remarkably similar to that used for the typical itinerary of the British Grand Tour from two to three hundred years before.

The *Satchel Guide*'s 1924 edition differs from its predecessor only in two minor respects. Belgium is included among the countries overrepresented, thus expanding the contiguous area of overrepresentation, a development similar to what happened some thirty years earlier when Austria proper was added to the overrepresented area of Switzerland and Italy. Hungary is incorporated in the 1924 edition among those fairly represented. (The latter has to do, along with a minimal increase in the country's coverage in the *Satchel Guide*, with the secession of two-thirds of the country's population with the 1920 Trianon Peace Treaty. The change had reduced the population percentage used as the control factor in the computation.) Finally, the next edition of the *Satchel Guide* in 1925 is the same as the previous year's, except that Nordic destinations are included.

In summary, the above reconstructions of the mental maps of Europe in some early North American guidebooks indicate that the emergence of leisure migration implied interest in the continent that was far from evenly distributed. Switzerland, Italy, Austria proper, and the British Isles received by far most (altogether always more than 50%) of the attention of guidebooks while practically the entire eastern half of the continent was consistently ignored. Guidebook data suggest that *the emergence of international leisure travel in Europe has involved a very uneven spread from the very beginning, with Eastern Europe invariably placed in a disadvantaged position.*

Denoting the Tourist

Languages

This part of the study determines the approximate time when concepts pertaining to standardized and normalized, commercial travel emerged throughout Europe. As the emergence and spread of concepts cannot be studied directly, the dynamics of conceptual change will be reconstructed from evidence pertaining to the formation and establishment of an appropriate set of lexical elements: the dates of the first written records of the equivalents of the English words *tourist, tourism,* and *touristic*.

These English terms, derivatives of the French word *tour* (*mouvement circulaire*, [Larousse 1960]), go back to an ancient Greek root denoting "a tool used to describe a circle" (Leiper 1979:391). Leiper argues that the most likely adaptation in English from French, circular movement,

was then reinforced by usage such as the Grand Tour and was popularized by Daniel Defoe's famous travel account entitled *A Tour Through
the Whole Island of Britain* (Leiper 1983:278).

All European languages for which information has been secured,
record a French-based loan word variant to denote the equivalents of
the terms 'tourist' and 'tourism.' (Equivalents of 'touristic' are missing
in Danish, Finnish, Irish, Lappish, Latvian, and Magyar, as these languages do not allow the simple adjectival form of that particular loan
word.) *Tourist*, *tourism*, and *touristic* are international loan words—that is,
their transfer from one particular language to another cannot be
unambiguously reconstructed by using linguistic-historical methods.
(These three words share this feature with such international loan words
in the popular culture of mass communication technology as telephone,
radio, television, computer, etc.)

Resistance to foreign linguistic influences, a key instrument in the
creation of national identities and hence an important feature of
nineteenth-century linguistic nationalism, often implied the invention of
indigenous alternatives to the acceptance of international loan words. In
German, an alternative to borrowing a French-based word in the pattern
of *tourism* (but not to *tourist*) was devised in the form of the word
Fremdenverkehr (literally, stranger[s]' travel). To be sure, the emergence
of this term did not wipe out *Tourismus* and *Touristik*, the originally
French-based international loan words, even from German. It is a somewhat ironical indication of the power of leisure migration's international
sweep that, although the term Fremdenverkehr emerged originally as
national alternative, it came in turn to be the subject of further foreign
adaptation itself: Several other national alternatives have been created
by imitating the German original.

Three Indo-Germanic languages—Danish, Dutch, and Norwegian—
along with (Finno-Ugric) Magyar, which all reflect various forms of
German political and cultural influence and direct contact with the
predominantly German-speaking area of the continent, have produced
their own versions of Fremdenverkehr by inventing its literal mirror
translations or calques. Of these, the Danish and Norwegian versions are
now considered obsolete, but the original German term and its equivalent in Dutch and in Magyar are still in use. For instance, the national
offices for tourism in Austria, the Netherlands and Hungary used this
equivalent in their names until recently. (Those names were, in 1989,
for Austria, Österreichische Fremdenverkehrswerbung, for the Netherlands, Vereniging voor Vreemdelingenverkeer, and, for Hungary,
Országos Idegenforgalmi Hivatal. The Austrian institution has since
been renamed Österreich Werbung.)

German and Magyar are, incidentally, in complete stylistic parallel in
terms of their usage of the available synonyms: The German word

Fremdenverkehr and its Magyar equivalent, *idegenforgalom*, are the preferred variants by officialdom and business. Both the German word *Touristik* and the Magyar's *turisztika* refer to the athletic-oriented aspects of leisure travel, such as hiking, trekking, bicycling, and so forth; while the German's *Tourismus* and Magyar's *turizmus* denote the phenomenon of leisure migration in an abstract sense. (*Turisztika* and *turizmus* are, obviously, loan words rather than calques in Hungarian.)

Timing of words

As Table 2.3 indicates, the equivalents of concepts related to leisure migration took more than 150 years to spread across the continent. The 'tourist' first appears in French in 1793 (Desvignes 1988:115) and in English in 1800, while its appearance in Serbo-Croatian, Ukrainian, and Turkish is estimated around the late 1950s. The material included in Table 2.3 is important sociolinguistic evidence concerning the dynamics of tourism's uneven development in Europe.

A general tendency reflected in Table 2.3 is movement from the concrete towards the abstract: Words denoting the 'tourist'—the most concrete element of leisure migration—tend to precede the more abstract concepts of 'tourism' and 'touristic.' (Two exceptions from this tendency are Swedish, in which the denotation 'tourism' appears to precede that of tourist by forty-nine years and Ukrainian, in which it precedes by a single-year difference.) The lag in time between the first written record of the denotation 'tourist' and that of 'tourism' is as much as eighty-five years in Danish, seventy-three years in Romanian, and sixty-four years in Dutch. This lag between the concrete and abstract aspects could be considered the period of solidification of concepts related to tourism.

The earliest first written records of 'tourism,' dispersed during the first half of the 1800s, are followed by a cluster of languages between the late 1870s and the turn of the century. There is another cluster during the interwar period, and the queue ends with the real late-comers after World War II. The distributions of the equivalent words for 'tourism' and 'touristic' differ from the pattern of the 'tourist.' The earliest written records (as in English, French, and German) are spread across a range of twenty to thirty years (approximately 1810 through 1840 for 'tourism' and 1845 through 1865 for 'touristic'), but the rest are quite evenly distributed over the entire twentieth century.

Map 2.3 is a visually more perceptible reproduction of the information contained in the first column of Table 2.3, and allows for a comparison with the guidebooks' mental maps above. This map displays the times in which the first written records of the equivalents for the term

Table 2.3. Years the Equivalents of Tourist, Tourism, and Touristic Were First Recorded[a] in European Languages[b]

	Tourist	Tourism	Touristic
Albanian	ca 1920	ca 1920	ca 1920
Armenian	b/f 1945	b/f 1945	b/f 1945
Basque			
Byelorussian	b/f 1928	b/f 1928	b/f 1928
Bulgarian			
Catalan	1970	1970	1970
Czech	1847	1864	1861
Danish	1824	1909	N.A.
Dutch	1847	1911	
English	1800	1811	1848
Estonian			
Finnish	1890	1917	N.A.
French	1793	1841	1846
Georgian	aft 1930	aft 1930	aft 1930
German	1834	1840	1865
Greek	b/f 1930	b/f 1930	b/f 1930
Icelandic			
Irish	1884	1922	N.A.
Italian	1877	1905	1904
Lapp			
Latvian	1886	ca 1920	N.A.
Lithuanian	1929		
Macedonian			
Magyar	1851	1886	N.A.
Norwegian	b/f 1892	b/f 1934	b/f 1947
Polish	1899	1922	1938
Portuguese	1885	1924	1939?
Romanian	1879	1952	1952
Russian	1897	1937	1940
Serbo-Croatian	b/f 1958		
Slovak	1894		
Slovene	1929	1929	1934
Spanish (Cast.)	b/f 1960	b/f 1960	b/f 1960
Swedish	1934	1885	1884
Turkish	b/f 1959	b/f 1959	b/f 1959
Ukrainian	1956	1955	1960
Welsh	1932	1964	1932

[a]For languages with more than one equivalent (e.g., German where Tourismus, Touristik, and Fremdenverkehr correspond to particular aspects of 'tourism'), the year of the first written record is included. Blank spaces indicate missing data. N.A. indicates a missing equivalent in the given language.

[b]See Figure 2.3 for a visual reproduction of the information contained in the first column of this table.

Sources: Dictionaries listed in the bibliography and research correspondence listed in the appendix.

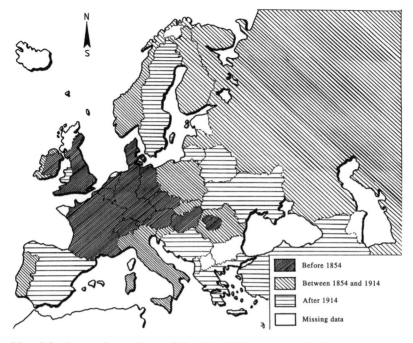

Map 2.3. Approximate Date of the First Written Record of the 'Tourist' in European Languages

'tourist' in the national languages of the continent. French, English, German, Dutch, Danish, Czech, and Magyar appear in the area marking the earliest records of the 'tourist.' At the other extreme, there are fourteen languages, ranging from Albanian to Welsh and from Finnish to Turkish, for which the first records of the equivalent of the 'tourist' are documented only for the period after World War I. East-central Europe appears to be under a recognizable impact associated with Austrian rule (and a concomitant influence by German): Czech, Magyar, Slovak, and Romanian register earlier records than their neighbors dominated by non-Austrians.

If we regroup the first written records of the equivalents of 'tourism' using the same cut-off points as in Map 2.3, we find only English, French and German in the earliest category, while the area of the first written records after World War I includes as many as nineteen languages. As to the timing of the representation of 'touristic,' the area of earliest written records is reduced to those of English and French. The area represented by records of first use in Swedish, German, Czech, and Italian constitutes a nearly perfect straight north–south line of first records between 1854 and 1914 splitting the continent in two halves. In the rest of the continent, the adjective 'touristic' was not recorded until after World War I.

The historical-sociolinguistic distribution of the three concepts related to tourism are variations on essentially the same theme. They convey a sense of the following temporal sequence: Equivalents of all of the concepts emerged first among speakers of French, English, and German—that is, in the area of today's France, Switzerland, Southern Belgium, England, Germany, and Austria. On the other extreme, the first written records of concepts related to tourism apparently did not reach into the Albanian, Byelorussian, Catalan and Castillian Spanish, Greek, Turkish, Serbo-Croatian, and Ukrainian languages until as late as World War I. The most concrete concept—the term for 'tourist'—traveled rather fast: It reached the Netherlands, Denmark, Bohemia, and Hungary well before the cut-off of 1854, and extended to several Slavic- and Latin-speaking areas (and Norway) before World War I. Equivalents of the two more abstract concepts appear consistently later, hence pushing a number of languages into the category of latecomers.

The temporal distinctions reflected in the language distributions suggest a spatial core-periphery structure: The earliest records are concentrated in a contiguous area on the west-central part of the mainland and the British Isles, while the latest arrivals are more or less towards the fringes. Inconsistency is found, typically, in the middle area. *The spread of concepts denoting leisure migration reflects a very uneven distribution suggesting spatial concentration with its center on the west-central mainland and England.*

Tourism and Capitalism

Mental maps and conceptual maps

The two sets of distributions in space and time, examined so far—the early tourists' mental maps of Europe and the reconstructions of the spread of words denoting 'tourists' and 'tourism'—are by no means identical. However, important points of similarity do merit attention. First, on the positive end of the distributions, the contiguous area connecting England with the continent's west-central mainland (including France, the Low Countries, Germany, Switzerland, and Austria proper) is privileged as a destination area and the region that marks the earliest development of concepts pertaining to leisure migration. In sharp contrast, the vast stretch of land east of the continent's north–south dividing line reflects unmistakable signs of touristic neglect and belatedness. A comparison of the two sets of distributions suggests that the uneven development of leisure migration has had two important features: England and west-central Europe enjoyed an advantaged, forerunner position, and the eastern portion of the continent suffered a consistently disadvantaged, latecomer status.

The only conspicuous inconsistency between the guidebooks' mental maps and the sociolinguistic dynamics of destination societies concerns Italy: Its attractiveness scores indicate a greater degree of inclusion in the international flow of leisure migration than was reflected in the speed at which concepts related to tourism had appeared in the language. A possible explanation would be to connect this result with Italy's peculiar touristic prehistory, which suggests its privileged destination status for the British Grand Tour. In this sense it appears tenable that the British Grand Tour had made a cultural impact on the destination choices of early British and North American tourists. This effect may have been reinforced by the spread of classical education highlighting Italy's past. A turn-of-the-century American source reflects the significance of Italy as a focal point of reference in the history of western civilization: "it will suffice to say (. . .) that Italy is *the goal*; and that, after Italy, you will understand everything else by the light of what you have learned in 'the cities of the soul'—Venice, Rome and Florence" (Allen 1899:33). The relatively belated appearance of the concept of the tourist in Italian could be explained as a result of the several centuries long, ceaseless inflows of Grand Tour travelers with Italy as their destination. It is conceivable that the transition from travel to tourism was not as clearly perceptible and dramatic in Italian as in other languages due to Italy's history of continued exposure to foreigners. This could have resulted in a slight delay in the emergence of separate terms for the 'tourist,' 'tourism,' and 'touristic.'

Uneven development: tourism and industrial capitalism

Thus far, this study has detected patterns of uneven development in the differential spread of leisure migration across Europe. This section compares those patterns to the spatiotemporal paradigm of the development of industrial capitalism to examine whether isomorphy can be demonstrated between the two.

Figure 2.1 plots the relative representation of individual countries in the *Satchel Guide*'s 1908 edition (note the use of data from the 1908 column in Table 2.2) by Bairoch's estimates (1976) of the per capita industrial production of various European countries expressed as percentages of the European average. Although the relationship is not strictly linear, Figure 2.1 implies a systematic association between per capita industrial output and per capita representation in the form of a negative and a positive censoring effect: No country with an industrial output below 70% of the European mean made it into the guidebook,

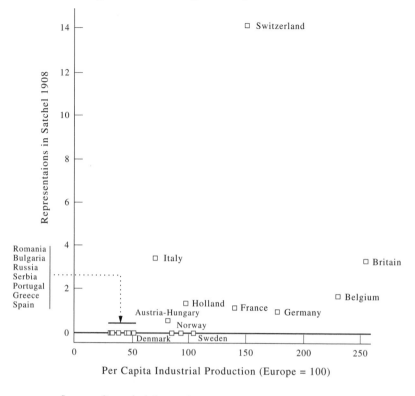

Sources: Own calculations and
Berend-Ránki, 1982:Table 7.2
quoting Bairoch 1976.

**Figure 2.1. Country Representations in Satchel 1908 (controlled for Popul-
ation 1910) by Per Capita Industrial Production in 1900**

and all countries with an output higher than 104% of the average are at
least mentioned. Overappreciated Italy and Switzerland are outliers in
terms of the degree of the relationship. The three Scandinavian countries
with data points of zero representation in the middle zone around the
100% mark were eventually included in the *Satchel Guide* but not until
seventeen years later.

Figure 2.2 plots the absolute representations of countries in guidebooks between 1889 and 1908 (based on data from Table 2.1) by
Bairoch's estimates (1973:14) of the shares of individual countries in the
total of European exports. Most countries with exports of less than 3%
of the total and Russia are characteristically absent from the guidebooks.
Again, the relationship is positive, nonlinear, and the two main outliers,
Italy and Switzerland, are overappreciated.

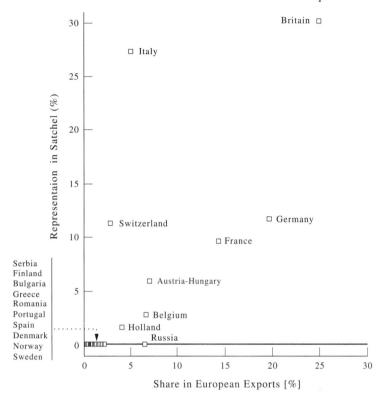

Figure 2.2. Country Representations in Satchel (1889–1908) by share of Countries in European Exports (1900)

An overview of the entire period of 1870 through 1912 suggests the remarkable stability of these patterns. Separate ordinary least square regression lines have been fitted to each of the guidebooks with different representation scores and their respective export-shares values: The slope of the four regression lines is practically identical. The correlation of the four consecutive datasets shows a slightly declining tendency. During the forty-two years under study, the correlation between guidebook representation and export-share values decreases from $r=.870$ (1870; 15 datapoints) through $r=.714$ (1877; 19) and $r=.709$ (1889–1908; 19) to $r=.663$ (1912; 19). This implies the presence of a nearly constant, positive relationship between shares in European exports and the degree to which individual countries have been represented touristically during the emergence of mass tourism in Europe. The strength of the relationship, however, appears to diminish slightly over time.

Arthur Schärli provides the following list of possible explanations for the record appreciation of Switzerland as a tourist destination country during the turn-of-the-century Belle Epoque of Swiss tourism: medicinal springs and baths; educational attractions (most markedly the University of Basel); Alpine nature and sport opportunities (Alpinism); the early development of Cantonal roads; lake steamboat shipping; festivals; travel writing by foreign authors, including Lord Byron, Cooper, Dickens, Daudet, Goethe, Michelet or Twain; favorable inclusion in Baedeker's guidebooks, Cook's organized package tours; and railroad development (Schärli 1984:6–11). All these factors, along with perhaps the popularity of mountain sanatoria in treating well-to-do patients with lung diseases, could have contributed to what Georg Simmel described as "the socialistic wholesale opening up of the Alps" (1991[1895]:95) and, in general, the emergence of Switzerland as a major destination country for tourism. These elements of attraction have certainly been reinforced by the country's location between the European centers of industrial-capitalist accumulation and Italy, the traditional Grand Tour destination.

In his book, *Cities and Economic Development* (1988), Paul Bairoch produces a table indicating the approximate time of the "take-off" of industrial capitalism, which he calls the "start of modern development," for several European countries and the United States. Figure 2.3 applies that table for this inquiry: It plots the first written record of the word tourist by Bairoch's "start of modern development." Again, the emerging, uneven structures of leisure migration and those of industrial capitalism show a strong positive association.

Evidence concerning the early spread of leisure migration in Europe reproduces structural patterns of the uneven development of industrial capitalism in two important respects: The earliest arrivals to industrial capitalism and consequently the most advanced industrial-capitalist societies tend to be those where tourism arrives first and takes the most massive proportions. In contrast, distinct latecomers in terms of capitalist-industrial development, especially in the continent's eastern part, show unmistakable signs of belated development in touristic terms as well. The findings concerning an underlying isomorphy between patterns of emerging leisure migration and industrial capitalism are not trivial: Commonplace images of nineteenth-century industrial capitalism could be taken to suggest that the spatial relationship between industry and leisure should be negative. An argument based exclusively on descending cultural patterns from the British aristocracy would have implied no association between the spatio-temporal patterns of leisure migration and industrial capitalism. The fact that some association has been found is an implicit refutation of that conceptualization as well. The positive geographical association is counterintuitive and should be taken very seriously.

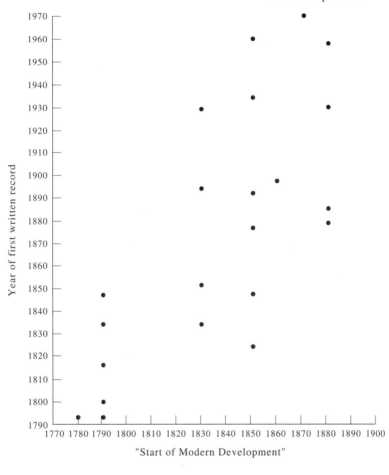

Sources: Own calculations
and Bairoch, 1988.

Figure 2.3. First Written Records of the 'Tourist' by "Start of Modern Development" (after Bairoch)

Travel-Capitalism

This chapter challenged the idea that contemporary tourism could be deduced as a popularized version of aristocratic patterns of travel. It has suggested that the notion of tourism as a transhistorical constant of human life is not very useful either. It has argued that, although the large-scale technological change of the European nineteenth century clearly does have to do with the emergence of mass tourism, the latter is hardly a simple consequence or effect of industrial development as an independent variable. The working thesis of this inquiry has been, instead, that the emergence of mass tourism is organically connected to the spread of industrial capitalism so that the production of tourists, hosts, and the commercial relationship between them, that is, the tourism industry, is a logical extension of the general principle of industrial capitalism to the realm of leisure. The findings indicate an underlying isomorphy between structures of emerging leisure migration and the uneven development of industrial capitalism. On this basis, it is possible to conclude this analysis by reconceptualizing tourism as travel-capitalism.

Building on Elizabeth Eisenstein's work on the impact of print, especially the mass production of books, on society (1968), Benedict Anderson introduces the concept of "print-capitalism" (1983:41–50) to address the direct, unmediated connection of ideological processes, technological change, and the structural transformation of the mode of production. The above study of the emergence of mass leisure migration in the context of industrial capitalism lends support to a similar conceptualization of leisure travel.

Industrial capitalism not only creates a need for massive flows of people away from their usual place of residence or work for leisure purposes, but it also creates its institutional frameworks, that is, the standardized, normalized, and commercial means necessary for the satisfaction of that need. Today, this process encircles practically all segments of advanced capitalist societies. Although class-based and national cultural patterns of leisure travel do vary, it would be difficult to restrict the conceptualization of leisure migration to certain cultures, the elites or the bourgeoisie. Partly an effect of working-class struggles for leisure, partly an outcome of the global tourism industry's marketing efficiency, large parts of the relatively deprived segments of advanced capitalist welfare societies engage regularly in leisure travel. As a result, the tourism industry is one of the biggest and fastest-growing sectors of today's world economy. The process also extends to those societies in which large groups cannot afford spending on leisure migration, let alone foreign travel. Ability to engage in leisure migration is often a potent marker of wealth and power in such contexts.

The conceptual relationship between leisure migration and earlier forms of travel for pleasure can be understood as structurally very similar to that between printing and previous forms of the production and distribution of knowledge. Tourism relates to earlier forms of travel for pleasure in the same way as printing, especially mass-produced book printing, has been the industrial-capitalist equivalent of the manuscript: An existing, small-scale, manufactural practice is taken over by the growth machine—the compelling logic of technological change and commercialization contained in the package of industrial capitalism. Printing and tourism represent but two aspects of a large-scale transformation in which complex institutional arrangements emerge as a result of the penetration of industrial capitalism into previously manufactural structures.

The essence of the tourism business is control over tourist experience and the flow of travel-related commodities, capital, and currencies and by managing the services for advertising, transportation, accommodation, attraction, and interpretation offered to traveling consumers on a commercial basis. Ultimately, the product marketed by the tourism industry is based on the very geographical, climatic, social, and cultural diversity of the global system itself. The transformation of global diversity into marketable product involves partial control by the tourism industry over the production and dissemination of the self-reflective images of global capitalism. In tourism, capitalism creates, sells, and buys its own images. These images are processed products which use the social distance between the tourist's context at home and the destination society as raw material. The processing of the tourist industry product involves the standardization, normalization, and commercialization of raw travel experience. As in the case of the messages, meanings, and knowledge transmitted through mass communication, the processing of tourist experience is also achieved by filtering through an institutional screen that Nelson Graburn calls the "environmental bubble" (1977). *The tourism industry is that branch of the mass media in which not only the message but the receiver is physically transported through the communicative channel.* Print, broadcast and travel media offer commercial ways in which curiosity— desire to know and be entertained—is satisfied. *Tourism is the leisure migration of industrial capitalism.*

Chapter 3

Comparative Tourism Growth: Austria and Hungary, 1870–1988

István Deák's fascinating monograph about the officers' corps of the Habsburg army describes various parts of the Austro-Hungarian Monarchy as a destination from the viewpoint of the often-relocated military personnel as follows:

> Up until 1859, a large part of the armed forces was stationed in northern Italy and in the monarchy's central Italian client states. (. . .) For the officers, [Italy] was a delightful place; it was clean and civilized, with a friendly population (. . .). The Alpine provinces and the Czech lands were likewise favorites (. . .). The best place was, of course, Vienna (. . .). Metternich's dictum that Asia began just east of Vienna was a view widely shared by the Habsburg officers. They found the hotels and inns in Hungary infested with bedbugs, the roads abominable, and the country gentry haughty and nationalistic. Still, garrisoning in that country had its rewards, both because of the legendary passion and beauty of its women and because of Hungarian hospitality (. . .). Transylvania and Croatia were viewed as less civilized parts of only moderately civilized Hungary; Bosnia-Hercegovina was a hardship post with the compensatory features of Oriental exoticism and military adventure; and the Bukovina, at the eastern confines of the monarchy, was surprisingly popular because of its rich cultural life and the extraordinary ethnic harmony of its mixed Jewish, Ruthene, and Romanian population. Finally, Galicia, where a large part of the army was stationed beginning in the 1880s, was perceived as a place of exile and the ultimate hardship post (Deák 1990:108–9).

This chapter makes a double effort. It replicates the previous chapter's study on the Austro-Hungarian empire, and outlines and compares the growth of leisure migration in Austria and Hungary from the last third of the nineteenth-century through recent times. To do this, it triangulates three different kinds of data referring to three partly overlapping time periods. It (1) pencils the mental map of the Austro-Hungarian

Dual Monarchy on the basis of American and German guidebook representations from 1870 to 1908; (2) examines the earliest available comparable statistical data concerning the actual presence of tourists and foreign tourists in Vienna and Budapest between 1874 and 1940; and (3) surveys and contrasts national-level time series data reflecting the exposure of Austria and Hungary to tourists and foreign tourists from 1909 through 1988.

Representations of the Empire 1870–1908

First attention is drawn to the mental construction of the Austro-Hungarian Dual Monarchy as a tourist destination. This state, the product of political power sharing created by the Compromise Agreement of 1867 between the Imperial Court and the Hungarian nobility and comprised, four years before its eventual dissolution in 1914, ca. 53 million inhabitants, occupying a land area of 677,000 square kilometers.

There are at hand four cases of guidebook representations of the Empire. Two of those—*Appleton's* (1870) and *The Satchel Guide* (1889–1908) are American guidebooks to Europe analyzed in *chapter 2*. This chapter will review two additional guidebooks focusing on the central portion of the continent.

Karl *Baedeker's Southern Germany and Austria, including Hungary and Transylvania*, published in 1883, was the fifth, "revised and augmented," edition of its kind. It is the English version of the nineteenth German edition of Baedeker's guide to southern Germany and Austria. In addition to standard "general travel information" primarily for British and American tourists and sections on the German provinces of Wurtemberg and Bavaria, it offers chapters on "Austria" (including material on five of the German-speaking provinces of the Empire but omitting Tyrol and Vorarlberg to which Baedeker had devoted a whole volume series), "Bohemia and Moravia," "Hungary and Galicia," and "Transylvania." The guide features 13 regional and 28 city maps.

For reference, Map 3.1 shows the administrative breakdown of the Dual Monarchy at around 1890. It consists of three large administrative units: (1) "The Perpetual Possessions of Austria" including the dominantly German-speaking western provinces plus Bohemia, Moravia, Silesia, Galicia, Bukovina, Carniola (Krain), the Littoral (Gorizia, Istria and Trieste) and Dalmatia, (2) "The Lands of the Hungarian Crown"—that is, the Kingdom of Hungary, Croatia, and the city of Fiume—and (3) Bosnia-Hercegovina, annexed in 1878 and thence jointly administered by the Hungarian and Austrian authorities until the breakout of World War I. The predominantly German-speaking provinces are also called "Austria proper": The territory of the Austrian Republic created in 1918 more or less corresponds

Map 3.1. Provinces and Principal Cities of the Austro-Hungarian Empire (1890)

to that area. "Hungary proper" or "Trianon-Hungary," on the other hand, was created in the peace treaty of Trianon in 1920 by reducing the state to roughly one-third of the territory of the "Lands of the Hungarian Crown": It comprises the middle section of the territory created by the secession of Croatia and the adjacent Bácska and Bánát regions (now Vojvodina province in Rump Yugoslavia), its northern part (now Slovakia), and Transylvania on its eastern extreme (now Romania). This analysis will focus only on the sections describing the Austro-Hungarian Dual Monarchy.

Baedeker's Austria-Hungary Including Dalmatia and Bosnia, published in 1905, is the tenth, "revised and augmented" edition of Baedeker's guidebooks about the Habsburg Empire. It "corresponds with the twenty-sixth German edition" (1905:v). In contrast to its predecessor above, it ignores southern Germany while including such destinations as the entire Austrian Alps (with Tyrol and Vorarlberg provinces), Dalmatia and Bosnia-Hercegovina. It contains 33 regional and 44 city maps of meticulous detail and superior quality.

Table 3.1 contains the numerical results of the reconstruction of the guidebooks' mental maps of the Empire. Most of the guidebook users' attention is focused on the Perpetual Austrian Provinces, the directly

Table 3.1. Representations of the Provinces of the Empire in Guidebooks, 1870–1909

	Population	Appleton 1870			Baedeker 1883			Satchel 1889–1908			Baedeker 1905		
	(%)	ll	%	ll/pop	pp	%	pp/pop	ll	%	ll/pop	pp	%	pp/pop
"Perpetual Possessions of Austria"	(55.34)	(2706)	(95.0)	(1.7)	(149)	(70.9)	(1.3)	(434)	(89.1)	(1.6)	(282)	(73.1)	(1.32)
Austria proper	(14.6)	(1468)	(51.5)	(3.5)	(94)	(44.7)	(3.1)	(402)	(82.5)	(5.7)	(181)	(46.9)	(3.2)
Lower Austria (incl. Vienna)	6.9	969	34.0	4.9	74	35.2	5.1	186	38.2	5.5	88	22.8	3.3
Upper Austria	1.6	78	2.7	1.7	8	3.8	2.4	54	11.1	6.9	15	3.9	2.4
Salzburg	0.42	92	3.2	7.6	6	2.9	6.9	42	8.6	20.5	16	4.1	9.8
Styria	2.8	76	2.7	0.96	6	2.9	1.0	32	6.6	2.4	16	4.1	1.5
Carinthia	0.77							4	1.0	1.3			
Tyrol and Vorarlberg	2.1	253	8.9	4.2	N.A.	N.A.	N.A.	88	18.1	8.6	42	10.9	5.2
Bohemia	13.9	920	32.3	2.5	37	17.6	1.4	30	6.2	0.48	47	12.2	0.94
Moravia	5.05	57	2.0	0.4	6	2.9	0.57				7	1.8	0.36
Silesia	1.5												
Littoral (incl. Gorizia, Istria, Trieste)	1.8	126	4.4	2.4	4	1.9	1.1	26	5.3	2.9	11	2.8	1.6
Carniola	1.1	35	4.7	4.7	1	0.5	0.5	6	1.2	1.2	4	1.0	1.0
Dalmatia	1.3							18	4.7	3.6			
Bukovina	1.5							1	0.26	0.17			
Galicia and Lodomeria	15.6	94	3.3	0.21				13	3.4	0.22			
"Lands of the Hungarian Crown"	(40.75)	(143)	(5.0)	(0.12)	(61.1)	(29.1)	(0.71)	(23)	(4.7)	(0.12)	(104)	(26.9)	(0.66)
Kingdom of Hungary	35.6	143	5.0	0.14	60	28.6	0.8	23	4.7	0.13	89	23.1	0.65
Fiume	0.09							1	0.26	2.9			
Croatia and Slovenia	5.06				1	0.5	0.09				2	0.52	0.1
Bosnia/Hercegovina	(3.9)	N.A.	N.A.	N.A.	N.A.	N.A.	N.A.				(12)	(3.1)	(0.79)
Total		2849			210			457			398		

Sources: Own calculations, Freytag 1914.
ll, lines; pp, pages; pop, population.

Austrian-ruled part of the empire. These provinces have population-controlled representation values of between 1.3 and 1.7, while the Lands of the Hungarian Crown are consistently, quite severely "underesteemed" (with representation values ranging between .12 and .71). Bosnia-Hercegovina is not even mentioned until the 1905 edition of *Baedeker* (twenty-seven years after its annexation to Austro-Hungary).

The moderate preponderance of the Perpetual Austrian Possessions, pointed out above, gives way to more extreme disparities once we compare Austria proper to the Kingdom of Hungary. The predominantly German-speaking provinces of Austria together are very highly appreciated at values of 3.1–5.7, while the relative unimportance of the Kingdom of Hungary as a tourism destination is, again, marked by underrepresentation values ranging between .13 and .80, almost identical to those above.

Maps 3.2, 3.3, and 3.4 reproduce some of the information detailed in Table 3.1 in a visually more perceptible form. Map 3.2 presents the

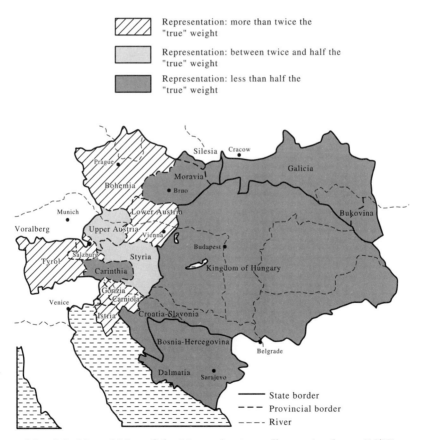

Map 3.2. Mental Map of the Monarchy According to Appleton (1870)

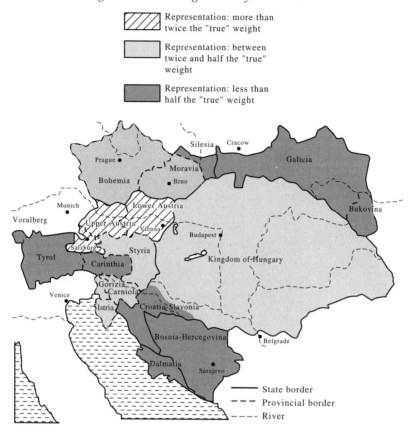

Map 3.3. Mental Map of the Monarchy According to Baedeker (1883)

mental picture of the Dual Monarchy as suggested in *Appleton's* (1870). The list of most appreciated regions comprises Salzburg, Lower Austria (including the imperial capital city, Vienna), the Alpine provinces of Tyrol and Vorarlberg, Bohemia, and the westernmost section of the Adriatic Littoral along with Carniola province. Except for the German-speaking province of Carinthia, underrepresentation is in the area east of a north–south dividing line separating the less fortunate parts from the most advanced one-third of the Empire.

The 1883 edition of *Baedeker*—reproduced on Map 3.3—favors the contiguous area of the provinces of Salzburg, Upper Austria and Lower Austria the most. Moreorless fairly represented portions of the Empire include Bohemia, Moravia, the Kingdom of Hungary and the western part of the Adriatic coastline. Underrepresentation is limited to Carinthia and the southern and northeastern extremities of the Empire—Croatia, Dalmatia and Bosnia-Hercegovina in the south, and Silesia,

Representation: more than twice the "true" weight

Representation: between twice and half the "true" weight

Representation: less than half the "true" weight

State border

Provincial border

River

Map 3.4. Mental Map of the Monarchy According to Baedeker (1905)

Galicia and Bukovina in the north and northeast. (The provinces of Tyrol and Vorarlberg are not underrepresented but intentionally excluded from this guidebook. Thus, those data are considered missing.)

Baedeker's 1905 edition—illustrated on Map 3.4—emphasizes, again, the provinces of Austria proper (this time including Tyrol and Vorarlberg). Now, for the first time, the Dalmatian coastline appears as a noteworthy component of the Empire's "mix" of tourist destinations. Bohemia, the western Adriatic Littoral with Carniola and Carinthia, as well as the Kingdom of Hungary and Bosnia-Hercegovina, appear on this map as represented "appropriately" in terms of their "true" weight. The list of "underesteemed" provinces is similar to those before: border areas of Moravia and Silesia in the north, of Galicia and Bukovina in the northeast, and of Croatia in the south.

Overall, it is noticeable that the two German guidebooks—the 1883 and 1905 editions of *Baedeker*—reflect a less discriminating sense of

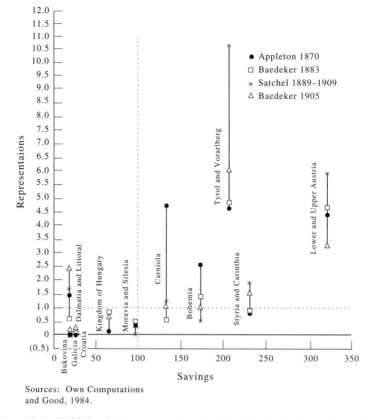

Sources: Own Computations
and Good, 1984.

Figure 3.1. Guidebook Representations by Per Capita Savings Deposits— Regions of the Austro-Hungarian Dual Monarchy, 1870–1909 by 1890

proportion than their North American counterparts: Albeit hardly free from region-specific emphases, Baedeker's regional descriptions tend to be apportioned more even-handedly than those of either *Appleton's* or *The Satchel Guide*. This contrast is especially apparent in comparison to *The Satchel Guide*: While the latter is almost completely preoccupied with the German-speaking Austrian provinces of Salzburg, Lower and Upper Austria—located alongside the Munich-Vienna railroad line, in the west-central administrative center of the Dual Monarchy—*Baedeker* appears to reflect an editorial effort to cover as much as possible of the large and multiethnic Empire.

The emphases of interest expressed in the mental maps of various parts of the Habsburg Empire by and large conform with the general conclusions of the previous chapter concerning Europe. The most appreciated territorial units of the Empire are those which had experienced the earliest transition to industrial-capitalist development, especially those in such central locations as Upper and Lower Austria. The least emphasized regions are those on the northern, eastern and southern fringes of the Empire—the areas hardest hit by the belatedness and unevenness of capitalist development.

Figure 3.1 helps examine this relationship by contrasting the findings concerning the relative degree of representation of individual provinces with a measure of capitalist economic development, namely Good's (1984:-157, Table 27) estimates of per capita saving deposits across the Empire. (Again, Appendix 2 contains the methodological details of this analysis.)

In Figure 3.1, each set of symbols representing the same province or set of provinces has been connected with a line. The lines so created embody estimates of the range of the approximate position of individual (sets of) provinces. Then, the figure is divided into four sections by two dividing lines: one for the "perfect" representation, and another for the Empire-wide arithmetic mean value of per capita savings deposits. The datapoints in the upper right section stand for provinces with above-average savings figures *and* overrepresentation in the guidebooks. Those in the lower left quadrant mark the regions with below-average amounts of savings *and* underrepresentation in, or complete absence from, the guidebooks.

On the basis of the findings of the previous chapter, one should expect that most datapoints will be located in either the upper right or the lower left quadrant. Overall, 34 datapoints confirm this expectation by appearing in the upper-right or lower-left boxes. There are 9 outliers: In some—but not all—of the guidebooks, Carniola, Bohemia, and Styria are less emphasized than would be expected on the basis of the savings rates, while Dalmatia and the western Littoral (Gorizia, Istria and Trieste) are "overappreciated" at times. The ordinary least square regression value of this dataset (43 datapoints) implies an increase of 1.38% in the relative degree of representation per every 1% difference in the mean per capita savings deposits. The strength of this positive relationship is marked by a correlation value of $r = .62$.

Data depicting the representation of the Austro-Hungarian Dual Monarchy in guidebooks lend further support to the previous chapter's conclusions concerning the nexus of the uneven development of industrial capitalism and the emergence of the international structural patterns of leisure migration. Guidebook data suggest that the German-speaking provinces of Austria proper (the soon-to-be Austrian Republic) arrived at the time of the Empire's dissolution with clear touristic advantages over all others. Of the relatively underdeveloped regions, only the Istrian peninsula and the Dalmatian coastline appear to have developed into tourist destinations of sorts during this early period. The "Lands of the Hungarian Crown," with their limited degree of capitalist development have achieved "fair" levels of representation in the two German guidebooks, although, even there, their population-controlled representation values have remained below 1. In contrast, the American guidebooks have remarkably little to say about the Hungarian half of the Empire. The Czech-speaking parts of the Monarchy have been approximately on par with Hungary. This implies relative underrepresentation considering their somewhat more advanced level of economic, especially industrial and urban, development. The two most agricultural, least urbanized, and most poverty-stricken provinces of the Monarchy—Galicia and Bukovina—have been conspicuously missing from or, at best, grossly underrepresented in, guidebooks around the turn of the century.

With the exception of the Adriatic provinces on the "positive" end and the Czech provinces on the "negative" extreme, an overview of the guidebook representations of the Austro-Hungarian Dual Monarchy suggests that the greatest levels of attention and attractivity are assigned to the economically most developed areas of the Empire, while there is a clear tendency to ignore or grossly underrepresent least advanced regions. The mental production of the Austro-Hungarian Dual Monarchy as an emerging tourist destination area implies *grave regional inequalities, approximately along the lines of the uneven development of late-nineteenth-century central European capitalism.*

The following sections of this chapter will examine evidence pertaining to a comparison of the dynamics of tourism growth in Austria and Hungary based on statistical data which concern the actual presence of leisure migration in the two societies. The descriptive sections will be preceded by a brief description of the measures.

Estimating Exposure to Tourism

The following sections will examine the four most fundamental social indicators of the exposure of a society or region to tourism. *Tourist Arrivals* (TA) record the annual number of tourists—defined as a travelers who spend at least one night away from his or her usual residence; those not staying overnight are categorized as *sojourners* (IUOTO 1963)—at a given destination. Every tourist arrival is counted once, regardless of the length of stay. Repeated visits by the same person are added to the total. TA is a measure of the size of a tourism destination market in terms of the number of people involved in it as traveling consumers.

In order to make possible comparisons across destination societies or regions of often different size, Høivik and Heiberg (1980) introduce a useful index—they call it the *Tourism Exposure Rate* (TER)—to control the population size of the country or region. TER is obtained by dividing the number of tourist arrivals by the appropriate population figure for the destination unit and converting the results into percentages. TER measures the relative weight of the presence of tourists *vis-à-vis* the "local" society at the destination in terms of percentages of the number of people involved.

Tourist Nights (TN) is a more accurate measure of the substantive presence of tourists in a given society. Beyond the number of arrivals, it also accounts for differences in the tourists' length of stay. TN is produced by multiplying the number of tourist arrivals by the number of overnight stays per tourist. It is a measure of the given destination market in terms of the number of overnight stays by traveling consumers in it.

The population-controlled version of this measure—the *Tourism Intensity Rate* (TIR)—was proposed by this author (Böröcz 1990) as an updated adaptation of Høivik and Heiberg's TER. It is constructed by dividing the number of tourist nights by "population nights" (i.e., the population size multiplied by 365) and converting the results into percentages. TIR measures the relative presence of traveling consumers at a given destination in terms of percentages of time.

States use two basic ways to obtain the touristic component of these measures. Historically, the first one developed from summaries of alien registration files compiled from information reported by hotels, inns, lodges, pensions, hostels, etc. In Austria, this has been the method of tourism statistical data collection since the onset of leisure travel until today. In Hungary, the Budapest Statistical Office used the same approach until the late forties. On the national aggregate level, however, the Hungarian Statistical Office utilized an alternative method which only focuses on *foreign* tourists. This involves estimates of group-specific border crossings and length-of-stay. Theoretically, the latter method is supposed to be more inclusive as it does not omit those who stay with friends, relatives, or in any other way outside the registration framework applied to commercial accommodations. Its accuracy, however, depends on the precision of a large number of border crossing estimates.

The methodological difference in obtaining these figures introduces a sense of unreliability in the application of the two measures for the comparison of postwar Hungary and Austria. However, for the purposes of this analysis—namely for estimating relative magnitudes—they represent by far the most reliable sources of data. To be noted is that any distortion of the data resulting from this particular discrepancy concerning the different methods of obtaining them would *under*estimate Austria's scores by missing those who stay at noncommercial accommodations.

Incoming Tourism: Vienna and Budapest, 1873–1940

Tourism growth, statistics and the state

Much in similarity with the development of the statistical "enterprise" in mid-nineteenth century Italy (see Patriarca 1992 and 1994), local statistical data production preceded national endeavors in both halves of the Empire. The earliest statistical data for tourism in Austria and

Hungary refer to Vienna and Budapest, the two capital cities of the Dual Monarchy. In assessing the relative exposure of the two countries to tourism during the earliest period of leisure migration, one must start out by examining data concerning the two capital cities. The main methodological implication of this fact is that population-controlled measures cannot be produced for the earliest period. Throughout this chapter, the purpose of controlling for population size is to tease out the relative tourist saturation of a society or region to be contrasted with structural conditions of uneven industrial capitalist development. Whereas the size of the population of a country or a region can be conceived as a relatively independent control variable, the size and the primacy of a country's main (i.e., capital) city is in and of itself an important indicator of the development of industrial capitalism and urbanization in the given country. Using population-controlled measures for the two cities would create a circular argument.

In Vienna, systematic statistical data collection and regular reporting of tourist traffic appears to have begun in 1873. The earliest data available for Budapest reflect the year 1885. (The city, defined geographically more or less as it exists today, was created in 1873 by the unification of the townships of Pest, Buda and Óbuda and designated as the official capital city of the Lands of the Hungarian Crown.) This implies a time lag of twelve years in terms of statistical measurement and reporting practices between the two cities.

The beginnings of statistical data collection on tourism coincide with the distinguishable onset of tourism development in the two countries. In his monograph (1984) on the history of Austrian tourism, Alois Brusatti emphasizes the importance of the 1873 Vienna World Exposition as the first massive event in Vienna's tourism history. The early 1870s also mark the creation of Vienna's famous Ringstrasse, an urban redevelopment project on par with Haussmann's reconstruction of Paris two decades earlier (Schorske 1961; Pound 1985). The first data on incoming tourism in Vienna reflect the year of the Vienna World Expo.

The date of the first tourism statistics of Budapest corresponds to the establishment of the first Hungarian tour operator travel agency called the "International Ticket Office of the Hungarian State Railways" ("Magyar Államvasutak Nemzetközi Menetjegyirodája") in 1884. This date approximately corresponds to the creation of the Nagykörút—the Budapest equivalent of the Viennese Ringstrasse. The establishment of the national travel agency followed an aborted attempt in 1861 (Szántó 1982).

The Imperial state played a decisive role in developing the basic conditions for incoming leisure migration in the Empire. The state's role manifested, first and foremost, in the operation of the railways and the Imperial and Royal Danubian Steam Shipping Company (commonly referred to, in its German acronym, as DDSG). The Erste K. und K.

Donau-Dampffschiffarts-Gesellschaft was established with some English capital in 1829. In order to become independent of foreign ship manufacturers, it opened its own shipyard—soon to be the biggest in continental Europe—in the Hungarian town of Óbuda (Althofen) in 1835. In 1875, the company operated 201 steamers and 750 river barges and became, by 1880, the world's foremost domestic shipping enterprise. As such, it was one of the mightiest corporations ever operating within the Habsburg Empire (Binder 1979).

Both the railways and DDSG had a sizeable state ownership component. By the mid-1880s, railways and (primarily Danubian) steam shipping became the main means of tourist transportation. During the first 17 years after the establishment of the Dual Monarchy in 1867, deligeance travel in Hungary declined from 39,000 to 10,700 passengers annually while, in the single year of 1883, DDSG had transported over three million passengers. Approximately three-quarters of those trips took place in the territory of the lands of the Hungarian Crown (Szántó 1982).

On the Hungarian side, the state was involved in running the incoming tourism business through the activities of the state-owned national travel office. The International Ticket Office was established in 1884, opened branch offices in Vienna and Constantinople in 1886, and connected to the British Cook's Tours system in 1888. It divorced from the railroads in 1902. It continued to function as a state-owned combination of "a tour operator, a travel agency, an ethnographic bazaar, a theater ticket agency, a shipping company, the lead representative of Hungarian [thermal and medicinal] baths, a [provider of] currency, check exchange and letter-of-credit services, an accident and baggage insurance company and an issuer of hotel coupons" (Csók 1969:21). It combined the travel business with a role as the government's national public relations agency.

A quick glance at the foreign linkages of the new Hungarian national travel office reveals a peculiar structural hierarchy, much in line with the country's "middle" position in the uneven development of industrial capitalism in Europe. The agency soon established its presence in those areas of Europe that were even less developed economically than Hungary and, as a consequence, had a relatively insignificant, mostly aristocratic, travel demand. Its own branch offices were opened in Saint Petersburg, Bucharest, Belgrade, Sofia, Constantinople and Thessaloníki. In contrast, the Hungarian national travel agency's connections to the strong and growing bourgeois tourist markets of the continent—i.e., its representation in Berlin, Nice, Paris and Vienna—were handled through a subordinate arrangement with a foreign company called Carl Stangen und Schenker.

By the time of the 1896 Millennium Exposition held in Budapest to commemorate the one-thousandth anniversary of the most likely date of the incursion of the Magyar tribes into the Carpathian Basin—the Hungarian national "replica" of the Vienna World Expo with a delay of nearly a generation—Budapest had a reasonably well established system of collecting and reporting tourism statistics. With the end of the year of the Expo, however, the city council suddenly canceled the minuscule financial support it had provided to its small office producing local tourism statistics (the equivalent of .4% of the amount spent by the city on cabs). That decision, in effect, terminated Budapest tourism statistics for a decade (Szerény 1900:73).

European tourism grew spectacularly during the second half of the nineteenth century. While the 1851 London World Exposition attracted "only" 6 million visitors (Szántó 1982) the Paris World Expo of 1889 was a soaring success with 33 million arrivals (ibid.). The Dual Monarchy as a whole was hardly the most important tourist destination in Europe around the turn of the century. In 1896, the number of tourist arrivals was 903,000 in Paris and 717,000 in Berlin (Szántó 1982) while Vienna showed a modest figure of "only" 358,000. In comparison, only 153,000 people visited Budapest during the same year—the year of the very heavily state-subsidized and widely publicized Hungarian Millennium Exposition.

Budapest was unable to imitate what seemed to have worked elsewhere. A sense of collective frustration over the failure of the Expo may explain the termination of tourism statistics in Budapest perhaps better than Szerény's suggestion (1900) of lack of recognition of the importance of tourism on the part of city officials. No doubt, the sobering experience of the Millennium Expo's failure had much to do with the Hungarian state's absence from subsequent infrastructural development for tourism. Local and regional efforts to channel state resources into tourism development were a crucial component of tourism growth in both rural and urban settings in the Austrian half of the Empire (Brusatti 1984). Instead of large-scale projects aimed to develop tourism infrastructure, the Hungarian state strengthened its control over its already existing, relatively small market via the national travel agency thereby attempting to "substitute" for the role played, in Austria, primarily by private capital.

Arrivals and foreign tourist arrivals

Figure 3.2 presents all the data that are available concerning the number of tourist and foreign tourist arrivals in Vienna and Budapest until 1940. Throughout the sixty-some year period covered by this graph, the number of tourists had been continuously and unambiguously higher in Vienna than in Budapest. By the early 1910s, the number of total annual tourist arrivals in Vienna exceeds 600,000 and, in 1913, the

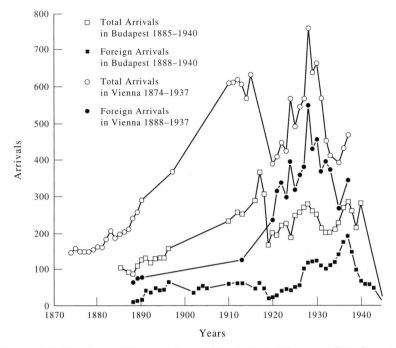

Figure 3.2. Tourist and Foreign Tourist Arrivals in Vienna and Budapest,
1874–1940

number of *foreign* arrivals in Vienna is over 100,000. In contrast, Budapest's total tourist arrival figures reach 300,000 only in a single year (1917), and the number of foreign arrivals wavers between 15,000 and 35,000 per year.

The curves depicting total tourist arrivals in the two cities can be described as combinations of two dynamics: a steady and moderate general growth pattern interrupted by sudden, sharp drops. The downturns coincide with three cataclysmic events in East-Central Europe's twentieth-century history: (a) World War I—1914 through 1919, (b) the Great Depression—1929 to 1934, and (c) World War II—from 1938 onwards. (1938 is the year of the *Anschluss*, Austria's "unification" with the Third Reich.) *Before World War II, the tendency of the development of incoming leisure migration in Vienna and Budapest had been stable, balanced growth, punctuated only by social and economic disasters of continent-wide or global magnitude.* Short of such catastrophes, the total volume of tourism had been rising steadily in both cities.

Comparing the dynamics of change in the magnitude of the two cities' exposure to incoming *foreign* tourism, two characteristics should be pointed out. First, the two curves clearly manifest the general tendency observed before: Vienna's unambiguous advantage. Second, the curves do not indicate any tendency of major growth until the immediate post-World War I period. Absence of data for the wartime years in Vienna preclude the identification of the exact time when Vienna's foreign arrival figures started increasing sharply. It is clear, however, that in 1920, Vienna registered 229,000 foreign arrivals, as opposed to Budapest's mere 15,000—a ratio of over 15 times. (This is in contrast to the last prewar year, 1913, when this ratio had been only 2.2 times. The differential of the two cities will not be reduced to its prewar level until 1935.) It appears that the war and its immediate aftermath (in Hungary's case, two revolutions, the creation and defeat of the Hungarian Soviet Republic, the country's foreign military occupation, and the subsequent period of ultra-right "White Terror") created conditions that were particularly unamenable for the reception of foreign leisure migration. Following this period, Budapest's foreign tourist arrivals scores continued moving more or less parallel with those of Vienna.

This difference may have had to do with the different statuses that the two cities had inherited from the time of the Empire. Up until 1867, Vienna was the Imperial capital of the Habsburg House. After the change in the state structure introduced with the Compromise Agreement, Vienna remained the seat of the Imperial Court and the capital city of the Perpetual Austrian Provinces of the Dual Monarchy. By the turn of the century, the city had grown into a major cultural, economic, and political center, in comparative proximity to the West European centers of capitalist accumulation, to Germany (with which it shared a national language and much of its cultural orientations), and, last but not least, located in easy reach from the most bourgeois and most prosperous regions of the Empire itself. Lower Austria, the province surrounding Vienna, had been the most advanced of all.

Vienna of the early 1920s was the direct descendant of the famous "Fin-de-Siècle" Vienna. It continued to radiate important cultural and economic influence on the entire region, notwithstanding the fact that it had just lost its role as an Empire's political center. With the dissolution of the Dual Monarchy, however, many of the traditional "domestic" visitors—i.e., those from Bohemia, Moravia, (by then, part of the newly formed Republic of Czechoslovakia), Hungary or Croatia—suddenly came to be *foreign* travelers in Vienna. This was bound to increase the number of tourists registered as foreigners. *Part of Vienna's touristic advantage during the early years of the Austrian Republic can be explained as continued processes of leisure migration "inherited" from the period of the Dual Monarchy.* This could help interpret the fact that the number of foreign arrivals in Vienna could increase from 119 thousand to 229 thousand while the total number of arrivals not only did not increase, but actually *declined* from 599 thousand to 382 thousand from 1913 to 1920. Due to the post-World War I rearrangement of state borders in Central Europe, many of those previously "domestic" leisure flows to Vienna suddenly became "international." It is a consequence of imperial realities that the dissolution of the Empire should produce the continuation of such flows. This implies that leisure flows have an important, historically stable social component whose pattern-producing capacity is less readily transformable than the political boundaries of states.

The loss of imperial political power affected the Hungarian part of the Dual Monarchy no less than Austria proper. Hungary had been, however, Austria's subordinate partner in the Dual Monarchy in virtually all relevant aspects. The implications of this uneven condition for the two cities' differences is captured by a sapient twin-metaphor offered, after Carl Schorske (1961), by Hungarian historian Péter Hanák in his essay (1988) on the comparative history of the two cities during this period. Hanák describes imperial and dominant Vienna as "The Garden," in contrast to royal yet subordinate Budapest—"The Workshop." Many features of the two cities substantiate this metaphorical distinction, ranging from such concrete aspects as the amount of urban space set aside for park use in the two cities and the physical presence or absence of dusty industrial establishments in their proximity (as following from the concentration of almost the entire industry of Hungary around the capital city) to such less tangible aspects as the forms and degrees of the proletarianization and embourgeoisement of their inhabitants, reflected in architecture, the availability and social control of public spaces, and the quality of the quotidian lives of citizens. "The Garden" may have been better equipped to attract tourists, especially foreign tourists, than "The Workshop."

The comparative disadvantages of Hungary and its capital city in economic and cultural terms should explain at least some of the apparent feebleness of its transformation into a tourist destination. Having been less of a tourist destination for "domestic" travel flows within the Empire than Vienna, Budapest had less of a legacy to continue benefiting from, once the Empire was dissolved. These effects were likely to have been exacerbated by the physical and social damage suffered in connection with the acts of war, upheavals, and violent reprisals in Hungary.

During the immediate post-World War I years, Vienna's tourism shows impressive growth. By the year 1928, the annual number of tourist arrivals in Vienna reaches 752 thousand. That record number is accounted for largely by foreign arrivals (541,000). Consequently, the effects of the subsequent Great Depression are also greater in Vienna than in Budapest: By 1935, Vienna experiences an almost 50% drop in the number of tourist arrivals while Budapest's figures decrease only by less than 20%, and the declining tendency is reversed a few years earlier than in Vienna. Data for Vienna cease with the year 1937. After the

Anschluss, statistical data are nowhere to be found until 1949. Data on Budapest continue until the end of 1940. (The following year marked Hungary's military involvement in World War II.)

Overall, the curves of the two cities appear moving much in accord. Incoming leisure migration in Budapest and Vienna, while showing unmistakable signs of relative underdevelopment on Budapest's part, appears to have been affected by much the same factors.

Tourist nights and foreign tourist nights

Figure 3.3 summarizes the data available on the substantive presence of tourists and foreign tourists in Vienna and Budapest for the period of 1908 through 1940. Sporadic as they are, the data allow the deduction that Vienna's relative touristic advantage, observed so far with respect to arrivals, is also reflected in the number of tourist nights in the two cities.

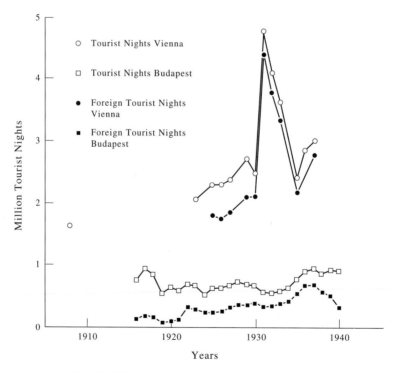

Sources: Brusatti, 1984, Austrian
and Hungarian Statistical Offices.

**Figure 3.3. Tourist Nights and Foreign Tourist Nights in Vienna and
Budapest, 1908–40 (million nights per year)**

In 1908—the earliest available datapoint for tourist nights in Vienna—the Austrian (and at the time also Imperial) capital saw 1.6 million overnight stays by tourists. Budapest never even approximates that figure during this period: Its tourist night scores have always remained below 1 million. The Austrian capital's advantages are even more pronounced in terms of foreign tourist nights: A consistently higher percentage of tourist nights was spent in Vienna than in Budapest by foreigners.

The year 1931 saw a spectacular upsurge in tourist night figures in Vienna, entirely made up of an increase in foreign tourist nights. While the number of tourist arrivals as well as specifically foreign tourist arrivals declined during that year, the number of tourist nights and foreign tourist nights suddenly increased nearly twofold. For German tourists—the most numerous group of foreign tourists in Vienna—whose average length of stay in Vienna increased from 5.5 to 10.5 days, longer stay may be explained by the introduction, by the German government, of a special "travel tax" on foreign tourism in the amount of 100 Reichsmark (Brusatti 1984:117). Instead of making several shorter trips, the special tax suggested a longer stay, once German travelers were abroad.

This does not explain, however, the even greater increase in the length of stay by other, non-German foreigners. (The mean length of stay for all foreigners increased from 4.9 to 12 nights.) This appears to imply that the main effect of the Great Depression manifested in (1) a decrease in the number of foreign arrivals—i.e., the pool of foreign travelers visiting Vienna has diminished—(2) more than compensated by much longer stays by those who actually traveled. That increase not only offset the loss but even increased the total amount of tourist nights spent in Vienna about twofold. Whatever the precise reason for the upsurge and subsequent drop of tourist night figures in Vienna, it suffices for our purposes to observe that *tourist nights scores also reflect Vienna's comparative advantage vis-à-vis Budapest*. The upsurge and subsequent drop of Vienna's tourist nights scores around the Great Depression affect only the magnitude of that differential.

In summary, this overview of statistical evidence concerning the emergence of incoming leisure migration in Vienna and Budapest suggests that, as far back in time as data allow, *the development of Budapest as a tourist destination had never been on par with that of its imperial and dominant counterpart. The emergence of leisure migration reflects symptoms of belated and uneven, yet largely parallel, development in the two cities.*

Incoming Foreign Tourism: Austria and Hungary, 1909–88

The earliest data for Austria that could be located for this study refer to the Perpetual Austrian Provinces (the territory of the would-be Austrian

Republic) for the immediate pre-World War I years. It is an indirect indication of the relatively greater importance of tourism in Austria than in Hungary that, while the Austrian provinces produced their own collective statistical summaries even before the dissolution of the Empire, the Hungarian state began nationwide tourism data collection as late as 1933—that is, with a time lag of 24 years. (Analyses of the impact of tourism in Hungary relied exclusively on figures for Budapest even in the late 1930s.) The time lag in the establishment of nationwide statistical data services itself reflects a more severe case of (1) *urban primacy* (i.e., uneven urban development manifested in the overgrowth of the capital city *vis-à-vis* other cities) and a sharper contrast between (2) *the capital city and the countryside* in the case of tourism development in Hungary than in Austria. (To be noted is that the post-World War I primacy of Budapest is partly an artifact of the loss of two-thirds of the territory of the Kingdom of Hungary. The seceded territory included relatively sizeable urban centers.) A perhaps even more telling indication of the comparative unimportance of tourism in Hungary is that, once established, *Hungarian tourism statistics do not provide nationwide total arrivals figures* at all. They only focus on the travel of incoming foreigners. This of course precludes Austrian–Hungarian comparisons of total arrival data.

Foreign Tourist Arrivals

Figure 3.4 includes data concerning *foreign* tourist arrivals in the two countries during most of the twentieth century. As far as the discontinuous data allow an inference, the pattern appears to be similar to that established for the two capital cities: growth interrupted by the two world wars and the Great Depression. Austria's scores are, again, always higher than those of Hungary.

The end of World War II signals the beginning of an entirely new period in the tourism history of the two countries. Both countries' foreign tourist arrivals figures indicate striking growth during this period. However, the particulars of those growth patterns reveal serious differences between the two countries.

First, the Austrian figures start climbing as early as in 1949 while Hungarian figures remain very low until the early sixties. This represents Hungary's delay of about 15 years.

Second, the growth pattern of foreign tourism in Austria is that of steady, near-perfectly linear increase. (The correlation of time and foreign tourist arrivals for the 41 datapoints during the postwar period in Austria is $r=.997$.) In contrast, Hungary's pattern is composed of sudden upswings interspersed with short periods of stagnation and even a serious setback during the early 1980s. (As a result, the correlation of

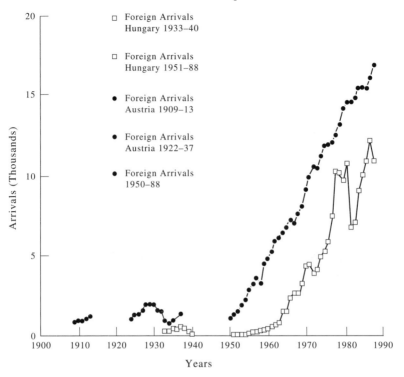

Sources: Austrian and Hungarian Statistical Offices.

**Figure 3.4. Foreign Tourist Arrivals in Austria and Hungary, 1909–88
(thousands)**

time and foreign tourist arrivals for the postwar period in Hungary is
somewhat lower than that of Austria: $r=.942$ with 38 datapoints.)

Third, incoming foreign tourism grew at a faster rate in Austria than
in Hungary: The steepness of Austria's increase in foreign tourist arrivals
is approximately 1.25 times greater. (The ordinary least squares
regression coefficient is $b=423.02$ for Austria and $b=337.2$ for Hungary.)

Foreign tourist nights

Figure 3.5 shows the number of annual tourist nights spent in Austria
and Hungary by foreigners. The shape of the two curves is similar to
the one before—i.e., the length of stay of tourists in the two countries is
not sufficiently different to cause decipherable differences in the growth
patterns. Two of the three comparative conclusions drawn concerning
changes in tourist arrivals above continues to be true for the tourist

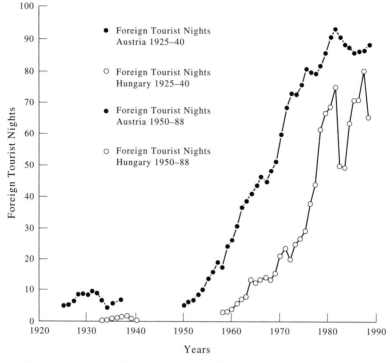

Sources: Austrian and Hungarian Statistical Offices.

**Figure 3.5. Foreign Tourist Nights in Austria and Hungary, 1925–88
(million nights)**

nights data as well: (1) Austrian figures start climbing about 15 years earlier than Hungarian ones and (2) the Austrian growth pattern is somewhat smoother. (The correlation figures between time and annual tourist nights for Austria and Hungary are $r=.976$ and $r=.941$, for 39 and 31 datapoints, respectively).

As far as the steepness of their growth is concerned, however, the two regression lines are exactly parallel: The ordinary least squares regression coefficient of both lines is $b=2.66$. As opposed to the previous dataset, Hungarian tourist nights data are missing until 1958. As a result, the latter graph includes data for only the growth phase in Hungary. (Put differently, the removal of the Hungarian data for tourist arrivals until the late 1950s would also produce greater regression coefficients.)

Exposure to incoming foreign tourism

As discussed before, population-controlled versions of the two indicators above produce more accurate descriptions of the presence of tourism in a given destination society. Figure 3.6 presents such information—the foreign TER—for the two countries during much of the twentieth century.

The foreign tourist exposure rate of the two countries before World War II shows extreme discrepancies: Austrian scores are between ca. 4 and 6 times higher than those for Hungary. In the last prewar peaceful year, 1937, the number of foreign tourists in Austria was equivalent to 19.1% of its population, as opposed to Hungary's figure of 4.2%. Austria's postwar recovery was also much faster: In 1950, Austria's score is already 13.6% while Hungary reaches that level only in 1965.

The shape of these curves is very similar to that of Figure 3.4 containing the "raw" tourist arrivals scores for Austria and Hungary. The only major difference is that the steepness of the post-World War II curve shows important divergence between tourism growth in the two countries. While Austria's TER increases by an average of 5.51% annually, the corresponding figure for Hungary is only 3.18%. This represents a 1.73 times higher rate of relative tourism growth in Austria.

As a combined result of the earlier beginning of its postwar tourism boom (noted above) and its steeper rate of tourism growth, Austria

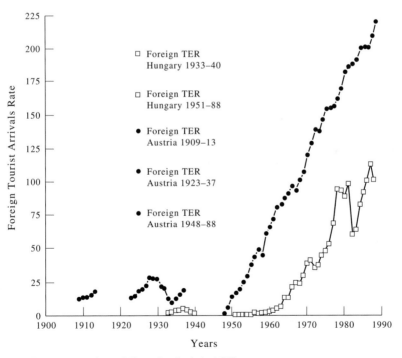

Sources: Austrian and Hungarian Statistical Offices.

Figure 3.6. Foreign Tourist Exposure Rate in Austria and Hungary, 1909–88 (%)

passed the 100% mark of tourism saturation in 1968. Hungary approximated that point in 1981; that is, with a time lag of 13 years. However, the high score of 1981 represents a local maximum, followed by a sharp downturn so that Hungarian TER scores do not climb back to the 100% level until 1986. By then, Austria's TER had already reached 200%. By the end of the period covered in this graph—1988—Austria has Europe's highest level of saturation by foreign tourists at an annual rate of 220% of its population size. During the same year, Hungary's figure is at 100% which places it somewhere in the middle of the West European spectrum. With that score, Hungary had become the most tourist-saturated state socialist country of the world by the late 1980s (Böröcz 1990).

The comparison of the foreign tourist exposure rates for the two countries indicates that (1) the proportion of foreign tourists to the local population has been consistently higher in Austria than Hungary and (2) the growth of this indicator has been somewhat steeper for Austria than for Hungary.

Intensity of incoming foreign tourism

The shape of the growth curves of the two countries' foreign TIR—portrayed in Figure 3.7—is also very similar to those before. Austria's foreign TIR scores always exceed those of Hungary. Up until World War II, Hungary's scores hardly reach the .05% mark. In contrast, the time spent by foreign tourists in Austria measures between .17% and .38% of the total "population nights." By 1954, the presence of foreign tourists in Austria exceeds the extent of the highest prewar year. The substantive presence of foreign tourists in Austria shows a tendency of continuous increase from .09% in 1949 to 2.95% in 1975. Since then, the level of foreign tourist presence in terms of time has leveled off at around the value of 3%. Hungary's first postwar scores indicate levels approximately the same as those before the war. Between 1958 and 1981, the substantive presence of foreign tourists in Hungary increased through monotonous growth. During the following year, tourist presence in Hungary declined from 1.91% to 1.26% of "population nights." During the following five years, the substantive presence of foreign tourists in Hungary climbed back to around the 2% level.

Just as in the case of all previous measures of the size of tourism in the two countries, the speed of increase of the substantive presence of foreign tourists relative to local "population nights" is higher in Austria than in Hungary: The ordinary least squares regression coefficient of foreign TIR shows an average annual growth of $b=.0928\%$ for Austria (for 40 datapoints between 1949 and 1988) in contrast to Hungary's estimate of an annual $b=.0687\%$ (for 31 datapoints between 1958 and 1988). The comparison of the two curves' steepness presents a 1.35 times more favorable result for Austria.

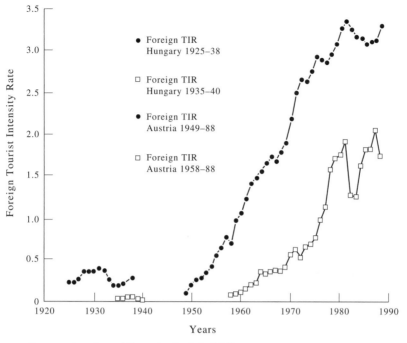

Sources: Austrian and Hungarian Statistical Offices.

Figure 3.7. Foreign Tourist Intensity Rate in Austria and Hungary, 1925–88 (%)

Comparative Tourism Growth, Austria and Hungary

Table 3.2 provides a comparative summary of this chapter's findings concerning the growth of incoming tourism in Austria and Hungary. The figures in the table have been produced by dividing the Austrian score by its Hungarian equivalent whenever appropriate pairs of indices could be secured, so that the numbers in the table indicate how many times higher the scores of the Austrian component are of its Hungarian counterpart. The guidebook representation scores of the directly Austrian-ruled "half" of the Empire (the Perpetual Austrian Provinces) are compared to those of the "Lands of the Hungarian Crown"; Austria proper is contrasted with the Kingdom of Hungary; Vienna's measures are divided by those of Budapest, and, finally, tourism indicators of the Republic of Austria are broken with those of Trianon-Hungary.

The first and most striking observation to be made is that there is not a single instance that the ratio of the corresponding scores would indicate Hungary's advantage. (All of the scores are $x > 1$.) Throughout the nearly 120-year period of the emergence of incoming leisure migration in the

Table 3.2. Comparison of Degrees of Comparative Advantage in Touristic Terms, Vienna vs Budapest and Austria vs Hungary, 1870–1988

Year	(1)	(2)	(3)	(4)	(5)	(6)	(7)	(8)
1870	14.2	25.0						
1883	1.8	3.9						
1885			1.9					
1887			2.3					
1888			2.8	7.8				
1889	13.3	43.8	2.3	6.7				
1890			2.3	5.3				
1897			2.4					
1905	2.0	4.9						
1910			2.7					
1912			2.5					
1913			2.5	2.2				
1920			2.0	15.3				
1921			2.2	14.0				
1922			2.1	9.7				
1923			1.9	7.6				
1924			3.1	10.8				
1925			2.0	7.1				
1926			2.2	7.2				
1927			2.2	3.9				
1928			2.8	4.9				
1929			2.5	3.8				
1930			2.7	3.9				
1931			2.7	3.7				
1932			2.3	3.0				
1933			2.1	2.6	5.3		6.9	
1934					3.9		5.1	
1935			1.7	1.9	2.9	5.9	3.8	6.0
1936			1.6		3.3		5.5	7.0
1937			1.6	1.8	3.2	4.5	5.6	6.8
1951					72.8		84.0	
1952					83.5		96.5	
1953					53.7		61.8	
1954						106.2		145.0
1955					52.2		75.0	
1956					24.5		33.5	
1957					44.9		61.1	
1958					20.3	27.1	27.7	9.9
1959					22.3	8.2	31.9	12.1
1960					18.9	6.9	26.3	10.5
1961					15.1	5.6	21.7	8.1
1962					12.3	5.1	17.5	7.4
1963					10.0	5.0	14.2	7.0
1964					4.8	3.1	6.8	4.4
1965					4.9	3.6	7.0	5.2
1966					3.3	3.5	4.7	4.9
1967					2.8	3.3	3.9	4.6

Continued

Table 3.2. (*continued*)

Year	(1)	(2)	(3)	(4)	(5)	(6)	(7)	(8)
1968					3.1	3.7	4.3	5.1
1969					2.6	3.4	3.6	4.7
1970					2.2	2.9	3.1	4.
1971					2.3	2.9	3.2	4.1
1972					2.8	3.7	4.0	5.2
1973					2.7	2.9	3.7	4.1
1974					2.3	2.9	3.3	4.
1975					2.3	2.8	3.2	3.9
1976					2.1	2.1	2.9	3.
1977					1.6	1.8	2.3	2.5
1978					1.2	1.2	1.7	1.9
1979					1.3	1.3	1.8	1.8
1980					1.5	1.3	2.1	1.9
1981					1.4	1.2	1.9	1.7
1982					2.2	1.8	3.1	2.6
1983					2.1	1.8	3.0	2.5
1984					1.7	1.4	2.4	1.9
1985					1.6	1.2	2.2	1.7
1986					1.4	1.2	2.0	1.7
1987					1.3	1.1	1.9	1.5
1988					1.6	1.3	2.2	1.8

(1) Representations in guidebooks, Perpetual Austrian Provinces vs Lands of the Hungarian Crown, controlled for population size.
(2) Representations in guidebooks, Austria proper vs Kingdom of Hungary, controlled for population size.
(3) Tourist arrivals, Vienna/Budapest.
(4) Foreign tourist arrivals, Vienna/Budapest.
(5) Foreign tourist arrivals, Austria/Hungary.
(6) Foreign tourist nights, Austria/Hungary.
(7) Foreign tourist exposure rate, Austria/Hungary.
(8) Foreign tourist intensity rate, Austria/Hungary.
Sources: Own Calculations; Vienna, Budapest, Austrian and Hungarian Statistical Offices, Grieszelich 1890, Szerény 1900, Hegedűs 1938, MGKI 1938, Markos (ed.) 1942, Brusatti 1984.

two countries, covered in this chapter, Hungary has never surpassed Austria in terms of any of the measures examined. The only variation to be interpreted is that of *the magnitude of Austria's comparative advantage*.

Apart from guidebook representations (where much of the variation has to do with Baedeker's more even-handed approach than the Anglo-American guidebooks), the magnitude of Austria's advantage appears to vary in a fairly systematic manner. The pattern that emerges from this table can be described by the following regularities:

1. In times of peace, the dominant tendency is a gradual decline in Austria's relative advantages in terms of foreign tourism. Between

1888 and 1913, the differential of foreign tourist arrivals in Vienna and Budapest decreased from 7.8 to 2.2. Scores of the same measure declined from 15.3 to 1.8 between 1920 and 1935. During the years of 1958 through 1988, the ratio of the two countries' foreign tourist arrival, tourist nights, TER and TIR scores was reduced from 20.3 to 1.6, from 7.1 to 1.3, from 27.7 to 2.2, and from 9.9 to 1.8, respectively. *Total* tourist arrivals figures, however, do not conform to this regularity: The ratio of the two capital cities appears to be fairly constant with values between 2 and 3 during most of the period of 1885 and 1937.

2. As the gaps of the above cited results indicate, the two world wars and the periods immediately thereafter are associated with sudden, sizeable increases in the magnitude in Austria's touristic advantages over Hungary. The Great Depression, however, appears to have exerted relatively little effect on the differential between the two capital cities' measures of incoming leisure migration: The ratio of their scores does not indicate a significant change except for an increase for the year 1924.

3. World War II and its aftermath had a much more devastating effect on the two countries' tourism-related disparities than World War I. The highest post-World War I differential is Vienna's over 15 times higher foreign tourist arrivals scores in comparison to Budapest in 1920. In contrast, the two countries' foreign tourist arrival and TER score differentials even exceeded the level of 100 times for a few years after World War II.

4. "Substantive presence" scores (tourist nights and TIR) tend to reflect a smaller degree of inequality than those pertaining to the number of incoming tourists. In other words, the lesser degree of Hungary's exposure to incoming tourists tends to be somewhat balanced by the slightly longer stay of those who do visit.

This chapter has examined various forms of data in order to reconstruct the dynamics of tourism growth in Austria and Hungary. It has found that patterns of uneven capitalist development have been largely reflected in emerging patterns of incoming leisure migration in the Dual Monarchy and the successor states of its two principal constituent units. This system of inequalities has produced the Empire as a highly structured tourism destination with great differences in the degree of relative attractivity and importance attached to its sociogeographical regions. The legacy of this pattern has placed Austria proper in a clearly more advantageous position than Hungary proper after the Empire's dissolution. Consistent belatedness and quantitative underdevelopment characterize pairwise comparisons of statistical data on incoming leisure migration, reflecting unequivocal relative disadvantages for Hungary.

It is just as important to recognize, however, that initial under-development "*per se*" does not sufficiently explain the dynamics of tourism growth in the two countries: Original discrepancies have shown a convincing tendency of diminishing during peacetime. Detectable instances of relapse in the degree of Hungary's relative under-development have been observed during the two world wars and their aftermath. The relative belatedness of Hungary's tourism growth has been reproduced repeatedly, at an ever increasing magnitude, by wars and subsequent periods of generalized political violence and abrupt political change in Hungary. In contrast, the recent interval of some thirty years of peace and relative political stability involved stable growth, resulting in Hungary's approximation of Austrian measures of incoming tourism. The comparisons examined in this chapter suggest that *the reproduction of relative underdevelopment in incoming leisure migration has not been a mechanical replay of historical backwardness. It appears to have been a combined effect of the legacy of underdevelopment activated and exacerbated by wars and generalized political violence.*

Chapter 4

Austria's and Hungary's External Linkages after World War II

The two preceding chapters analyzed a wide range of comparative-historical data, and detected an isomorphy between the emerging spatial and temporal patterns of international tourism and the uneven development of international capitalism. *Chapter 2* observed this relationship on the level of the European continent as a whole; *chapter 3* replicated the analysis using data on the Austro-Hungarian Empire and its two main successor states since the 1870s until today. Leisure migration was conceptualized as an intrinsic component of the development of industrial capitalism whose ideological–political, economic–structural, and technological components constitute a single process. By and large, changes in the gross volume of international tourism in Austria and Hungary mirror world tourism's tendency to dynamic growth. The comparison also suggested that the reproduction of relative under-development in incoming leisure migration was exacerbated by such macrostructural factors as wars and generalized political violence.

Another main aspect of the contextual conditions under which inter-national leisure migration takes place today has to do with the post-World War II bifurcation of the interstate system. The cleavage between state socialism and capitalism bears on the analysis of the sociospatial patterns of international leisure migration in two ways. It refers to two distinct sociopolitical systems—two sets of state-entities with partly different internal characteristics—and two sociopolitical blocs—relatively distinct sets of state entities characterized by partly different types of linkages among them. This chapter draws a brief outline of the parallel histories of the postwar reconstruction and transformation of the Austrian and Hungarian states and economies in terms of their external linkages.

Austria's and Hungary's Linkages

Political linkages

World War II found both countries in the Axis Powers' camp. With its *Anschluss* to the Third Reich, the independent statehood of Austria was suspended in 1938. Although Hungary was not occupied militarily by Germany until the Spring of 1944, it, too, belonged squarely in the German sphere of great-power interests as a subordinate partner. Austrian conscripts were integrated in the *Wehrmacht* (the military force of Nazi Germany) and fought the war as regular military personnel. Hungarian troops participated in the war in national units under Hungarian command, first launched on the Soviet front in 1941.

Great-power decisions concerning the fate of the two countries began well before the Allied victory. The Allied Powers' Moscow Declaration is often quoted as the foundation for the reconstruction of Austria's statehood after the war: "Acting on a draft introduced by Anthony Eden, Churchill's Foreign Secretary, Great Britain, the United States and the Soviet Union declared on November 1, 1943, that 'they wish to see re-established a free and independent Austria' " (Jankowitsch 1981:361 quoting the Moscow Declaration 1943). The Moscow Declaration also pronounced Austria as the first victim of Nazism.

Designs for Hungary's future were formulated in a starkly different tone. The Allies' plans for a set of countries on the Balkan peninsula (Bulgaria, Greece, Romania, and Yugoslavia) reveal a distinctly colonial mode of deliberation. At the Yalta conference, Churchill jotted down on a half sheet of paper the West's bargaining position concerning future political influences over these states, in relative percentages of Western versus Soviet leverage, and passed it on to Stalin. The British Prime Minister recalls the subsequent events of historic significance for the future of the Balkans and Central Europe in his memoirs:

> There was a slight pause. Then [Stalin] took his blue pencil and made a large tick upon it, and passed it back to us. It was all settled in no more time than it takes to set down (Churchill 1953:226–7, reprinted in Stokes, 1991:31–2).

Under the conditions of 90% Soviet predominance in Romania, and "Western" control over Greece of the same magnitude, the note proposed a fifty–fifty division of power over Hungary and Yugoslavia between the two blocs.

The events that followed did not conform even to the suggested formula of "equal" sharing of political influence over Hungary. Control over the Hungarian state and, consequently, the nature of the political system of the state, was determined by such clearly imperial considerations as the military events of the last year of the war. With the retreat of the Axis Powers from the Soviet theater, the front passed through Hungary in the course of about five months so that the war was over for Hungary by early April, 1945. Lacking an Allied offensive on the Balkans, it was the Red Army alone that defeated the joint German and Hungarian forces in Hungary, so that the country was placed under Soviet military occupation. Direct military government was established by the Soviet forces, under largely symbolic oversight by an Allied military committee devoid of any significant power. A few weeks after the hostilities ended, the situation normalized somewhat, and the Soviet authorities banned all spontaneous forms of democratic self-government called "national committees" ("Nemzeti Bizottságok") and reorganized public administration to mirror the Soviet pattern. Then power was handed over to the new authorities, called, henceforth, "councils" ("tanácsok"). Soon the Allied observers left the country. (The world *soviet* means "council" in Russian.)

The Soviet political leadership exercised increasing influence on the shape of the political systems of the countries it occupied. In Hungary, all "bourgeois" political parties were eliminated in the course of three years, and the rule of the Communist Party, a close subordinate of the Moscow center, was established with full force. Soviet political, military, security and economic advisors were placed in key decision-making positions in the Hungarian state and party bureaucracies. The country's borders with its non-Soviet-dominated neighbors—Austria and Yugoslavia—were sealed by barbed wire fences, mine fields, and a several-kilometers-wide, high-security border zone. Entry visa obligation was established for all foreign visitors except those from the Soviet bloc, and western radio broadcasts were jammed. Travel abroad by Hungarian citizens was severely restricted. The military *status quo* dissolved into political conquest: Hungary was effectively recast in the Stalinist mold.

In contrast, the Austrian part of what was in early 1945 still the Third Reich was occupied not only by the Soviet Union but also the Western Allies. The country was divided into four territorially separate zones of military control by the Allied powers. Political, administrative, and practical controls over Austria had been, from the defeat of the Wehrmacht during the Spring of 1945 onwards, substantively shared among the Allies. The provisional government of newly-independent Austria was set up under Soviet supervision, and consisted of representatives of the socialist, communist and Christian democratic parties. After about five months, the legitimacy of this provisional arrangement was accepted by the western Allies. National elections were held in November, 1945. Although "the Austrian government was given a large measure of authority by the Allied Control Authority on June 28, 1946" (Keefe et al 1976:22), the presence of foreign occupying troops made the exercise of state sovereignty difficult. With the proliferation of the Cold War, power sharing among the Allies came to be plagued by increasingly sharp conflicts. Audrey Kurth Cronin (1989) for instance mentions Soviet-proposed "draconian economic penalties" and Yugoslav territorial claims against Austria as major stumbling blocks that prevented a compromise between the Soviet Union and the western Allies concerning Austria.

The tug-of-war concerning Austria's place in the new European order of political and military alliances—known in the history of international relations as "the Austrian question" (Jankowitsch 1981:361)—lasted for ten years. During this period, Austria was not allowed to have a military force of its own (Spannocchi 1981:381). The compromise eventually reached concerning the external political alliances of Austria was codified in the formula of "active neutrality" proposed after the Swiss model by the then Austrian Secretary of State, Bruno Kreisky, and negotiated successfully by Austrian government officials with Moscow (Jankowitsch 1981:363). This compromise is to be understood against the background of the intensifying Cold War, West Germany's refusal in 1954 to observe the postwar ban on its remilitarization—a move obviously supported by the western Allies—the pronouncement of the Soviet-occupied eastern part of Germany as a fully sovereign state by the Soviet authorities, and, finally, the establishment of the Warsaw Pact in 1955, with all Soviet-occupied countries of east-central Europe as its founding members (Roberts 1976).

The foreign occupation of Austria concluded in 1955 with the enactment of the Austrian *Staatsvertrag*—literally, the 'State Treaty' signed by the Foreign Ministers of the Allied Powers, which proclaimed Austria as a sovereign, independent, and democratic state. It restored the country's pre-1938 borders, enunciated its neutrality, and expressly forbade its unification with Germany as well as entry into any military alliance (Eppel and Lotter 1981:113). The American, British, French, and Soviet troops departed from Austria in less than six months, and the construction of a new Austrian military force was permitted again. The day after the removal of all foreign troops from Austrian soil, Parliament enacted a new constitutional law. Before year's end, Austria was accepted for membership in the United Nations and the international conflict known as the "Austrian question" was over. In the following year, Austria joined the Council of Europe. During the decades that followed, Austria specialized, on the basis of its externally guaranteed hence very stable neutrality, in diplomatic mediation between various blocs and alliances. Today Vienna is one of the permanent seats of the United Nations and hosts many international organizations, including the Organization of Petroleum Exporting Countries and the International Atomic Energy Agency.

The withdrawal of the Soviet occupational forces from northeastern Austria in 1955 removed the only remaining justification for the stationing of Soviet troops in neighboring Hungary in terms of international law. (Up until then, the Soviet military presence in Hungary was rationalized in terms of the logistical necessity of providing them access between the mother country—the Soviet Union—and their positions in northeastern Austria. By expressly ending the occupation of Austria, while conspicuously omitting any provisions concerning the Soviet troops' withdrawal from Hungary, the Austrian State Treaty *de facto* reinforced politically, legally, and psychologically, the Hungarian state's sense of helplessness *vis-à-vis* the Soviet Union.) This situation was solidified further by the formal establishment of the Warsaw Pact which tied Hungary as well as all other states of east-central Europe in the Soviet orbit.

Hungary's anti-Stalinist uprising of 1956 was extinguished by the Soviet military forces which at that point experienced their first engagement in combat since World War II. At stake in the 1956 uprising were the two main structural determinants of Hungary's sociopolitical future: Its relationship to external political powers, namely the Soviet Union, and the future of its political system. On both counts, the crushing of the uprising left behind a severe sense of collective frustration. After the suppression of the uprising, about 200,000 people, or 2% of the country's total population, emigrated from Hungary through the borders that were open for about four months between October, 1956 through January, 1957. Austria played an extremely important role in processing these masses of asylum-seekers. Hungarians thus initiated a role for Austria as a gate of emigrés from east-central and eastern Europe as well as, more recently, from elsewhere in the world.

As a former ally of the Axis Powers, Hungary's international reputation suffered after World War II. The Stalinist transformation of the country's economic, political and social fabric came to be one of the many points of tension between the Soviet Union and the western powers. The forcible removal of the revolutionary government of 1956, the creation of a puppet government installed by the Soviet Union, and the subsequent execution or imprisonment of tens of thousands of participants of the uprising, made Hungary's diplomatic recognition in international fora extremely difficult. The "Hungarian question"—the western powers' refusal to grant Hungary membership in the United Nations—continued to plague East–West relations until the solidification of the *status quo* and the first signs of a political reconciliation inside the country. Hungary was admitted to the United Nations six years later than Austria, only in the year of the famous Kennedy–Khrushchev talks (held in Vienna), in 1961.

The dynamics of superpower rivalry placed Austria and Hungary in very different positions after World War II. The formal reconstruction of Austria's independent statehood took ten years to establish, and can be causally attributed to changes in military strategy due to nuclear parity between the NATO and the Warsaw Pact. The removal of the foreign occupational forces from Austria involved reciprocal arrangements on both sides of the "Iron Curtain." As Hungary was occupied by a single foreign power, an end to its foreign occupation would have required a unilateral concession on part of the Soviet Union—something which did not take place until a few months before the eventual collapse of the Soviet state itself in 1990.

Austria arrived on the threshold of the sixties as a country positioned firmly in between the two military and political blocs, whose neutrality, democratic politics, and independence was jointly guaranteed by an explicit agreement between the main powers of the two blocs. Hungary, on the other hand, started the sixties as the ominous empirical evidence of Soviet imperial ambitions in central and eastern Europe. The eventual acceptance of the Hungarian government in international fora thus represented the admission on part of the Western powers of their limited interest in, and circumscribed ability to exercise influence over, matters "internal" to the Soviet bloc so that the principles of neutrality, democracy and independence remained unsettled as far as those countries were concerned. To apply an elegant distinction borrowed initially from Lewis Coser (1956) by Adam Przeworski (1986:56), the main difference between the ends to the Austrian and the Hungarian "questions" was that the former was resolved while the latter problem, similar to the situation of many of the Soviet-dominated areas of Europe, was terminated. As Przeworski points out, "[c]onflicts are rarely resolved, but under democracy some states of affairs are recognized as temporarily binding in the sense that they are alterable only by going through the same rules by which they were brought about" (Przeworski 1986:56).

Austrian statehood was restored through a diplomatic compromise that restricted the Austrian state's military freedom but re-established all other elements of the sovereignty of the state as a multiparty democracy. The postwar restoration of Hungarian statehood involved the large-scale transformation of the character of the state into a one-party system, tightly integrated within the Soviet sphere of military alliance, political influence, and direct control, thereby leaving serious questions concerning the sovereignty of the state.

Economic linkages

The two countries' position in the emerging economic order of postwar Europe became just as disparate as their place in the interstate system. Although both economies suffered tremendous losses of both fixed and human capital during the war, their reconstruction took very different paths. Those differences can be best outlined by two dimensions: (1) the two countries' different reactions to the Marshall Plan and, hence, sharply differential access to financing their reconstruction projects, and (2) the subsequent reorganization of their external economic linkages, solidified through their membership in distinct international systems of economic integration.

It is customary to identify the initiation of the European Reconstruction Project in US Secretary of State George C. Marshall's famous speech at Harvard University on June 5, 1947. In that address, Marshall identified the root cause of the seemingly perpetual crisis of Europe in "the dislocation of the entire fabric of European economy" due to the abnormal conditions created in Europe by Nazi rule, and preparation for, and fighting of, the war (Marshall 1984[1947]:271). Marshall pronounced that, as Europe's economic viability was "essential to political stability and an assured peace, the interest of the United States lay in providing economic assistance" (Brown and Opie 1953:126).

Except for the Soviet Union, all European countries reacted with great interest to Marshall's proposal. The Soviet leadership, involved in transforming the political and economic fabric of its satellite states, interpreted Marshall's aid proposal as a disguised manifestation of the Truman Doctrine. The Truman Doctrine, attributed to President Truman's justification for aid to Greece and Turkey, was proclaimed a few weeks before the announcement of the Marshall Plan. It urged that infusions of American monetary assistance should have political strings attached to them, and that their main purpose should be to support the United States' worldwide fight against the "Russian Communist threat" (Brown and Opie 1953:124).

The Soviet Union thus attended the first conference concerning particulars of the large-scale European Reconstruction Program only to voice its reservations. As Brown and Opie summarize, the Soviet delegates:

> (. . .) opposed the idea of a common recovery plan on the ground that it would mean outside interference in the economies of small countries and the destruction of the existing framework of bilateral trade agreements. [The Soviet Union] alleged that the primary reason behind the offer of the United States was to increase American exports (Brown and Opie 1953:133).

Soon the Soviet Union and all the countries it occupied refused participation in subsequent talks. The satellite countries' refusal was clearly under Soviet pressure: "On July 7, [1947], for example, Czechoslovakia announced that it would be represented at the [next] conference, but on the 10th, after [Czechoslovak] Premier Gottwald had talked to Stalin in Moscow, it reversed its stand" (Brown and Opie 1953:133). The

Hungarian government was also unable to resist Soviet pressure, and renounced the Marshall Plan as an imperialist ploy.

The creation of the international organization to administer the aid package of the Marshall Plan—the Organization for European Economic Cooperation (OEEC)—prompted the establishment of a symmetrical economic integration on the Soviet side, the Council for Mutual Economic Assistance (CMEA) in 1949. For lack of access to substantial amounts of capital, what this Soviet-centered counterpart to the economic organization of the Marshall Plan provided for its members was exclusive access to the member states' economies through bilateral political negotiations concerning exchange rates, terms of trade, and the "harmonization" of national economic plans. This integration of the various economies was achieved through the establishment of annual delivery quotas in natural terms, thus eliminating the necessity of scarcely available convertible currencies with exchange rates controlled from the outside of the state socialist bloc.

To insure the exclusivity of access to each other's economies and to protect the state socialist bloc's nonconvertible-currency trade, all previously existing external linkages of the participating economies were brought under the substantive control of the imperial state apparatus. Connections between the CMEA-member countries and the rest of the world were severely reduced, and ties among the participating economies were transformed. These arrangements provided the external component of the state socialist transformation of these economies. The main internal component of the state socialist formula—the large-scale confiscation and placement under "planned," bureaucratic management by the state of the main means of production—took place simultaneously with the rejection of the Marshall Plan and the formation of the CMEA.

Large-scale takeover by the state of the major means of production in itself is not a sufficient condition for an economy's transition to state socialism. This is illustrated by the very example of Austria where, März and Szecsi point out, the Nationalization Acts of 1946 and 1947, enacted jointly by socialist and conservative members of Parliament, established state control over:

> the extractive industries [. . .], practically the entire steel industry, and most of the large enterprises in the field of machinery, chemicals, and electrical equipment. At the same time the three largest banks of the country, which in turn held considerable industrial assets, were nationalized. Full public property was also established in the field of electric power generation (März and Szecsi 1981:128).

These measures can be understood in light of the Potsdam Conference which granted control over all German property in Austria to the occupying powers. Given the heavy historical influence of German capital, solidified by the Anschluss and subsequent large-scale German industrial investment activity, in Austria:

> the domestic political consensus in the question of state take-over reflected
> fears that, in the absence of such measures, a very significant proportion of
> the Austrian economy would slip out of the hands of the Austrian government
> for a long time, or perhaps even forever (Richter and Székffy 1986:15).

Even with large-scale "preventative" confiscation by the Austrian state,
252 industrial and 140 agricultural firms, with altogether ca. 45,000
employees, were under Soviet control during the first ten years after
World War II (Richter and Székffy 1986:15 quoting Austrian sources).

   The implementation of the Marshall Plan had at least two effects. First,
it provided, along with other less comprehensive aid packages, an important boost to the war-torn, investment-hungry economies of the non-
Soviet-dominated part of Europe. Austria, for instance, received,
during the first ten years of the postwar reconstruction of its statehood,
US$1580 million in foreign aid, 87% of which came from the United
States alone (Nemschak 1955:27). Of that sum, about US$956 million
were donated to Austria through the Marshall Plan, officially called the
European Reconstruction Project (ERP) (Nemschak 1955:28). Austria—
with about 2.35% of the total population of the non-Soviet-controlled
part of Europe at the time (United Nations 1950)—received between an
annual 4.7% and 6.1% of the drawing rights of the total European
Recovery and Defense Support Programs financed by the United States
government between April 1948, and December 31, 1951 (Brown and
Opie 1953:222). Over two-thirds of the ERP funds were provided as
direct aid, pumped into the Austrian economy through a revolving fund
called the "counterpart account." The essence of this arrangement was
that, once the basic sum was remitted to the Austrian government, the
countervalue of the aid was issued at subsidized rates as business credit
to enterprises. Revenues from the repayment of those credits were then
channeled back into the same fund. The rest of the Marshall Aid to
Austria was spent: "to cover deficits in the balance of trade, first on a
bilateral, later on a multilateral, basis in the framework of the European
Payments Union" (März and Szecsi 1981:127).

   Another important effect of the Marshall Plan was the creation of the
basic framework of the reconstruction of an integrated European market
through international organizations. That development, in turn, split the
continent in the middle. The Soviet rejection of the Marshall Plan
worked to detach the Soviet-controlled economies of the continent from
the rest of the world economy. This accelerated the consolidation of the
state socialist bloc as not only a military and political alliance, but also a
trading bloc and an international organization of economic integration,
resulting in the large-scale structural transformation of the economies
involved.

Table 4.1. Proportion of Austria's and Hungary's Foreign Trade with the State Socialist Countries, Selected Years, 1937–89

	Austria		Hungary	
	Imports	Exports	Imports	Exports
(1937–8)	(40.6)	(33.7)	(22.5)	(12.6)
1948	27.2	20.0	—	—
1954	11.8	13.6	65.5	70.9
1960	13.5	18.3	68.9	69.8
1970	11.1	19.3	64.2	65.3
1980	10.7	19.3	50.6	55.1
1989	7.8	11.7	43.1	47.3

Sources: Computed from United Nations, 1956–89. For comparison's sake, the row of 1937–38 was included to describe trade with the countries that would make a transition to state socialism after the war. Austria's figures are for 1937, and Hungary's ones are for 1938.

Time series data on the transformation of the composition of Austrian and Hungarian foreign trade by groups of countries illustrate this point. As Table 4.1 indicates, Austria had, in the last year of its prewar independence, a substantial proportion of its foreign trade with the countries that would constitute, after World War II, the bloc of socialist states. In 1937, over 40% of Austria's imports came from those countries, and one-third of its exports were directed there. These figures are 1.8 and 2.67 times higher than the corresponding prewar figures for Hungary. The divergence of the two countries' postwar paths is clearly visible in the subsequent rows of Table 4.1: By 1954, the relative proportion of Austria's trade connections with the state socialist countries declined sharply, falling to between 11.8 and 13.6%. In contrast, Hungary's dependence on its state socialist trade linkages increased three-to-fivefold: From the early 1950s onwards, about two-thirds of its exports and imports were made up by transactions with other state socialist economies. These contrasting tendencies clearly reflect the separation of Austria's and Hungary's positions in the economic fiber of a continent torn in the middle by the two sociopolitical blocs exactly on the border between the two countries.

The external economic linkages that the two countries inherited from the prewar period were broken up by this arrangement. Before World War I, Austria proper—the more affluent and more industrialized of the two countries—had had an important sense of involvement in the east-central European economies as an exporter of capital and technology. With the destruction of the Empire after World War I, remnants of that role remained, notwithstanding the adjustment crisis of the country which had just lost all of its imperial realm, as it entered the period of the Great Depression of 1929–34. (With the breakup of the Habsburg

Monarchy, the very economic viability of Austria proper as a country was seriously questioned by experts and statesmen alike.) Historically, east-central European exports to Austria have consisted mainly of agricultural goods. As a former imperial center of a large part of central Europe, Austria had also played, until the Anschluss, an economic middleman role between the eastern and western halves of Europe, most prominently Germany. An important consequence of the Anschluss was Austria's inclusion in the German military economy, marked by sizeable direct German investment in the Austrian heavy industry. The stagnation following World War I and the subsequent dismantling of the Habsburg Empire was hence followed by a brief period of expansion during which "unemployment radically decreased and the growth rate went into the double digits" (Richter and Székffy 1986:13).

No doubt, the disruption of much of its trade with the less advanced economies of the Soviet-dominated part of Europe and its detachment from a defeated and divided Germany caused, again, economic adjustment problems for Austria after World War II. However, this time the adverse effects of the forced reorganization of Austria's external economic ties were counterbalanced by two main processes; namely, the infusion of subsidized investment credits through the US-led aid programs and the country's access to the new west European institutions of economic integration.

As a recipient of the Marshall Aid, Austria became a member of the OEEC by default. The OEEC was later broadened to encompass a few non-European economies and renamed Organization of Economic Development and Cooperation (OECD). As its neutrality prevented its formal entry into the European Economic Community (EEC), Austria became a founding member—along with Switzerland and Sweden—of the European Free Trade Association (EFTA). Concerted efforts aimed at providing some kind of avenue to attain integration with the EEC were rewarded by a free trade agreement between Austria and the EEC. Hence, Austria enjoyed a doubly advantageous position in terms of its external economic relations: First, it eventually achieved a high degree of association with the most developed economies of Europe while, second, it enjoyed a preferential position in trade with the Soviet bloc.

Austria's successful integration with western Europe through a series of financial and economic agreements took place just in time for Austria to benefit from postreconstruction economic growth. Stephan Koren's data indicate that Austria's growth was one of the steepest after the signing of the State Treaty. Between 1955 and 1974, the real gross national product of the European members of the OECD increased by a mean value of 132% while Austria's economy grew by 156% during the same twenty-year period (Koren 1981:178). That growth rate was the third highest in Europe.

As a technologically advanced neutral country, Austria had comfortable access to orders from the state socialist economies for commodities that the Soviet-bloc states could not, or, for political reasons, would not, purchase in the EEC. Similar to Finland, the Austrian economy specialized in mediation between the state socialist economies and the capitalist world. This phenomenon was clearly reflected in the rising percentages of the shares of the state socialist economies in Austria's *exports*. By 1960, Table 4.1 suggests, trade with the state socialist economies surpassed the magnitude of half of those countries' share in Austria's prewar structure of exports, and stabilized around that figure. By the late seventies, Austria was second only to Finland in the non-CMEA-member part of Europe in terms of the proportion of its trade with the state socialist countries (Butschek 1981:145). This "interbloc" mediation was, however, rather one-sided; the state socialist economies' exports have never reached more than one-third of their prewar market share in the Austrian economy. Their export percentages have reflected a tendency of monotonous decline since 1960. Austria's recent "eastern" trade reflects a classic core-semiperiphery pattern. The state socialist economies, primarily the Soviet Union, have supplied about 35–40% of Austria's energy. Nine-tenth of the Austrian exports to Hungary have been manufactured goods, while manufactures have comprised only about one-third of Hungarian exports to Austria (after Richter and Székffy 1986:191–2).

With its simultaneous access to the EFTA-, EEC- and CMEA-areas, Austria transformed into a vibrant economy. Austria's earlier middleman role between two areas of Europe, characterized by radically different degrees and forms of industrial capitalism, was replaced in the more complex postwar period—marked, for instance, by the accelerated, state socialist industrialization of east-central Europe—by a new kind of middleman role, this time between the two political blocs. Under the peculiar conditions of the Cold War, and due to its own idiosyncratic position between the two blocs, the Austrian economy has evolved from a bi-directional middleman between the more and less developed parts of Europe into a major exporter of goods of west European quality to the state socialist bloc.

Dual Dependency

The postwar reorganization of international power integrated the countries of east-central Europe in the framework of the Warsaw Pact and the CMEA, while erecting serious barriers to their access to west European markets. The system of dependencies to which the societies of the Soviet-controlled part of Europe came to be subjected was a direct reflection of this ambiguous relationship. (For more detail, see Böröcz 1992.) Ambiguity originated from the fact that their local imperial power represented a grandiose, albeit eventually frustrated, attempt at the creation of a (politically integrated) state socialist world empire implanted within a world market. (The term "world empire" refers to the Wallersteinian concept and denotes a politicoeconomic system wherein multiple states are integrated principally through the power of an overarching suprastate. The east-central European imperial arrangement implied the partial displacement of state sovereignty from the local to the imperial center.)

The creation of a state socialist bloc radically redrew the web of dependencies connecting the societies of east-central Europe to the global system. This new web was conceptually more complex than that of the less developed capitalist societies. The mode of incorporation of east-central Europe involved, over the entire state socialist history of the region, a strong sense of "dual personality." Structurally speaking, the place of the east-central European socialist states can be conceptualized as a mixture of two constitutive elements: (1) a partially constructed, hence "imperfect," and primarily *political* form of dependency on an imperial center which was created by military means and maintained via imperial methods; and, combined in intricate ways with this, (2) an essentially *economic* form of dependency on core actors—capital, states, etc.

This thesis can be extended. For all societies that have undergone a state socialist transformation after the founding of the Soviet Union, the parallel presence and continuous interplay of the political and economic aspects of external dependency on two distinct sets of actors have been the "differentia specifica" of their mode of incorporation in the world economy. To be noted is that what is unique here is not the combination of political and economic elements *per se*—that is obviously present in all other forms of external dependency—but the fact that those two constitutive elements are separated not only analytically but also empirically, as historical forms. East-central Europe's experience suggests that political and economic components of external dependency can be fixed on two distinct sets of actors as long as the two nuclei are locked into a partly antagonistic relationship with each other. As a result, east-central Europe's experience with dependency differs in important qualitative respects from that of other semiperipheries.

The cruelest, Stalinist form of dual dependency was characterized by the overwhelming dominance of the imperial-political component. During the period that followed Stalinism—starting, in Hungary's case, around the early 1960s—the two components of dual dependency came into some kind of precious equilibrium. Although Stalin died in 1953, the beginning of post-Stalinism is marked in Hungary so late because of the protracted disturbances during and following the uprising of 1956. It was not until the early 1960s that political prisoners were released and a host of symbolic as well as substantive gestures were made by the Kádár-regime, signalling an end to the openly violent form of rule under state socialism. For precision's sake, it should be noted also that Romania and Albania represent exceptions from the general tendency of de-Stalinization by never effectively exiting from the Stalinist model of state socialism. Rather than inching toward softer compromises after the Hungarian revolution, the Romanian and Albanian forms of government became more and more rigid and, by the mid-sixties, both countries saw the emergence of the harshest form of despotism, only to be overthrown by the Romanian uprising and coup of December 1989, and the Albanian crisis of 1991 and early 1992.

Once Hungary's anti-imperial revolution of 1956 had been extinguished, the imperial state's claims to direct "manual" controls receded substantially. By the early 1960s, certain important forms of direct core-dependency reappeared, especially through technological follow-up dependency on, and large-scale state borrowing from, core actors. This order represented a sophisticated compromise whose stability can be understood as the outcome of a complementary arrangement: Relatively moderate yet undoubtedly extant political oppression suited well the lenders' demand for internal stability in the debtor country, while infusions of hard currency worked to quiet the political climate inside the state socialist bloc.

The period following Stalinism was marked by the large-scale transformation of the structure of Hungary's external linkages. The relaxation of the previous regime's rigid restrictions on cross-border contacts and flows became a fundamental component of the period's soft, "winking dictatorship." The early 1960s compromise, however, did not mean in any way a complete surrender of linkage-restrictions as such. The new system of external ties was worked out through conflict and gradual, often very hesitant and lopsided, "reforms" introduced over the period lasting from the early 1960s through the late 1980s.

Hungary's transition from the Stalinist linkage system to the subsequent, more relaxed version of state socialism can be summarized, schematically, as a combination of three main elements: (1) the partial reorientation of the state's own external linkages, (2) a careful opening-up of the first economy (that sector of the state socialist economy which is substantively controlled by the state through direct ownership, planning, and/or bureaucratic management) toward the European core of the world market and for horizontal linkages with other east-central European state socialist states, and (3) the slow and gradual process of extending tacit political-economic concessions developed in the domestic second economy (all income earning activities outside the realm of state control through ownership, planning, and/or bureaucratic management) to external linkages as well.

First, the state's own linkages were rearranged. Day-to-day imperial controls over the local state were replaced by a more efficient, "strategic" regime of control. The state re-established bilateral contacts and flows with the neighboring small state states of the region. The early 1970s general atmosphere of *Realpolitik* and *détente* provided access for the post-Stalinist state to large sums of state credits mostly from private lenders: Between 1970 and 1979, the Hungarian state's gross foreign debt redoubled at the average speed of three years, and reached the level of US$17.7 billion by 1987 (Világgazdaság, 1989 quoting the National Bank of Hungary). In essence, foreign capital came to valorize Hungarian labor by lending to the socialist state during the period after the fall of Stalinism.

Austrian capital was involved in this process in two important ways. First, major Austrian banks played a key role in organizing the credit packages offered to the Hungarian government. Second, they also participated in lending to the Hungarian socialist state in very significant ways themselves: Between 1974 and 1986, the share of the Austrian banks in the external debt of Hungary increased from 10.3 to 18.4% (Richter and Székffy 1986:196). By the mid-1980s, the share of Austrian capital in the Hungarian state's foreign debt was about twice as high as Hungary's share in Austrian exports. Richter and Székffy point out that three-quarters of Hungarian debt to Austria was incurred in currencies other than the Austrian Schilling (ATS). These loans were "extended mostly on the basis of the activities of the Austrian banks in the Euromarket, that is, they were freely usable finance credits" (Richter and Székffy 1986:195). They were not tied to Austrian exports to Hungary. In essence, the Hungarian government, excluded from direct access to the European financial markets, utilized Austrian financial services following the old middleman pattern.

The intercourse of the Hungarian first economy with formal sectors in the core produced a growing trade in investment goods as well as consumption items. Traditionally strong Hungarian products were reintroduced in West European markets, and some actors of the Hungarian first economy were able to make modest technological adjustments with such revenues. The Hungarian economy reoriented itself toward trade with the world outside the state socialist bloc. The share of hard currency deals in Hungary's total foreign trade increased from its lowest point of 30% in imports and 29% in exports in 1960 to 38% and 39% in 1970, 50% and 57% in 1980, and 57% and 58% in 1988, respectively (computed from KSH 1965; 1970; 1975; 1980; 1989a). Trade with such non-CMEA-member state socialist countries as Yugoslavia or China has always been on hard currency accounting. In addition, some strategically crucial items of Soviet-Hungarian commerce—such as oil, for instance—were exempted from Soviet-Rouble-based accounting, and have been on a US$-basis since the aftermath of the oil crisis of the early 1970s. These considerations explain the discrepancy between these figures and Table 4.1.

In 1990, the share of hard-currency transactions in Hungarian commerce climbed to 70% in both exports and imports, (hvg 1991) and approximated the level of 100% on January 1, 1991, when nonconvertible currency trade was officially abolished. By contrast, Austria's official economy of course never exited from hard-currency accounting.

Cross-border labor migration also re-emerged—especially from Hungary to the German Democratic Republic and from Poland, Vietnam, and Cuba to Hungary—under careful control and close supervision by the state and party organs of the participating countries. From the early 1970s onwards, Hungarian workers were sent to East Germany with the aim of alleviating some of the structural tensions of the Hungarian industrial labor market and training Hungarian labor in the more advanced East German industry. The total number of Hungarians having worked in the German Democratic Republic under the umbrella of this agreement is estimated at ca. 40,000. The placement of Polish labor—especially miners and construction workers—in Hungary was agreed upon in foreign trade accords whereby Poland's mounting debt to Hungary would be decreased by the direct exportation of skilled labor from Poland to Hungarian companies. The Cuban and Vietnamese arrangements had been of similar character to the Hungarian–East German bilateral state agreement, combined with provisions for training and technology transfer.

Labor flows from Hungary to the west European and north American labor markets, unmediated by the state, were relatively insignificant due to the "short stay versus no return" character of travel arrangements during the post-Stalinist period: In order to be able to spend an extended period of time abroad, Hungarian labor had to "defect," i.e., leave Hungary with a regular tourist exit visa and claim political asylum in the destination core country. The combination of a limited freedom of leisure travel with the state's ban on entering into legal employment abroad precluded return to Hungary until a new citizenship had been obtained. That price was high enough to dissuade much of potential spontaneous labor emigration so that relatively few Hungarians have resorted to this solution, notwithstanding the availability of that option since the gradual easing of exit visa restrictions from the mid-1960s until the late 1980s.

It is in this context of political, economic and social relaxation that Hungary's increasing exposure to international tourism, demonstrated in the preceding chapter in the rising numbers of foreign tourists, occurred. By the early 1980s, Hungary had become the state socialist country with the world's highest per capita foreign tourist presence, measured both in terms of arrivals and tourist nights.

In summary, different constellations of the same set of external forces produced sharply different outcomes in terms of the postwar political and economic reconstruction of the two countries. Austria was restored as an almost completely sovereign state under strong external guarantees. Hence, Austria managed to find a niche that more than compensated for the external constraints on its military power within a role as a relatively independent, "actively neutral" state actor in the international arena, and a successful commercial middleman in a world market bifurcated by the state socialism–capitalism divide. On the other hand, the reconstruction of Hungary's statehood and economy placed the Hungarian society in the Soviet orbit, restricted its state sovereignty, and locked it into an economic integration with the Soviet Union and the latter's other satellites. Between the early 1960s and 1989, the more compromising post-Stalinist period can be characterized as a process of gradual opening and abatement of tension whereby the severity of the enforcement of state socialist linkages was reduced but the fundamental pattern of dual external dependency was not repealed.

Chapter 5

Austria and Hungary as Destinations, 1960–84

This chapter, first, briefly examines the aggregate total statistical effects of two structural properties of the capitalist world system—the uneven development of the world economy and the splitting of the interstate system into political blocs—on geographical patterns of leisure migration by observing global and European data on tourist flows. Then it develops a set of propositions concerning the relative likelihood that foreign tourists from various countries of origin visit Austria and Hungary, and tests them on detailed statistics of country-specific foreign tourist arrivals and foreign tourist nights in the two countries for the period of their longest undisturbed parallel tourism growth, i.e., between 1960 and 1984.

Global and European Evidence

The best compendium of national and international tourism statistics available to date—Raymond BarOn's *Travel and Tourism Data* (1989) combines information from national tourism statistics and estimates by such international organizations as the World Tourism Organization (WTO), the Organization for Economic Cooperation and Development (OECD), and the United Nations, and accounts for different methodologies of data collection and estimation. Data drawn from this source suggest that the worldwide distribution of tourist arrivals and overnight stays is very uneven: Of the 215 countries included in the statistics, 10 countries, with 13% of the world's population, recorded altogether 56% of the total of 385 million arrivals in 1985 (BarOn 1989:Table 2). Reordered by tourist night equivalents, the top ten countries, with 12% of the world population, registered 59% of the total of 3248 million tourist nights (BarOn 1989:Table 2).

BarOn (1989) only focuses on tourism statistics as recorded at destinations. It offers some information on the national origin of tourists at destinations but those data are neither exhaustive nor reliable, and directly comparable worldwide data on international tourist departures are impossible to come by. Hence, this overview will only focus on the effects of uneven development on the worldwide distribution of tourists among destinations. Some material concerning European travel will be examined later, and this matter will be taken up in the final segment of this chapter where the Austrian and Hungarian cases are analyzed.

Figure 5.1 plots the distribution of worldwide per capita foreign tourist arrivals in 1985 by per capita gross domestic product in 1982 for 118 countries (with data from BarOn 1989:Table 5). Scarcity of data

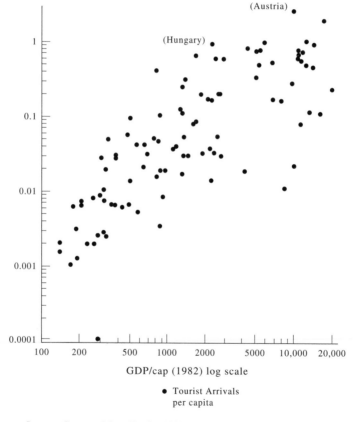

Source: Computed from BarOn, 1989, and World Bank, 1985.

Figure 5.1. Per Capita International Tourist Arrivals by Per Capita Gross Domestic Product

restricted the selection of the countries for these graphs. The main difficulty had to do with the absence of reliable national product or income information for 1982 for the smallest states and for the state socialist bloc except for such World Bank member countries as China, Hungary, Romania and Yugoslavia. As neither GDP/cap nor GNP/cap figures are available for the entire set of 215 countries for which BarOn (1989) offers tourism statistics, Figures 5.1 and 5.2 use GDP/cap scores (from IBRD 1985) for 100 countries, appended by GNP/cap scores (from IBRD 1991) for Antigua and Barbuda, the Bahamas, Bahrain, Barbados, Belize, Bhutan, Bulgaria, Fiji, Guyana, Iceland, Iran, Luxembourg, Malta, Poland, St. Lucia, St. Vincent, the Solomon Islands, and Suriname. As the difference between GDP/cap and GNP/cap figures (for countries where both are available) typically does not exceed the magnitude of 5%,

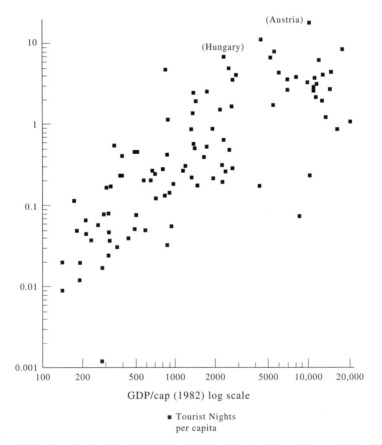

Figure 5.2. Per Capita Tourist Nights by Per Capita Gross Domestic Product

the mixture of two kinds of measures on the horizontal axis should not impair the accuracy of Figures 5.1 and 5.2.

As expected from the findings of *chapters 2* and *3*, by and large the greater the economic wealth of a country, the more likely it is to receive foreign tourists. The metric Ordinary Least Squares (OLS) regression coefficient of the relationship, using the logged version of the dependent variable, is $b=.219$, that is, every US$1000 difference in the per capita GDP, is statistically accompanied by an 21.9% expected difference in log per capita foreign tourist arrivals.

Figure 5.2 replicates the inquiry of the previous graph, presenting per capita foreign tourist nights figures on the vertical axis. Again, the relationship is positive and logarithmic. For log per capita foreign tourist nights, the Ordinary Least Squares regression procedure yields a metric slope coefficient of $b=1.471$; that is, for every US$1000 difference in per capita GDP, the expected difference in the number of log per capita foreign tourist nights is 147%. Although the distribution by destination country of the tourists' length of stay is far from homogeneous, the latter relationship is almost as tight as the one for foreign tourist arrivals. Both measures of foreign tourist presence leave over 80% of the variance unexplained after the introduction of a predictor variable pertaining to economic backwardness.

For reference, both graphs indicate the data points representing Austria and Hungary. The two figures help outline the two countries' position in the system of international tourism; both are positioned on the upper edge of the distribution. Austria is clearly among those most saturated by leisure migration both in terms of arrivals and tourist nights (it is only surpassed, on both graphs, by the Bahamas), while Hungary, with its substantially smaller per capita GDP, also occupies a fairly high position on a per capita basis.

The same set of data also allows direct comparisons between the state socialist bloc and the rest of the world in terms of their exposure to foreign tourism. Computations from BarOn's data, summarized in Table 5.1,

Table 5.1. Foreign Tourist Arrivals and Foreign Tourist Nights by Sociopolitical Blocs, 1985

	(1)	(2)	(3)	(4)
State Socialist Countries	50.7	333.5	0.033	0.216
Capitalist Countries	334.3	2,914.5	0.101	0.885
World Total	385.0	3,258.0	0.080	0.673

(1) Foreign tourist arrivals (million arrivals).
(2) Foreign tourist nights (million nights).
(3) Per capita foreign tourist arrivals (%).
(4) Per capita foreign tourist nights (%).
Source: BarOn, 1989:Tables 2 and 5.

indicate that, in 1985, the European and Asian state socialist countries and Cuba together received about 13.2% of all foreign tourist arrivals and registered ca. 10.2% of all foreign tourist nights. Data controlled for population size, included in columns (3) and (4), suggest that the societies of the state socialist bloc were between three and four times less exposed to foreign tourism than the rest of the world. Global data inform that tourist flows reproduce patterns of not only uneven development, but also those of the capitalist–socialist divide, with the state socialist societies less exposed to incoming foreign tourism.

Country-to-country matrices of tourist travel are even less available than aggregate arrival and tourist night statistics. Robert Senior's *The World Tourism Market* (1983) allows some inference concerning the magnitude of international leisure migration within and between the two sociopolitical blocs, based on estimates of European tourist arrival data from 1979. In 1979, over two-thirds of all annual international tourist arrivals worldwide occurred in Europe, a continent with about 18% of the world's population (computed from Senior 1983). Table 5.2 summarizes the findings of this inquiry.

In 1979, over 254 million foreign tourist trips were registered in Europe. Eighty-five percent of the travelers were citizens of the capitalist countries, and only 17.5% of all trips had state socialist destinations. Over three-fourths of all international tourist travel in Europe took place among capitalist countries, while trips within the state socialist bloc comprised a mere 11.2% of the total. The total number of "cross-Iron-Curtain" trips was about one tenth of all trips. The smallest number of travelers is found in the cell for the citizens of the European socialist states who visited a capitalist country; with fewer than ten million such trips, they made up a mere 3.8% of the European total.

Table 5.2. Tourist Departures and Arrivals in Europe by Sociopolitical Blocs, 1979 (thousands)

	To		
From	Capitalist Bloc	State Socialist Bloc	Total
Capitalist Bloc	200,251	15,851	216,102 (85.0%)
State Socialist Bloc	9,714	28,534	38,246 (15.0%)
	209,965 (82.5%)	43,385 (17.8%)	
Total			254,350

Source: Computed from Senior (1982:68, 162, 167).

Table 5.3. Tourist Departures and Arrivals in Europe by Sociopolitical Blocs, Controlled for Population Size at Sending and Receiving Areas (10⁻⁶), 1979

From	To		
	Capitalist Bloc	State Socialist Bloc	
Capitalist Bloc	1.293	0.101	549.1
State Socialist Bloc	0.0612	0.181	96.3
	533.5	109.6	

Right marginal: International tourist departures per 1000 population at sending area
Bottom marginal: International tourist arrivals per 1000 population at receiving area
Source: Computed from Senior (1982:67–8, 162, 167).

A more precise measure of the relative magnitude of international tourist travel within and across the boundaries of the two sociopolitical blocs can be obtained by controlling for the size of both the sending and the receiving areas. The measures obtained in this way reflect the relative likelihood that such particular kinds of international trips would take place. The results of these computations, presented in Table 5.3, reveal the existence of severe inequalities in leisure travel by sociopolitical blocs. In 1979, international leisure flows were over seven times more likely to take place among the capitalist countries than within the state socialist bloc. Table 5.3 also reveals that the boundary between the two sociopolitical blocs was over 1.6 times more likely to be crossed by citizens of the European capitalist countries than the other way around. Among the visitors of the state socialist societies of Europe, citizens of other state socialist countries were 1.87 times more likely to be found than those of the capitalist bloc. Of those who entered the capitalist countries as foreign tourists in 1979, citizens of other capitalist countries were more than 20 times more likely to be found than those of the state socialist societies.

Spatial patterns of international leisure migration are systematically related to the two most fundamental global systems of inequality. The above overview of global data indicates that *the higher the per capita GDP of the destination country, the more likely it is to receive incoming foreign tourists.* Meanwhile, *membership in the socialist bloc reduces the likelihood of a country's participation in international tourism both as a sending and as a destination country.* Finally, *within-bloc travel is more frequent than crossing the two sociopolitical blocs' boundaries.* However, neither of the two global systems of inequality explains fully the patterns of cross-border leisure flows. A large proportion of the variation in worldwide tourism destination statistics is left unexplained when regressed on national product or income measures, and the cases of Hungary, Yugoslavia, and, for outgoing travel, Poland, suggest that the state socialist bloc has hardly been monolithic in terms of blocking cross-border tourist movements.

Large Structures and Foreign Travel to Hungary and Austria

Propositions

Although the international distribution of tourist flows has long been recognized as uneven, patterned, and relatively stable (e.g., Morgenroth 1927; Williams and Zelinsky 1970), the literature on tourism offers only a few pointers concerning those patterns. This section uses those, along with empirical considerations from earlier parts of this study, to develop a set of propositions on the expected distributions of foreign tourism in Austria and Hungary.

A geographically-inspired stance concerning patterns of leisure flows—labelled by its practitioners the "gravity" thesis—posits, as John Kelly (1982) summarizes, that "[h]owever the cost is calculated, the use of any recreation site is decreased greatly by distance from it" (1982:302). Although Kelly uses travel cost as its intervening mechanism, it is not necessary that the argument be restricted to that intervening variable. In essence, the gravity thesis is an application of the traditional human ecological approach (e.g., Bogue 1978:502; Petersen 1978:555) that assumes "that distance and the attractiveness of the resource work to determine use" (Kelly 1982:308). Kelly's model, however, lumps together all explanatory factors beside distance into the catch-all category of "attractiveness", akin to the use of an exogenous concept "taste" in the rational-choice framework. The rest of the propositions concerning determinants of leisure flows to Austria and Hungary can be considered an attempt to decompose Kelly's economic-reductionistic concept of "attractiveness."

Shin and Lee (1983) also hypothesize that distance is the main determinant of leisure travel patterns by suggesting that "[t]he more distance there is between two points, the higher the level of travel-cost and the less the population flow" (1983:64). On this basis it is expected that, all other things being equal, *the greater the distance between a country of origin and the two destination countries, the less likely tourist flows are*. The effect of distance is expected to be negative for both countries.

Lloyd Hudman (1979) argues that the size of sending and destination areas is an important determinant of tourist flows:

> [t]he smallness of the countries has two effects. It limits, in most cases, the variety and, to some extent, the number, of internal tourist attractions. Also, the location and size of each country allow quick access to other countries (Hudman 1979:46).

Hudman's point goes beyond a methodological warning concerning the fairly obvious idea that comparative analyses of leisure flows should control for the size of both sending and destination areas. It suggests that the effect of size is nonlinear, so that it should manifest itself even when size is controlled for. Thus, it is expected that, all other things being equal, *the larger the country of origin, the smaller the likelihood of travel* to Austria as well as Hungary.

Kelly (1982) observes also that "[t]he most evident difference that sets apart the leisure of the rich is that they go farther to do it" (1982: 301). This position is in accordance with what Yoel Mansfeld (1990) describes summarily as the "radical 'political economy' " approach. These analysts argue, on the basis of evidence from some Third World societies flooded with foreign tourists from the better-off parts of the world—which creates a distinctly neo-colonial condition—that "tourist flows emanate from the desire of affluent classes in metropolitan countries to travel to dependant and deprived countries" (Mansfeld 1990:375 quoting Lea 1988). This latter thesis in effect includes two propositions. First, tourist flows would be more likely to take place from better-off origin countries and, second, the more backward a destination economy is, the more likely that flows will be directed to it. The second component of this thesis is amply refuted by the findings of *chapters 2* and *3*—which demonstrated the association of emerging tourism with industrial capitalism both on the European level of analysis and in an Austro-Hungarian comparison— and the overview of contemporary global data, presented in the first part of this chapter—which indicate that there continues to be a positive association between levels of incoming tourism and relative development. The analysis of incoming tourism in Austria and Hungary allows for testing the first part of this proposition. All other things equal, it is expected that *the higher the sending country's relative level of socioeconomic development, the more likely it is that its citizens will visit* Austria and Hungary. The effect of relative economic development on the likelihood of incoming foreign tourism is expected to be positive in both countries.

The literature suggests contradictory speculations concerning the magnitude of the positive effect of the level of socioeconomic development of the leisure travelers' home society in Hungary and Austria. Walter Christaller (1955, 1963) proposes a starkly geographical-determinist model of leisure flows, suggesting that the main feature of tourism is an urge of escape from industrialization and urbanization. Therefore, for Christaller, "the bigger the agglomeration and the greater the population density, the greater the propensity to travel during holidays: to the seaside, to the mountains, and to the country" (Christaller 1963:103). Hofmeister and Steinecke (1983) summarize Christaller's position concerning the main motivation of leisure travel in the formula: "Drang zur Peripherie" (1983:7), i.e., approximately, a "drive toward the periphery."

As leisure flows are depicted as motivated by a desire to flee from "central places and the agglomerations of industry" (Christaller 1963:95), Christaller's thesis suggests that the effect of the relative development of the tourists' society of origin should be stronger in the *less* industrialized of the two countries, that is, in Hungary. In contrast, the findings of the earlier chapters of this study, and implications of the analysis presented in Høivik and Heiberg's work on "core-periphery tourism" (1980), which demonstrated the predominance of "core-to-core" travel, suggest that travel among the most affluent societies should prevail over that from rich to poor areas of the world. With Austria being clearly wealthier than Hungary throughout their recent history, it is expected on the basis of the latter argument that, all other things being equal, *the magnitude of the effect of the socioeconomic development of the tourist's sending country is higher in Austria than in Hungary.*

Previous treatises offer surprisingly little by way of formal conceptualization, or explicit analysis, of the effects of the two blocs on leisure travel patterns. Most of the work in this field talks about international leisure flows as if the state socialist bloc of states did not exist; in effect, they assume zero flows across those states' boundaries *en bloc*. The Hungarian case—marked, as shown in *chapter 3*, by an increase in the number of incoming foreign tourists equal in steepness to that of Austria and by a level of exposure to foreign tourism that surpasses the west European average—strongly contradicts that simplistic assumption, and urges that both the uneven development of capitalism and the bifurcation of the interstate system be taken into account when modeling international tourist flows.

Kushman, Groth and Childs (1980) approach the problem of the effects of the two blocs on leisure flows from the point of view of comparative political science. They apprehend the specificity of the state socialist bloc in what they call the "Marxist–Leninist" character of their political regimes, and consider observed obstructions of flows across those states' borders as corollaries of that condition. After testing their proposition about the effects of descriptive political distinctions between "Marxist–Leninist" polities, "polyarchies," and a residual category of "others," on leisure travel patterns, they conclude that "political considerations play an important and predictable role in social behavior toward travel which is evident at the state level" (Kushman et al 1980:614). This is in harmony with the findings of the preceding section of this chapter concerning bloc-to-bloc inequalities of European leisure flows. Thus, it is expected that, all other things equal, *the political bloc-affiliation of incoming tourists affects the likelihood of travel* to the two countries.

Chapter 4 of this study argued that, by the early 1960s, the political and military bloc-affiliation of the two societies had become strikingly different. Austria had become an "actively neutral" country, positioned outside of military alliances, integrated in west European networks of commerce, and an important trading partner of the Soviet-bloc states. In contrast, Hungary entered the 1960s as a country under foreign military occupation, and a member of all Soviet-centered military, economic, etc. organizations. Hence, the external linkage structures of the two societies were bound to be markedly different. As a result, it is expected that *the bloc-affiliation of the tourists' home state affects the likelihood of travel in the two countries differently.* More specifically, it is expected that, all other things being equal, the Warsaw-Pact-membership of the country of origin of incoming foreign tourists increases the likelihood of their travel to Hungary and decreases the probability of their travel to Austria. This effect is somewhat ambiguous. As Hungary had received, from the introduction in 1968 of its economic reform policies onward, consider-able positive publicity as the most "liberal" country within the Warsaw Pact, there have been a number of tourists from the capitalist countries who chose, at least once, Hungary as a travel destination precisely because they wanted to experience directly "really existing socialism"—with the least amount of "risk" or inconvenience involved. In a border survey of young foreign tourists arriving in Hungary in 1981, this author (excerpted in Böröcz 1983), found that most of those from the nonstate-socialist societies had no prior experience in Hungary or any other state socialist country, and that their attitudes towards their expected experience in Hungary can be characterized as a mixture of intense curiosity and a sharply critical outlook. It is expected, nevertheless, that the effect of political discouragement is stronger than political curiosity. Conversely, if the tourist's home state is a member of the NATO, that is expected to lessen the likelihood of travel to Hungary while not affecting the probability of travel to neutral Austria.

During the 1960–84 period, political bloc-affiliation has had impor-tant bearings on the freedom of leisure travel. For analytical purposes it is expedient to separate these administrative constraints from other effects of political blocs. There are three kinds of administrative constraints that are relevant for predicting leisure flows to Austria and Hungary.

First, all state socialist societies had imposed severe restrictions on the travel abroad of their own citizens during their initial, Stalinist period. There has been great variation in the degree to which, and the time when, those restrictions have been lifted after 1960. During the period under study, the socialist states of east-central Europe had widely varied exit visa regulations for travel abroad for purposes other than business: The Soviet Union, Bulgaria, Romania, and the German Democratic Republic severely restricted the travel of their citizens. Even for travel within the bloc, Soviet and Bulgarian authorities clearly privileged *package tours* and settled, prepaid vacation holidays, where surveillance of the travelers was more feasible. Romanian and East German regulations had been more permissive in this regard, and allowed for individual trips within the state socialist bloc. Tourist travel to the West by citizens of those countries was practically unthinkable. During the early 1960s, Czechoslovak regulations were relatively lenient, and severe travel restrictions were not introduced until 1968. Thereafter, travel to the West was permitted only with special exit visas granted on a case-to-case basis to a relatively small number of people, privileging package tours and prepaid holidays to other trips. (A typical denial of an exit visa would cite "shortage of convertible currency" as a reason.) Czechoslovak citizens could travel to destinations within the state socialist bloc without any special permit. Polish and Hungarian regulations represented a step further in the permissive direction, especially from the early 1970s onwards. Governmental decrees determined the frequency of travel to the West that would be allowed—usually once every three years, except for package tours and personal invitations that would be granted more often. The denial of an exit visa would be a rare event, used only as a form of punishment for political dissidence. Except for East Germany, for all countries mentioned above, travel to Yugoslavia was considered a trip within the state socialist bloc, obstructed only by problems concerning the availability of hard currency (as the Yugoslav Dinar was not a member of the CMEA Clearing Rouble club.) Finally, the Yugoslav state imposed virtually no restriction on the foreign travel of its own citizens during this period. It is important to underscore, however, that, notwithstanding all the restrictions, travel by people in societies subjected to these restrictions has never come to a complete halt. It is expected that if citizens of a particular state need exit visas from their own authorities to leave their country, then this constraint will decrease their opportunity to travel abroad and, by implication, it will reduce the number of their arrivals in Hungary as well as Austria.

Second, regulations concerning the travel of the citizens of the "socialist" states have often differentiated between travel to the "west" (to which category Austria has always been assigned) and travel to such Soviet-bloc countries as Hungary. It is expected that, all other things being equal, *the necessity of obtaining special exit visas for travel to Austria not only abates travel to Austria* but, at the same time, augments the likelihood of travel to Hungary, a textbook example of what Hungarian economist János Kornai (1983) describes as the forced substitution of scarce goods: Kornai shows that, along with increased search, postponement and forced savings, forced substitution is one of the few alternative strategies available to customers under conditions of endemic shortage.

Third, it is reasonable to argue that the requirement of an entry visa increases the bureaucratic burden associated with travel—entry visas require preparation, there are monetary and time costs attached, etc., so that the entry visa obligation diminishes the likelihood of travel. Thus, it is expected that, all other things equal, if the citizens of any given country have to go through the procedure of obtaining entry visas, they are less likely to travel to that particular destination state which imposes such requirements. Throughout the period under study, visa-free entry to Hungary was restricted to citizens of CMEA-member states, along with Finland and Austria. Citizens of all other countries were required to obtain entry visas. The bureaucratic hustle associated with obtaining entry visas to Hungary was gradually eased so that, by the early 1970s, the entry visa obligation was widely considered as a mere formality and a form of revenue for the Hungarian foreign service: In the year 1987, for instance, 1.763 million foreigners—or 9.5% of all foreign arrivals— entered Hungary with passports that required an entry visa (KSH 1989: 16.) In contrast, Austria had abolished visa obligation with most nonstate-socialist travel partners by the early 1960s. Of the state socialist societies of Europe, only Yugoslavian, Polish and Hungarian citizens were allowed entry to Austria without a visa from the mid-1960s onwards.

The effects of sociopolitical bloc-affiliation and uneven economic development on travel patterns to Austria and Hungary may not be independent from each other. It could be argued that the dynamics of economic development are bloc-specific, so that they do not apply to the state socialist and capitalist societies in the same way. What lends a certain sense of credibility to such an argument is the point, referred to in the introduction to the preceding chapter, concerning the specificity of state socialist societies in the particular role played by the political realm in integrating them as social "systems." Thus, it is expected that, all other things equal, the interaction between political blocs and uneven development contributes significantly to explaining the likelihood of travel. Furthermore, this implies that, all other things equal, the effect of the interaction between political blocs and uneven development is different for Austria and Hungary as the two are marked by different bloc affiliations themselves.

As the earlier part of this chapter has found the total association of uneven development and political-bloc-affiliation with leisure travel patterns to be moderate, it may be plausible to consider the effects of other large structural aspects on leisure flows to the two countries. One particularly poignant consideration concerns what could be called the *longue durée* hypothesis of region-specific development, proclaiming the specificity of east-central Europe as a historical constant. Hungarian historian Jenő Szűcs (e.g., 1983 and 1986) has argued that the east-central part of Europe has been separated from the rest of the continent by two clearly defined lines which have shown remarkable persistence over time. Relying on an overview of the spatial patterns of the historical spread of parishes of various denominations, Romanesque and Gothic art, the Renaissance and the Reformation, city autonomies and corporate liberties, feudalistic and other social structural and behavioral features, Szűcs insists that there exists an underlying deep-structural pattern which is essentially invariant since about the twelfth century: The east-central European region is distinct from both the eastern and the western endpoints of the European spectrum.

Szűcs' argument implies that east-central European patterns of interethnic and intersocietal contact (trade, the dispersion of information and knowledge, population dislocation, labor migration, and leisure travel flows) are distinct from those of the other two regions. An extension of Szűcs' magnum hypothesis is to expect that, all other things equal, east-central Europeans are overrepresented in comparison to both west and east Europeans *in contemporary leisure travel in Hungary*. Austria appears in Szűcs' argument as part of the easternmost reaches of western Europe, socioculturally distinct from east-central Europe where Hungary is located so that, given the "westernness" of Austrian patterns, all other things being equal, west Europeans are expected to predominate among foreign tourists in Austria.

Data and methods

This analysis focuses on annual data of tourist arrivals and tourist nights in Austria and Hungary for those origin countries which sent at least 10,000 tourists to Hungary in 1984. This method of selection excludes part of the sending countries, and results in the loss of some important variance in the data. However, problems with the availability and comparability of data in the lower range of the distribution force this type of selection.

This includes 25 years' scores for 23 countries—all of them European except the United States and Canada. Austrian data include foreign tourist arrivals and foreign tourist nights information for the same set of countries, net of Austrian travelers and appended by scores of Hungarian tourist arrivals and tourist nights. The two sets of datapoints were then pooled and treated as populations of occurrences to be predicted statistically by hierarchical regression models.

Table 5.4 presents a list of the variables used in the analysis, along with their short definition, and their mean and standard deviation scores for both countries. The criterion variables are based on annual tourist arrival and tourist night figures collected from the archives of the Tourism Section of the Austrian and Hungarian Central Statistical Offices. Once raw numbers of arrival and length of stay scores had been obtained, the criterion variables were constructed as follows:

Table 5.4. Definitions, Means, and Standard Deviations of Variables Used in the Regression Models

Variable	Definition	Austria		Hungary	
		Mean	S.D.	Mean	S.D.
Criterion variables					
Likelihood of travel	Number of foreign tourist arrivals from a given country of origin as % of the population of the country of origin	1.38	2.46	1.13	2.97
Probability of overnight stay	Number of annual tourist nights spent in destination country by 1% of the population of the country of origin	8.18	18.8	9.57	21.8
Predictor variables					
(1) Autocorrelation & distance					
Year	Year of observations [1960–84] [last two digits]	71.5	6.94	71.5	6.93
Minimum distance	Minimum distance [in thousand km] of country of origin	1.01	1.97	1.12	2.12
(2) Administrative constraints					
Exit visa to Hungary	1 = Exit visa is required by traveler's own state for travel to Hungary			0.192	0.392
Entry visa	1 = Entry visa is required by destination state for travel	0.253	0.435	0.736	0.441
Exit visa to the west	1 = Exit visa is required by traveler's own state for travel to the west (but not to Hungary)	0.289	0.454	0.275	0.447
(3) Sociopolitical blocs					
NATO-member state	1 = Citizen of a NATO-member state	0.499	0.500	0.477	0.500
Warsaw Pact state	1 = Citizen of a Warsaw Pact state	0.274	0.446	0.261	0.440
(4) "Longue durée" patterns					
"Eastern Europe"	1 = Citizen of an "East-European" country	0.181	0.386	0.174	0.379
"Western Europe"	1 = Citizen of a "West-European" country	0.590	0.492	0.564	0.496
(5) Uneven development					
GNP/cap/US	GNP/cap of country of origin as fraction of the US figure	0.433	0.242	0.442	0.235
(6) Interaction: bloc *underdevelopment					
GDP/cap by Warsaw Pact	Interaction term of GNP/cap/US and Warsaw Pact membership	0.067	0.116	0.070	0.128
GDP/cap by NATO	Interaction term of GNP/cap/US and NATO-membership	0.263	0.318	0.252	0.316

First, the number of annual tourist arrivals from a country of origin was divided by the population of the sending country and transformed into percentages. The resulting indicator is interpreted as the likelihood that a citizen of a sending country participated in tourism in the destination country during the given year. This indicator is the sending-country-specific equivalent of the Tourist Exposure Rate analyzed for Hungary and Austria in *chapter 3*.

Second, the number of annual tourist nights spent in Austria or Hungary by citizens of each country of origin was divided by home population size and transformed into percentages. This indicator can be interpreted intuitively in either of two ways: (1) the number of annual nights that 1% of the sending country's population spent in the destination country, or (2) the probability that a citizen of the country of origin spent 1 night in the destination country as a tourist during the given year.

The first indicator, "Likelihood of travel," reflects how widespread the experience of traveling in Hungary and Austria is in each sending society. The other, "Probability of overnight stay," more accurately reflects the extent of the presence of tourists, and is the sending-country-specific equivalent of Høivik and Heiberg's Tourist Intensity Rate analyzed in terms of its gross volume in *chapter 3*.

Comparing national product and income statistics across political-economic systems poses a difficult methodological problem: Capitalist and socialist states have had quite different statistical data-gathering and -reporting practices. That is especially true for GDP which is widely accepted as an indicator of a country's overall position in the world economy, and has often been used in international comparisons. Most of the state socialist societies appearing in the data are not included in the World Tables or other international compendia of data on national economic performance. After consultations with leading Hungarian econometricians specializing in the problem of comparisons between state socialist and capitalist economies, a decision was made to use time series estimates developed by the product-output-based Jánossy-method by researchers at the Institute for World Economy in Budapest. (This was first formulated in Jánossy, 1963. An English description and real-data application is included in Ehrlich, (1971). The country estimates used in this study were provided by Gyula Pártos. They consist of a series of percentages of the US figures for selected years. Scores for the intervallic years not directly provided in the estimates were computed through logarithmic intrapolation.) To control for bias caused by dollar-inflation over time, the GDP-scores included in this analysis indicate each country's GDP per capita as a fraction of the US figure for the corresponding year.

The hierarchical model was constructed in such a way as to maximize the comparability of the results (1) for foreign tourist arrivals and foreign tourist nights within each country, and (2) for the appropriate criterion variables between the two countries. The predictor variables are introduced in the model in six consecutive steps. First, year of the observation, minimum distance of the country of origin, and the land area of the country of origin are entered, both to filter out linear autocorrelation effects and to estimate variation due to such geographical conditions as distance and country size. The minimum distance of the country of origin is calibrated in thousand kilometers, and the land area of the sending country is represented in million square kilometers. The second block of variables estimates the additive effects of such administrative constraints on travel as exit visa requirements to Hungary, exit visa obligation for travel to the "west," and entry visa regulations. (Obviously, the variable for "Exit visa to Hungary" is only relevant in the Hungarian models. The fact that it is only entered in the Hungarian equations is the only discrepancy between the models used for the two countries.)

The variables representing each of these constraints are dichotomous, and are coded $x=1$ if the given constraint exists during the given year for the citizens of the given country of origin. Third, two dummy variables are introduced to represent the political-bloc-membership of the tourist's country of origin. They are designed such that the status of neutrality—i.e., citizenship of a state that is outside of both the NATO and the Warsaw Pact—is used as the point of reference. (Neutral countries are those coded $x=0$ on both variables.) Fourth, Szűcs' overarching trichotomous regional typology of Europe (i.e., western, east-central, eastern) is introduced through two dummy variables. Here, the east-central European position—i.e., neither east, nor west European status—is used as the basic reference. Fifth, the additional effects of relative economic development are entered, using the estimated per capita gross domestic product of the sending country, expressed as a percentage of the corresponding year's US score, as its measure. This is a single variable, measured on the level of a ratio scale. Finally, the interaction effects between membership in sociopolitical blocs and the degree of economic wealth are introduced by way of two variables: (1) The product of the GDP/cap/US score and the Warsaw Pact dummy, to be interpreted as the independent effect of GDP/cap/US if the sending country is a member of the Warsaw Pact, and (2) the product of the GDP/cap/US score and the NATO dummy—understood as the independent effect of the GDP/cap/US if the sending country is a member of the NATO. Again, neutral countries serve as the basis of comparison.

Findings

Although Austria and Hungary are neighboring countries with a long-shared history, the list of the main actors on their foreign tourist scene could hardly be more different between 1960 and 1984. There is no overlap among the first eight most represented countries on the parallel lists of top foreign tourists in the two countries. The lists are produced by dividing the mean annual number of foreign tourist arrivals in each country during 1960 and 1984 by the population size of the sending country.

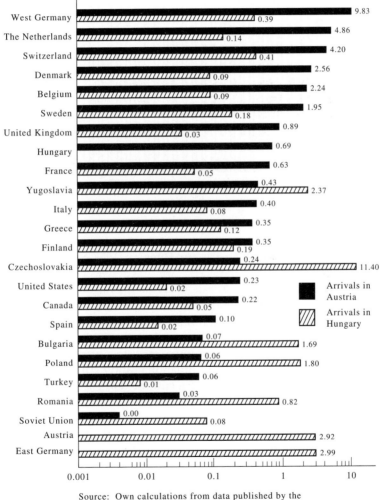

Source: Own calculations from data published by the Austrian and Hungarian Statistical Offices.

Figure 5.3. Foreign Tourists in Austria and Hungary 1960–84 (mean annual foreign tourist arrivals per population of sending country, log scale)

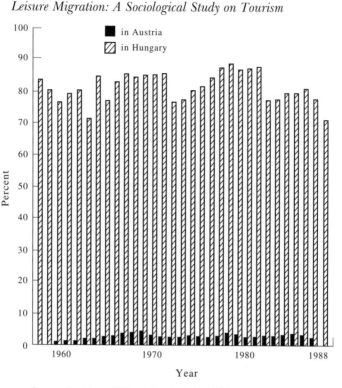

Source: Austrian and Hungarian Statistical Offices.

Figure 5.4. Percentages of Foreign Arrivals by Residents of State Socialist Countries in Austria and Hungary (1958–88)

West Germany, the country on the top of Austria's list with the equivalent of, on average, almost 10% of its population visiting Austria annually, occupies the ninth place on Hungary's tally, with less than .4%. Conversely, Czechoslovakia, the country most involved in tourist travel to Hungary with over 11% of its population visiting Hungary every year during the same period, is only fourteenth on Austria's list with a score of .24%.

The two societies' touristic exchange is strongly unequal. While Austrians are the third most highly represented group in travel to Hungary with roughly 3% of their population visiting, Hungarians occupy only the eighth place in Austria with scores below 1%. On average, thus, Austrians were 4.23 times more likely to visit Hungary than Hungarians Austria; when the length of stay is taken into account (as in Figure 5.4), that ratio of inequality increases to 8.03 times.

An important finding concerning the impact of the sending country's position in the world economy on travel to Austria and Hungary is revealed even before performing the statistical tests: Turkey is the only economically underdeveloped, peripheral society which "made it" for selection among the twenty-some top tourist-sending countries, and its presence is minuscule in both countries: In Hungary, Turkish citizens registered annual mean values of .01% and .05% while, in Austria, they are recorded at .06% and .12%. Even those low scores are likely to be artifacts of the high exposure of the West German economy to Turkish guestworkers who use Austria and, to a lesser extent, Hungary, as transit countries when traveling to and from Turkey. This is also suggested by their short stay in both countries, especially in Austria (ca. 5 nights in Hungary and ca. 2 nights in Austria). The difference in length of stay also suggests that the travel of Turkish citizens in Hungary implies a bit more of a touristic content than in Austria. However, to be noted is that even the longer mean length of stay figure—5 nights—of Turkish citizens is shorter than the average length of stay of foreign tourists in Hungary, estimated between 7 and 8 nights per trip.

Figure 5.5 portrays the distribution of tourist arrivals in Austria and Hungary by deciles of the per capita GDP (expressed in percentages of the respective year's US figure) of the tourists' country of origin. The two curves reveal normal distributions skewed in opposite directions. The median of foreign tourist arrivals in Hungary is in the fourth decile of the GDP/cap/US measure, followed by the third, while the Austrian

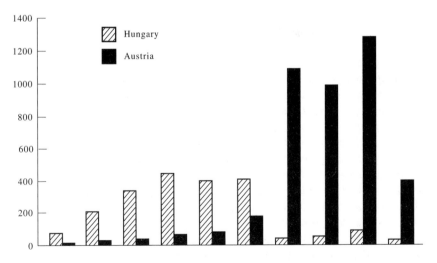

Source: Own Computations from data from the
Austrian and Hungarian Statistical Offices.

Figure 5.5. Annual Mean Foreign Tourist Arrivals, Hungary and Austria by GDP-Decile of Emitting Country, 1960–84 (thousand arrivals)

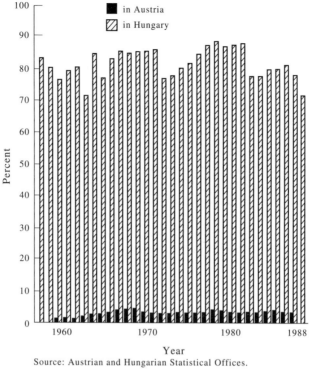

Year

Source: Austrian and Hungarian Statistical Offices.

Figure 5.6. Percentages of Foreign Arrivals by Residents of State Socialist Countries in Austria and Hungary (1958–88)

data present a distribution peaking three deciles higher, in the seventh decile, followed closely by the sixth. A comparison of the pool of foreign tourists visiting the two countries reveals a clear bias toward travelers from wealthier countries in Austria, and for those from poorer countries in Hungary.

Figure 5.6 offers a similar comparison, examining the annual percentages of foreign visitors from the state socialist societies in the two countries. Although Hungary's percentage scores do fluctuate, between the low seventies and the high eighties, the contrast with Austria is clear: The proportion of citizens of the state socialist societies never reaches the 5% mark in the latter. During the period under study, foreign tourists from the state socialist countries have dominated Hungary's touristic development while they have played only a minuscule role in Austria.

Data in Tables 5.5 through 5.8 reproduce the results of the hierarchical regression model of the large-structural predictors of the likelihood of tourist arrivals and tourist nights in Austria and Hungary,

Table 5.5. Hierarchical Regression Model Predicting the Likelihood of Travel to Hungary by Foreigners, 1960–84

Block coefficient	(1) metric	(2) metric	(3) metric	(4) metric	(5) metric	(6) metric	(6) Beta
(1) Autocorrelation & distance							
Year	0.094**	0.032*	0.037*	0.047*	0.027	0.021	0.049
Minimum distance	-0.249**	-0.083	-0.046	-0.015	-0.183*	-0.166*	-0.118
(2) Administrative constraints							
Exit visa to Hungary		-4.59**	-5.95**	-5.49**	-5.49**	-4.64**	-0.615
Entry visa to Hungary		-1.32**	-0.418	-0.053	-0.085	-0.174	-0.026
Exit visa to the West		4.67**	2.70**	2.09**	2.25**	1.60**	0.241
(3) Sociopolitical blocs							
NATO-member state			-0.664*	-0.292	-0.239	-1.19	-0.201
Warsaw Pact state			3.59**	3.26**	3.08**	-1.58*	-0.234
(4) "Longue-durée" patterns							
"Eastern Europe"				-1.54**	-1.14**	-0.889*	-0.113
"Western Europe"				-1.85**	-2.48**	-2.08***	-0.347
(5) Uneven development							
GDP/cap/US					3.16**	0.832	0.066
(6) Interaction: bloc * underdevelopment							
GDP/cap by Warsaw Pact						16.1**	0.691
GDP/cap by NATO						1.83	0.195
R^2_{inc}	0.080**	0.345**	0.063**	0.033**	0.016**	0.047**	$R^2_{tot}=0.584$

*$P<0.05$
**$P<0.001$

Table 5.6. Hierarchical Regression Model Predicting the Probability of Spending One Night in Hungary by Foreigners, 1960–84

Block coefficient	(1) metric	(2) metric	(3) metric	(4) metric	(5) metric	(6) metric	(6) Beta
(1) Autocorrelation & distance							
Year	0.659*	0.701**	0.740**	0.808**	0.566**	0.438*	0.108
Minimum distance	-1.73**	-0.190	-0.065	-0.062	-2.10	-0.363	-0.038
(2) Administrative constraints							
Exit visa to Hungary		-32.3**	-43.3**	-38.1**	-38.0**	-25.3**	-0.450
Entry visa to Hungary		-9.48*	4.64	7.73	8.00	3.30	0.074
Exit visa to the West		29.4**	20.6**	19.6**	23.2**	15.6**	0.337
(3) Sociopolitical blocs							
NATO–member state			-2.90	-1.43	0.976	11.2	0.256
Warsaw Pact state			31.9**	31.1**	30.1**	-9.99	-0.212
(4) "Longue–durée" patterns							
"Eastern Europe"				-8.67*	-5.62	-10.3**	-0.164
"Western Europe"				-5.86	-14.2**	-10.4*	-0.238
(5) Uneven development							
GDP/cap/US					39.6**	25.3*	0.269
(6) Interaction: bloc *underdevelopment							
GDP/cap by Warsaw Pact						129.2**	0.829
GDP/cap by NATO						-20.9	-0.319
R^2_{inc}	0.061**	0.354**	0.113**	0.010*	0.039**	0.074**	R^2_{tot}=0.650

*P<0.05
**P<0.001

Table 5.7. Hierarchical Regression Model Predicting the Likelihood of Travel to Austria by Foreigners, 1960–84

Block coefficient	(1) metric	(2) metric	(3) metric	(4) metric	(5) metric	(6) metric	(6) Beta
(1) Autocorrelation & distance							
Year	0.066**	0.063**	0.063**	0.067**	0.021	0.016	0.046
Minimum distance	−0.232**	−0.359**	−0.405**	−0.462**	−0.939**	−1.24**	−0.996
(2) Administrative constraints							
Entry visa to Austria		−1.13**	−1.21**	−0.058	1.07*	0.710	0.126
Exit visa to the West		−1.38***	−0.840	0.617	0.514	−0.816	−0.150
(3) Sociopolitical blocs							
NATO-member state			1.06**	1.24**	1.04**	−2.79**	−0.567
Warsaw Pact state			0.230	0.096	−1.46	−0.857	−0.156
(4) "Longue-durée" patterns							
"Eastern Europe"				−0.257	−0.267	0.646*	0.101
"Western Europe"				2.26**	−0.736	−1.69**	−0.338
(5) Uneven development							
GDP/cap/US					8.66**	6.20**	0.611
(6) Interaction: bloc *underdevelopment							
GDP/cap by Warsaw Pact						−3.85	−0.182
GDP/cap by NATO						7.66**	0.992
R^2_{inc}	0.070**	0.154**	0.026**	0.073**	0.129**	0.052**	$R^2_{tot}=0.505$

*$P<0.05$
**$P<0.001$

Table 5.8. Hierarchical Regression Model Predicting the Probability of Spending One Night in Austria by Foreigners, 1960–84

Block coefficient	(1) metric	(2) metric	(3) metric	(4) metric	(5) metric	(6) metric	(6) Beta
(1) Autocorrelation & distance							
Year	0.417**	0.396**	0.396**	0.429**	0.133	0.053	0.020
Minimum distance	−1.54***	−2.34***	−2.85***	−3.24***	−6.29**	−9.10**	−0.953
(2) Administrative constraints							
Entry visa to Austria		−5.83*	−6.94*	1.74	8.85*	9.26*	0.215
Exit visa to the West		−9.44***	−3.88	6.10	5.40	−6.13	−0.148
(3) Sociopolitical blocs							
NATO-member state			11.7**	13.2**	11.9**	−24.7**	−0.659
Warsaw Pact state			3.17	1.77	−8.13*	−16.0*	−0.381
(4) "Longue-durée" patterns							
"Eastern Europe"				−3.27	−3.21	4.38	0.090
"Western Europe"				15.1**	−4.10	−11.7*	−0.307
(5) Uneven development							
GDP/cap/US					55.3**	30.0**	0.387
(6) Interaction: bloc *underdevelopment							
GDP/cap by Warsaw Pact						8.13	0.051
GDP/cap by NATO						73.4**	1.24
R^2_{inc}	0.050**	0.100**	0.053**	0.063**	0.091**	0.069**	$R^2_{tot}=0.426$

*$P<0.05$
**$P<0.001$

as specified above. Step (1) regresses both criterion variables for each country on a baseline model composed of measures designed to filter out linear autocorrelation effects and to estimate the relative importance of distance and the size of the country of origin. Steps (2) and (3) introduce administrative constraints and other effects of sociopolitical bloc membership. Block (4) estimates the relative importance of *longue durée* patterns. Finally, step (5) examines the effects of socioeconomic (under)development, and step (6) scrutinizes the additive effects of any interaction between sociopolitical bloc affiliation and world-system position.

The statistical tests included in Tables 5.5 through 5.8 give ambiguous answers to questions concerning the demonstrability of the statistical effects of such geographical factors as distance and the size of the country of origin. When first entered on their own, they all point in the expected direction; that is, the results suggest that the longer the distance and the larger the country of origin, the less likely international tourism is to take place—and most of them are statistically very significant. The effect of distance, however, diminishes in the Hungarian model with the introduction of further variables, which appears to indicate that distance is a proxy for more sociological explanations. Meanwhile, the Austrian equations retain distance as a very significant negative predictor of the likelihood of travel: *The Austrian analysis supports, the Hungarian data reject, the "gravity"-model of international tourist flows.*

The reverse is true for the expected effects of the size of the sending country. The Hungarian analysis retains size as a moderately important, independent and negative predictor of the likelihood of travel, while its importance attenuates in Austria's case. *The Hungarian data are consistent, the Austrian ones are inconsistent, with Hudman's thesis predicting the effect of the size of the country of origin.*

To make more transparent the comparison of the effect of the consecutive steps in explaining variation in the criterion variables, Table 5.9 reproduces in a single list the increment R^2 of each step—included

Table 5.9. Increment Explained Variance Due to Each Step, by Criterion Variables

	(1)	(2)	(3)	(4)	(5)	(6)
Likelihood of travel						
to Austria [R^2_{tot}=0.507]	0.085	0.141	0.026	0.073	0.129	0.054
to Hungary [R^2_{tot}=0.591]	0.084	0.352	0.063	0.024	0.019	0.049
Probability of spending 1 night						
in Austria [R^2_{tot}=0.429]	0.059	0.090	0.053	0.063	0.091	0.071
in Hungary [R^2_{tot}=0.660]	0.069	0.354	0.113	(0.005)	0.043	0.077

Parentheses mark the increment that is not significant at the $P<.001$ level.

in the bottom of Tables 5.5 through 5.8—in all of the four models. This comparison reveals, first, that, although all of the models have reasonably good overall levels of explained variance, the hierarchical model does not provide an equally complete explanation for all four dependent variables. Its fit with Hungarian foreign tourist arrival and foreign tourist night scores is clearly better than with the Austrian data.

A major contributor to the better fit of the Hungarian models is the introduction in step (2) of administrative constraints as partial explanations of the variation in the likelihood of foreign travel to Austria and Hungary. The contrast between the Hungarian increment R^2_{inc} scores of .352 and .354, and their Austrian counterparts of .141 and .090—a difference of between 2.5 and 3.9 times—suggests that, during the period under study, administrative constraints played a more important part in influencing the distributions of foreign tourists in Hungary than in Austria, although the fact that the Austrian increment R^2 statistics are also very highly significant is a reminder that the effect of administrative constraints cannot be ignored even in Austria.

Tables 5.5 through 5.8 reveal the specifics of the direction and magnitude of those effects. The Hungarian models of per capita foreign tourist arrivals and foreign tourist nights indicate that the statistical effect of exit visa requirements for travel to Hungary work as a negative predictor of extreme strength. The regression coefficient of the dummy variable representing exit visa requirements for travel to Hungary is consistently negative, and it is unaffected by the introduction of other explanatory variables. (This variable does not appear in the Austrian models.)

The effects of entry visa requirements are somewhat more equivocal. Initially, they indicate a statistically significant effect in all of the four models, in the expected, negative, direction. In the Hungarian models, their relevance decreases, and their effect dissolves in other predictor variables. In contrast, in the Austrian models, the initial, statistically significant negative effect of an entry visa obligation recedes first (at the introduction of the *longue durée*-bloc), into nonsignificance and, finally, it transforms into a statistically significant, positive effect. The latter change occurs at the introduction of the GDP-measure which implies that, in the case of Austria, entry visa requirements are statistically too closely associated with relative underdevelopment to be separable in a regression model. This outcome suggests, furthermore, that Austria's relative price levels exert a stronger discouraging effect on people from poorer countries than the requirement of an entry visa for admittance to Austria.

Exit visa requirements to the "west" make a clearly negative initial effect on the likelihood of travel to Austria, but their influence loses statistical strength with the introduction of other predictors. In the case of Hungary, the analysis confirms strongly the expectation of a forced *substitution effect*: The presence of exit visa requirements to the west strongly, consistently and independently increases the likelihood of travel to Hungary.

The incremental explained variance scores in column (3) of Table 5.9 suggest that the statistical effects of sociopolitical bloc-affiliation—net of administrative constraints on travel—are stronger in the case of foreign tourism in Hungary than in Austria. When first introduced, the R^2_{inc} figures of the bloc-membership variables for Hungary are about twice as high as those for Austria. For both countries, the explanatory power of bloc-affiliation is greater for tourist nights than for tourist arrivals. For Hungary, the initial negative effect of NATO-membership (significant for arrivals and not significant for tourist nights) on the likelihood of travel is retained for tourist arrivals, and dissipates in the case of tourist nights. For Austria, NATO-membership never registers a statistically significant effect on tourist arrivals, while it shows a consistently significant, positive effect up till the introduction of the interaction term of bloc member-ship and economic development (see below). On the other hand, the Warsaw Pact membership of the tourist's home state makes consistently significant, positive statistical effect on the likelihood of travel to Hungary (again, affected only by the interaction term), while assuming the expected negative effect on the likelihood of travel to Austria only after the introduction of the GDP/cap/US measure. Step (5)—which includes all predictor variables except the interaction term—supports the expectation that sociopolitical bloc-affiliation has a statistically significant, but substantially different, effect on the likelihood of travel in the two countries. Warsaw Pact membership increases the likelihood of travel to Hungary and makes no or slightly negative statistical effect on the probability of tourism in Austria. Meanwhile, NATO-membership is, as revealed by the same step in all of the four models, largely irrelevant as a predictor of the likelihood of travel to Hungary while it has a strong positive effect on the probability of travel to Austria. The latter finding contradicts the expectations built on a speculative basis above.

Table 5.9 suggests that the effects of Szűcs' *longue durée* patterns are either minuscule—marked by an $R^2_{inc} = .024$ for tourist arrivals—or even statistically nonsignificant, on the Hungarian models. However, their effect on the likelihood of travel in Hungary is in the expected direction, that is, east-central European background does have a barely perceptible but extant, independent, positive effect on the likelihood of travel to Hungary. Further, that effect does not attenuate with the introduction of such further predictors as the GDP/cap/US of the country of origin or the combination of sociopolitical bloc-affiliation and economic back-wardness. In the case of Austria, the initially very significant effect of *longue durée* patterns dissolves or changes directions with the introduction of the subsequent predictors. These suggest that, in Austria's case, *longue-durée* patterns work as summary proxies for economic development and combinations of development and bloc-membership. This relationship implies that the more subtle, but detectable effects of *longue durée* patterns are more important in that society—Hungary—which has experienced less economic development than its western neighbor.

The inference that the degree of socioeconomic wealth of the country of origin is relatively more important in predicting the likelihood of travel to Austria than to Hungary is strongly supported by evidence from step (5) which reflects the statistical effects of the introduction of GDP/cap/US. Column (5) in Table 5.9 reveals that the increment explained variance attributable to this step is between 2.1 and 6.8 times greater for Austria than for Hungary. With this in mind, the statistical results produced by the models for the two countries can be interpreted as suggesting that, *while administrative constraints and, to a lesser extent, other considerations pertaining to the travelers' sociopolitical bloc-affiliation have been the main determinants of travel to Hungary, the likelihood of travel to Austria is more clearly demarcated by the relative wealth of the travelers' home society.*

Statistically, the socioeconomic wealth of the tourists' country of origin has a highly significant, unambiguously positive effect on the likelihood of travel to both countries. All else being equal, the wealthier the tourists' home society is, the more likely they are to travel to Austria as well as to Hungary. The magnitude of the relationship is stronger for Austria— another function of the observation concerning the strength of the effect above.

Finally, the analysis enters a step for two interaction terms to test the nonlinear effects of the combination of bloc-membership and GDP/cap/US on the likelihood of travel. The increment explained variance due to this step is significant in all of the four models. This step appears to predict the probability of foreign tourist nights more strongly than the likelihood of foreign tourist arrivals. For Hungary, the combination of Warsaw Pact membership and GDP/cap/US is a much stronger predictor than the interaction between NATO-membership and economic development. This finding can be interpreted as suggesting that, for tourists from Warsaw-Pact-states, the effect of the relative income level of their home economy is a stronger predictor of the likelihood of their travel to Hungary than for others. The Austrian data suggest the obverse inference: The Warsaw Pact membership of the travelers' home state does not affect the likelihood of their travel to Austria as determined by their country's relative wealth. Meanwhile, for NATO-members, there is a strong association between economic development of the home country and the likelihood of travel to Austria, above and beyond the overall effects of economic development. For tourists from NATO-member-states, the effect of the relative income level of their home economy is a stronger predictor of the likelihood of their travel to Austria than for others. (To be noted is that the introduction of the term for the interaction between NATO-membership and economic development creates a multicollinearity problem in the analysis. After the introduction of eleven predictor variables in six steps, the residual correlation between NATO-membership and economic development is very high, notwithstanding the relatively moderate level of zero-order correlation of $r=.393$ between NATO and GDP/cap/US in the Austrian model. This explains the statistically significant, sudden sign change in the independent effect of NATO-membership from step (5) to step (6) in the Austrian models presented in Tables 5.7 and 5.8.)

Discussion

The above test used a single conceptual model, translated into a series of hierarchical regression analyses, to predict statistically the likelihood of travel to Austria and Hungary, expressed in sending-country-specific percentages of foreign tourist arrivals and foreign tourist nights. It demonstrated that explanations of international leisure flows based solely on human ecological and geographic-determinist models provide only partial solutions. It also showed that there exists a strong statistical association between various large-structural properties of the contemporary world economy and patterns of tourist flows, which very significantly improves the explanatory power of predictive models. It revealed that, of those large-structural properties, both economic wealth and political-bloc-affiliation are valid and meaningful predictors of the directions of tourist flows. The levels of explained variance achieved in these analyses caution, however, that geographical and large-structural explanations together only account for between one-half and two-thirds of the observed variation in tourist flows.

The analysis above helped identify that set of predictor variables which affect the likelihood of foreigners' travel in both societies in the same way, and it produced another set of predictors which affect both countries but affect them differently, or affect only one of them. Exit visa restrictions and the relative economic wealth of the country of origin are the only two predictor variables whose effect is not only detected in both countries, but is also of the same direction. All other things equal, if citizens of a given country are required to obtain special exit visas to leave, they are less likely to travel no matter whether their supposed destination is Hungary or Austria. Similarly, all other things equal, the higher the level of wealth in the tourists' society of origin, the more likely it is that they will visit Austria as well as Hungary. The latter result is consistent with Kelly's proposition, as well as the first half of Mansfeld's summary of the "radical 'political economy' " approach, above, concerning the connection between wealth and the distance of leisure travel.

All of the remaining statistically significant effects reflect mechanisms that work differently in the two societies. To recapitulate,

1. Austrian data support, Hungarians reject the "gravity"-model of international tourist flows;
2. the size of the country of origin is an important predictor of travel to Hungary while it is of minor consequence for Austria;
3. the effects of the sociopolitical bloc-affiliation of the tourists' state of origin are different—Warsaw Pact membership increases travel to Hungary and has little effect on tourism in Austria, while NATO-membership is a strong, positive predictor of foreign tourism to Austria although it is of little importance for Hungary;
4. *longue-durée* regional background is a meaningful predictor of travel to Hungary especially as regards the overrepresentation of east-central Europeans, while it is not an independent predictor of travel to Austria;
5. and, finally, the combination of membership in the Soviet bloc with economic development has a strong positive effect on the likelihood of travel to Hungary, while a similar interaction effect is observable, in Austria's case, between NATO-membership and the level of the per capita gross domestic product.

The statistical tests performed above therefore revealed a comparative feature that is of utmost importance concerning the interpretation of the two countries' tourist development since the 1960s. The analysis suggests that while essentially the same set of large-structural conditions has operated in both countries, different constellations of various aspects of those conditions have produced substantively different social outcomes that shape the insertion of international tourism in the two societies in different ways. The identical slopes of growth in the gross volume of incoming foreign tourism in the two countries during the 1960–84 period demonstrated in *chapter 3* are, consequently, to be interpreted as the products of disparate social processes. While the deep-structural determinants at work have been largely the same, the outcomes produced by them have been very different, due to the two societies' different historical positions in the uneven development of global capitalism and in the bifurcated world of the postwar interstate system.

The geographical, economic, political, and social profiles of the main actors in international tourism in the two countries clearly diverged. Tourism in Hungary came to be dominated by tourists from the better-off "northern tier" of the CMEA-bloc countries like Czechoslovakia, East Germany and Poland, while Austria became a prime tourist destination for the population of some countries that are among those most oriented toward outgoing tourism in the world, including West Germany and the Netherlands. Among the latter, the role of West Germany has been particularly important due to its size, economic power, and its historical ties to German-speaking Austria. In light of those regularities, the relatively sizeable presence of Austrians in Hungary—marked by third place on Hungary's list—and, to a lesser extent, that of Hungarians in Austria—ranked eighth—is a substantively important exception.

Simple push–pull theories, as borrowed from the human ecology and neo-classical economics of labor migration are not satisfactory in the area of leisure migration. Neither in capitalist Austria, nor in state socialist Hungary has the tourists' relative wealth (i.e., an implicit measure of the tourists' relative advantages in the world market) completely determined the dynamics of leisure flows. The effects of cultural and political factors as well as the workings of an underlying, historical path dependence have been amply demonstrated. A complex model of destination choice—represented statistically by the technique of multivariate regressions—is fully justified by these results.

Chapter 6

The Splitting of International Leisure Migration in Hungary

The preceding chapters established that the two countries' historical legacies, patterns of participation in the interstate system, and insertion in the world economy made a strong impact on their position and mode of participation in the international system of tourism destinations. Behind the parallel rates of tourism growth, the many details of intuitively appealing resemblance, and even the often noted, pervasive sense of jovial "elective affinity" between these two neighboring societies, lies a system of sharp underlying differences; the national composition of the foreign leisure migrants appearing on the borders is just one of those profound disparities. It would be extremely surprising if such broad divergences did not appear in the more general social and cultural context surrounding tourism in the two countries. The remaining empirical chapters are devoted to outlining some basic features of those socioeconomic and sociocultural aspects of international leisure migration.

An important and widely noted distinguishing feature of the state socialist countries' mode of insertion in the world economy of leisure travel lies in the realm of economic rules and regulations and, specifically, in their treatment of the most important, because most liquid, form of economic linkage, money. This chapter adopts some conceptual tools from institutional economic sociology and anthropology to describe the mixed-currency regime of Hungary's state socialism in contrast to the exclusively hard-currency arrangements in Austria. It summarizes the fundamentals of state socialist policy controversies regarding incoming international tourism. Then it presents some original field material to show how the mixed nature of the currency regime of Hungary's international tourism sector was reflected in political and popular representations of foreign tourists and international tourism in Hungary.

These tasks require a brief detour into some basic aspects of the economic sociology of money.

Monies and International Tourism

Political "special monies"

A key conceptual instrument that helps understand the monetary arrangements under which international tourism gained massive proportions in post-1956 Hungary as distinct from Austria can be obtained by examining Viviana Zelizer's (1989) Polányian analysis of "special monies." (The very concept of "special monies" is a variation on Polányi's notion of "special-purpose money" [1957].) Zelizer argues that the neoclassical portrayal of money as a universal means of exchange is incomplete and incorrect. While acknowledging the existence and importance of "market money"—described as a perfectly quantitative metaphor of exchange-value equivalence, or, as in Simmel (1978[1907]), "pure means"—she emphasizes that any exclusively utilitarian description of money is inadequate. Money, of which "there are a plurality of different kinds" (1989:351), "also exists outside the sphere of the market" (1989:351) so that the functioning of market money is not universal. It is "constrained." (There is no compelling theoretical reason for conceptualizing the qualitative aspects of money exclusively as a constraint. The quality of money is a constraint only *in relation to* the purported standard of "free"—i.e., "unconstrained"—exchangeability, assumed in a utilitarian framework. Qualitative aspects of money can also operate as emancipatory means.)

Zelizer's analysis is imprecise at the point where she contrasts the concept of "market money" to that of "extraeconomic factors" (1989:351). This is by relying on Karl Polányi's work, a main insight of which is the point that the substantive concept of the economy is broader than that of the market. The direct juxtaposition of the "market" with "extraeconomic factors," as done by Zelizer, ignores forms of nonmarket economic integration as potential counterpoints to "the market." The confusion is exacerbated where Zelizer identifies "extraeconomic factors" with those associated with constraints due to "culture and social structure" (1989:351)—a rather restrictive conceptualization overlooking, to point out the obvious, the political dimension, i.e., the threat or actual use of direct coercion as distinct from symbolic, value- and/or network-based forms of coercion implied by Zelizer's reference to "cultural and social-structural" constraints.

As Zelizer focuses on a gender-structured example of special monies in the family, those imprecisions do not pose an insurmountable problem in her empirical analysis. For extending her main ideas to the subject matter of state socialist currencies, however, it is necessary to reconsider "special monies" explicitly in terms of Karl Polányi's "mosaic-typology" of modes of economic integration, as the case of the state socialist economies suggests that nonmarket economic processes and especially political power can modify the exchangeability of money in important ways.

The thrust of Polányi's argument in his seminal paper (1957) is that the three forms of economic integration—reciprocity, redistribution and exchange—presuppose the existence of three specific patterns of social institutions—symmetry between groups or individuals, a central authority, and a price-setting market, respectively. He further describes three forms of exchange: "operational exchange," defined as "merely locational movement of a 'changing of places' between the hands" (1957:254), counterpoised by two versions of appropriational exchange: "decisional exchange," proposed as "appropriational movement of exchange [. . .] at a set rate" (1957:254–5), and, finally, "integrative exchange," which takes place "at a bargained rate" in a price-setting market (1957:255). The latter two are distinguished from one another by the feature that price-setting markets imply "a distinctive antagonistic relationship between partners" (1975:254), while the set rates under which decisional exchange operates allow the existence of a less inimical nexus among actors as they involve "no more than the gain to either party implied in the decision of exchange" (1957:255).

Money is present in all of these instances. It is used, under social-institutional arrangements characterized by linear symmetry, as an object passed on through interpersonal or intergroup reciprocity. It is subjected, under centralized authority (or, focal symmetry), to redistributive action both on the macro and the micro levels. Finally, money is the object of all three forms of exchange—operational, decisional and integrative. The utilitarian concept of money applies only to the last subcategory: integrative-appropriational exchange in a hostile, price-setting market.

Konrád and Szelényi's Weberian-Polányian essay classic on the macrosociology of state socialism (1979[1974]) describes state socialism's dominant *domestic* mode of economic integration as characterized by rational redistribution, whereby a central authority—the party-state—collects, and then redistributes, the value produced by society according to a pre-established, rational, and universal pattern called the plan.

The core element of this insight is suggested by Polányi himself where he refers to the Stalinist experience of the Soviet Union as "an extreme instance" of societal-scale redistribution (1957:256). With the benefit of hindsight, it can be reasoned, as it has been proposed in a variety of ways in the 1980s' literature on the economic sociology of east-central

Europe, that the monopoly of the redistributive state eroded during the post-Stalinist, softer version of state socialism, so that the redistributive mechanism of the second period can be described as displaying a certain sense of segmentation and specialization in comparison to the "central authority" pattern of Stalinism. This consideration opens up the relationship among those oligopolistic elements of redistributive authority, marked by combinations of symmetric-reciprocal, centralized-redistributive, operational, decisional and market-based exchange processes, as a challenging theoretical subject itself. A more detailed analysis of this problem would, however, exceed the bounds of this study.

Konrád and Szelényi's formula of state socialism does not address the external linkages of the socialist state or of state socialist societies at all. For an assessment of that problem it is necessary to merge an examination of the state socialist societies' external linkages with Polányi's original conceptualization of the modes of economic integration.

What makes rational redistribution practicable on a macrosocietal scale, according to Konrád and Szelényi, is the existence of an overarching, integrative political actor—the rational-redistributive socialist state—as a dominant political institution. (The defining characteristic of this institution is political so that it cannot be subsumed under Zelizer's rubrics of "cultural" or "social-structural" constraints, notwithstanding the fact that the socialist state has its clearly recognizable cultural and social structural correlates.) The dual dependency thesis of the insertion of the socialist states in the world economy suggests that the existence of such a single, omnipotent state actor cannot be documented unambiguously *on the interstate-level*. Soviet control over the satellite societies has never developed into a completely centralized and planned, rational-redistributive state socialist world-empire (Chase-Dunn 1984). By the early 1960s, the CMEA was constituted as a set of bilateral relations marked by an annual series of pairwise negotiations among all rational-redistributive states of the region, offering a clear example of Polányi's *decisional exchange*. The CMEA-arrangement reveals a set of state entities characterized by redistributive internal integration, connected to one another through interstate mechanisms of decisional exchange, and held together by imperial military and political coercion reinforced by the bipolar splitting of the global interstate system.

Zelizer argues that no money is purely or exclusively market money; it is, in all of its forms, a qualitative entity, over and beyond any quantitative aspects. Among her many illustrations of qualitatively distinct monies, she quotes Thomas and Znaniecki's classic description of the "primitive" Polish peasant household economy where "[a] sum received from selling a cow is qualitatively different from a sum received as a dowry, and both are different from a sum earned outside" (Zelizer 1989:349 quoting Thomas and Znaniecki 1958[1918–20]:164–5).

The currencies of the CMEA countries can be described as strikingly similar to qualitatively organized, "primitive" peasant money with a single distinction: The social institution which supported the state socialist currencies was neither the village community, nor the extended family, but the decisional exchange mechanism of the bloc of rational-redistributive socialist states. The main distinguishing feature of the CMEA monetary system was the politically negotiated character of virtually all aspects of its monies. With this specification, Zelizer's description of "special monies" applies perfectly to state socialist monies. The four-and-a-half decades' experience of the state socialist economies demonstrate that political factors indeed:

> systematically constrain and shape (a) the *uses* of money, earmarking, for instance, certain monies for specified uses; (b) the *users* of money, designating different people to handle specified monies; (c) the *allocation* system of each particular money; (d) the *control* of different monies; and (e) the *sources* of money, linking different sources to specified monies (Zelizer 1989:351).

Mutual acceptance by the state socialist economies of each other's goods and currencies was guaranteed by political means so that political power came to be the "generalized means of exchange" within and among the economies of the state socialist bloc. This explains why the allegedly gold-based, synthetic general currency unit of the CMEA—the so-called "Transferable Rouble"—had been consistently relegated to use in bilateral trade and "plan-harmonizing" negotiations, merely as a basis of comparison on which the terms of trade can be determined by the politicians of a given pair of countries. The "Transferable Rouble" was a currency designed for decisional exchange between pairs of socialist states within the CMEA mechanism.

Consumer monies within the CMEA

Domestic consumer finances in the CMEA-countries had remained, throughout their state socialist history, predominantly cash-based, with few exceptions of limited scope. Guaranteed, often state-subsidized, low-interest consumer credits were available, especially for purchases of durable household goods (but not automobiles) and for housing construction or purchases. Except for East Germany since the early 1980s, consumer checking remained wanting. Consumer credit cards had been completely absent, and transfers between bank accounts had been used mainly by urban consumers paying utility bills and other periodically recurrent household expenses. Direct depositing and automated teller machines had not appeared until 1989. Salaries and wages were, with no exception, paid exclusively in cash, and so were all monetary transactions among private citizens, including even such major purchases as real estate. The most obvious substantive and methodological consequence of these conditions is that exclusive attention to recorded transactions in the official, formal, and openly observable realms of economic life is incapable of offering an exhaustive depiction of monetary processes.

Monetary regulations of within-bloc tourism were a combination of the CMEA-principle of interstate decisional exchange and cash-based domestic arrangements under very limited convertibility. The immediate acceptance of foreign currencies in exchange for goods or services was forbidden for establishments as well as private citizens. Direct money transfers for touristic purposes were possible, but almost never used, due to the administrative complexities involved. Incomes earned abroad, e.g., through guest labor arrangements, represented the only noteworthy exception as long as regulations pertaining to such labor flows stipulated that specific proportions of such salaries had to be processed through the official banking institutions.

Bilateral agreements kept the exportation and importation of cash below a rather low threshold introduced in order to make it possible for tourist banking service providers to moderate flows of cash by avoiding bilateral imbalances of shortages and overabundance of these nonconvertible national currencies. There was, of course, significant variation. Soviet law, for instance, expressly forbade the exportation of Soviet Roubles, irrespective of quantity, so that the Soviet state was even forced to provide savings bank outlets on its borders specialized in catering for those—mostly foreigners—who were leaving the country but were planning to return through the same route. (This was, for instance, the case with the Soviet–Finnish border, which was crossed often by travelers from east-central Europe to Finland and back, because of the cheapness of the Soviet transit train fare system for them.) Small amounts of the other European CMEA-currencies were allowed to be exported. There was variation in the degree to the severity with which such regulations were enforced, with the East German and Soviet authorities being most feared for their ardor and, according to common knowledge in the region, Polish and Hungarian customs were considered the least inquisitive.

The exportation of cash required "tourist cash export permits" that served as proof that the currency was obtained from "official" sources. As the acceptance of foreign currencies was forbidden, the cash exported could only be used after having been exchanged to local currency upon arrival; this exchange was made at the centrally-set rates which state monopoly-owned tourist money changers administered.

Larger amounts of money—sufficient for more than ca. two days' stay in the destination country—could only be taken in the form of CMEA-currency-specific travelers' checks, exchanged to local currencies at rates slightly lower than cash. Trade in such travelers' checks was clearly favored by the banks and the authorities because they did not pose imbalance problems in a physical form for the banks as cash did, the movement of currency could be kept under closer surveillance, they provided a certain margin of profit due to the fees imposed on them, and because travelers' checks were lumped together with other trade items so that an economy of scales reduced their handling costs. Within-bloc travelers' checks worked as the consumer-level equivalent of the CMEA's means of decisional exchange, the "Transferable Rouble."

Given the differential regulations concerning the travel of the citizens of the various states of the CMEA, the member states' different developmental patterns, degrees of industrialization and education, the different levels of material wealth available for the populations, and the bilateral framework of trade negotiations which treated consumer travel and consumer spending abroad as residual areas much less significant than commodity trade, a source of constant tension was the seemingly stable and predictable system of decisional exchange at set terms. The very stability and predictability of customer finances in within-CMEA tourism turned into rigidity and created, given the steep growth of international tourism, a multiplicity of complicated processes of informal money transactions.

Mixed-currency regimes and political dilemmas

As shown in the tourist arrival figures presented in *chapter 3* above, it was the Kádárist "normalization" of the early 1960s that reopened Hungary as a tourist destination country for foreigners. Levels of exposure to foreign tourism soon exceeded those of the prewar period. With the simultaneous presence of citizens of other CMEA-member-states and travelers from the capitalist countries of Europe, the Hungarian practice of incoming international tourism soon produced a system of intricately interconnected compromises in the realm of policies concerning tourist finances.

The simultaneous presence of tourists with hard currencies and those without—the latter including tourists from the CMEA-states as well as domestic tourists—split the Hungarian tourist market into two, qualitatively increasingly different parts. The splitting of the Hungarian tourist market was intensified by the fact that stark differences in income levels were associated with the two fields.

The incomes of the CMEA-member countries which sent the greatest number of tourists to Hungary (Czechoslovakia, the GDR, and Poland) approximated those characterizing personal incomes prevalent in the Hungarian economy—as long as the comparison was made on the basis of incomes from the official sector, using official exchange rates. This implies that, "officially speaking," travel to Hungary did not imply any major change in terms of the price levels as compared to the CMEA-tourists' conditions at home. Differences in the degree to which informality played a part in the CMEA-economies, however, make the picture more complex. Furthermore, "black market" rates devalued all CMEA-currencies *vis-à-vis* the Hungarian Forint, which, in turn, put CMEA-tourists at a disadvantage in their tourism in Hungary by default.

In contrast, tourists from hard-currency countries found themselves to be beneficiaries of clearly unequal relationships. With their home currencies in great need in Hungary by the party-state machinery and a large number of enterprises as well as by the population at large, even the official exchange rates were usually very favorable for them so that they could obtain touristic services of comparable quality for a fraction of the price that they would have to pay for them at home.

Given the mixed-currency arrangement of the country's external linkages, official Hungarian regulations concerning hard-currency tourism were formulated in the space of two separate sets of political considerations. (I will summarize these political positions on the basis of a series of conversations held with officials in Hungary's state bureaucracies in charge of tourism policy.) The two dimensions can be labelled as (1) the post-Stalinist dilemma and (2) the controversy between the "heavy-handed" versus "light-handed" approaches to securing the profitability of incoming international tourism.

The post-Stalinist dilemma involved determining the degree to which Stalinist isolationism would be abolished. On the hardline-Stalinist pole, the large-scale exposure of Hungary to incoming foreign tourists with a strong purchasing power in hard currency was seen as a threat to the consistency of the state socialist arrangement. The demonstration effect of the consumption patterns of hard-currency tourists, along with the gross wealth differential in their favor, was seen as a force that would work to "loosen up" the work discipline and increase the consumption-orientation of the state socialist labor force. In addition, the extra demand placed by "western" tourists on Hungary's tourism infrastructure, especially on the country's scarce capacity in tourist accommodation, was seen to threaten forcing out Hungarian and other CMEA vacationers whose service had been posited by the orthodox state socialist dogma to be the calling of the tourism industry of a state socialist country.

In contradiction to this view stood what could be described as a more permissive "reform-Communist" perspective, which saw a gradual process of transformation toward a more consumer-oriented pattern as a promising avenue of development for Hungarian state socialism. The hardline-Stalinist versus reform-Communist conflict over incoming international tourism hence reproduced the main political strife of the state socialist political regimes of the early 1960s. The focus of this debate was the question of whether the terrain of tourism should continue to be made up of a single redistributive structure or a sense of plurality should be tolerated in this field.

A second political dimension rested on the realization that incoming hard-currency tourism would be a potentially useful instrument for the socialist state as a major earner of national income. This policy controversy was focused, once the idea of the potential usefulness of tourism as a legitimate industry was accepted, on the ways in which maximum revenue effectiveness could be achieved from the viewpoint of the socialist state.

Adherents of the "heavy-handed" extreme urged the launching of the local monopoly of the socialist state to set exchange rates so as to drive the Hungarian Forint's rates *vis-à-vis* hard currencies as high as possible. They pushed for the introduction of stern law enforcement measures to ensure that as high a percentage as possible of tourism revenues be received and retained at state-owned establishments, and to guarantee that tourism cash exchange take place exclusively at "official" money changers (state-owned banks and travel agencies). This logic was the driving force behind many other state socialist destination countries' tourism development projects, including Romania's and Bulgaria's hard-currency-only resorts on their Black Sea shores and Soviet policies catering for Finnish tourism in Leningrad and Estonia.

In opposition to that stance, an increasingly vocal group of professionals, party-state bureaucrats and enterprise managers suggested a more "light-handed" approach. Recognizing that attractiveness in a competitive international tourism industry is a delicate matter, they warned that such stern measures would backfire as they would continue to deplete hard-currency demand for tourism in Hungary as they did during the 1950s. These actors argued, instead, that it was crucial that the monetary arrangements made for foreign tourists be sufficiently convenient so that Hungary could be placed "on the map" of West European tourism again. The latter perspective was tacitly reinforced by a peculiarly Hungarian political consideration, namely the Kádár regime's desire to dissipate the country's negative publicity as a newly recolonized state socialist society. Catering to hard-currency tourists from the wealthy European capitalist societies thus became a central element of the Hungarian state socialist regime's self-image as projected before western audiences. The second polemic can be reinterpreted as taking place between those who strived to use the socialist state to place local political constraints on the convertibility of hard currencies in Hungary, and those who realized the unpracticability and/or the political dangers of such attempts.

Three of the four polar perspectives to incoming international tourism tended to favor a particular institutional genre of tourism, namely, prearranged group travel in package tours. They did so for completely different reasons. The Stalinist approach, ideologically opposed to the very idea of allowing the entry of large numbers of hard-currency tourists, endorsed package tours as the "organized," planned, in all respects more "socialist" form of tourism as opposed to the blatant individualism of other forms of travel. This approach has been described, after the name of the official Soviet travel agency, as the "Intourist" pattern, allowing for the efficient surveillance of foreign tourists, and lending control for the receiving state in influencing what is shown to foreign tourists in the destination country. (This is the reason why, until the collapse of the Maoist government in 1990, Albania was accessible for foreign tourists almost exclusively in package-tour groups. For more on the Stalinist arrangements of incoming international tourism, the Intourist pattern, and on Albania, see Hall 1990.) The package tour was preferred by this group as the "next best" alternative to complete isolation, a touristic equivalent of the combination of a touristic policy of "containment" and of media censorship.

Proponents of the "heavy-handed" approach to using tourism as a hard-currency earner felt that package tours helped minimize contacts between the tourists and the locals. They advocated package tour group travel because it lessened the likelihood that foreign currency would "leak," from the state's point of view, through the hands of the Hungarian citizenry at large.

Finally, the technocratic devotees of a more sophisticated approach to opening up to tourism realized, upon examining practices in the tourism industry of the capitalist world, that package tours provided the highest margin of profit and therefore should be encouraged in any way possible. For them, the main attraction of the genre of package tours was that it helped minimize costs through bulk purchases, and increased sales through the massive standardization of travel experience.

The only political alternative that did not insist on making prearranged package tours the dominant genre of tourism was that of the reform-Communists who envisaged the spread of individual, fragmented tourism all over Hungary as a potentially positive agent of the country's continued transformation in the direction of a more relaxed, consumeristic, "petty bourgeois" version of state socialism. This conjuncture of so distinct political considerations made package tours to be the heavily preferred form of tourism on the level of policy rhetoric. The social process of tourism, however, produced a different outcome.

The tug-of-war between the extremes in both dimensions, represented by different groups of politicians, enterprise management interests and experts—both in and outside the state socialist party and state bureaucracy—created a near-balance of political forces. Slowly drifting state policies regulating hard-currency tourism in the direction of the hesitant and gradual introduction of increasingly permissive official regulations counterpoised the increasingly relaxed enforcement of existing regulations concerning the relationship between foreign tourists with hard and soft currencies and the Hungarian economy. As a result, no prescribed pattern, not even the preferred package tour model, was implemented with full force. Instead, patterns of incoming international tourism were shaped by the needs of, and relations among, travelers and the host society.

Hence, Hungary's history of official regulations for hard-currency tourism during the Kádár-period can be summarized briefly as follows: Initially, travelers from hard-currency countries were required to exchange a certain minimum amount of hard currency—approximately US$8–10 per day—at official money changers. This requirement was enforced by the Hungarian customs officers at the border upon departure; those hard-currency tourists who were not able to produce a receipt for their official exchanges received a small fine. Later on, fines were replaced by a verbal warning that next time they should "keep their exchange receipts". However, foreign tourists complained vigorously about the compulsory minimum exchange so that, ten years after the economic reform efforts introduced in 1968, the Hungarian state abolished the official harassment of hard-currency tourists on its borders for the minimum exchange requirement.

Up until the late 1960s, the official pricing mechanism of Hungarian commercial accommodations had also reflected the duality of the Hungarian tourist market. A legacy of the "heavy-handed" strategy of maximizing state incomes from incoming hard-currency tourism, prices had often been four-to-six times higher for hard-currency travelers than for "others". This dual system of pricing was also abolished as part of the economic experiments of the late 1960s. The mid-to-late-1960s also saw the liberalization of the regulations concerning the compulsory police registration of foreigners by reducing the formalities to match German and Austrian procedures. All things considered, about five to ten years after the curve of foreign tourist arrivals in Hungary had started to pick up, the country offered itself as the most "liberal" CMEA-member destination country for western tourists while being easily accessible for citizens of the CMEA-states as well. It is the combination of those two considerations with the relative cheapness of the country for hard-currency tourists that explains the fact that Hungary became the world's most tourist-saturated state socialist country, surpassing even Yugoslavia, by the early 1980s.

Hungary's tourist economy during the post-Stalinist period can be hence described as a *mixed-currency regime*, characterized by the parallel infusion of substantial amounts of hard currency and large sums of state socialist currencies. The concept of "money regime" ("*régime de la monnaie*") has been proposed by French philosopher Jean-Joseph Goux to capture minimal acts of payment as "a coherent mode of social institution," revealing practices of money in "structural relation to the law, the state, to that which is private and public, to representation, to reality, to materiality and ideality exposing itself every time." Inspired by this conceptualization, I use the summary term "currency regime" to capture the totality of institutional arrangements concerning practices of money on a macrosocietal scale.

The mixed-currency-regime emerged under conditions of the severe technological and organizational underdevelopment of consumer banking in Hungary's almost completely cash-based domestic economy. All of these factors point in the direction of increasing the propensity to circumvent "official," state-owned, state-operated, or state-recorded channels.

Hoping to avoid excessive imbalances in their trade with Hungary, many CMEA-countries placed quantitative limitations on the amount of money they allowed their citizens to exchange for CMEA-currencies officially. State limitations on the amount of money available for outgoing tourists are of course not a state socialist or CMEA-specialty. Most peripheral and semiperipheral countries of the world use such measures to control the leakage of their currencies. Major examples from Europe include Greece, Portugal and, until relatively recently, even France. Those limitations, however, have not made a significant structural impact on the shape of international tourism in Hungary as their level was set such that they did not restrict perceptibly the potential purchasing power of tourists from those countries in Hungary.

As a result, the within-CMEA consumer demand for Hungarian Forints soared, especially toward the second half of the period, when Hungary's standard of living increased discernibly in comparison to the other CMEA-countries, creating a comparatively attractive supply of goods and services in the area of direct individual consumption. Thus, the conditions for large-scale cross-border informal trade in nonconvertible currencies was in place, with the Hungarian Forint playing the role, in relation to the other CMEA-currencies, of a quasi-hard currency.

In summary, the mixed-currency-regime of incoming international tourism emerging, as it did, in Hungary during the post-Stalinist period, had the following basic consequences: First, *tourism to Hungary did not require access to hard currencies*. In fact, as seen above, most foreign tourists in Hungary were people whose travel alternatives were severely limited by the restrictions placed on their travel by their own states, and participated in Hungarian tourism precisely for that reason.

Second, *the field of incoming international tourism in Hungary was split according to the kinds of currencies to which the tourist had access.* This cleavage also entailed a marked difference in terms of the visiting tourists' purchasing power in quantitative terms, with those from hard-currency countries in a clearly advantageous position. Travel to Hungary required one of two alternatives: Access to such convertible "market monies" as the leading west European or North American hard currencies, or access to special monies whose acceptance was guaranteed through political means for citizens of the CMEA-countries.

Third, the sizeable influx of hard currency, coupled with the Hungarian citizens' loosely restricted travel to the capitalist countries, created *a two-dimensional system of inequalities between tourists and hosts*, placing Hungarians in an intermediate position: disadvantaged vis-à-vis tourists with hard currency and advantaged in comparison to those without. The hard-currency segment of incoming tourism to Hungary represented an interaction between guests—whose money, in its simple form, as earned in the home society, was universally useable everywhere in the world—and members of the host society, who had extremely limited official access to such hard currencies. All those conditions, coupled with the relative relaxation of the Hungarian state's restrictions on its citizens' travel to the capitalist world, steeply increasing consumer demand due to the economic reforms and the general sense of liberalization in Hungary, and the state's success in preventing domestic private capital formation by allowing luxury consumption to vent excess incomes, created an acute consumer hunger for hard currency not nearly satisfiable within the confines of the state-controlled official economy.

Mixed Currency Regime and Split Representation

The distinct intermediate position created by these arrangements of tourist finances acted as a powerful determinant of the patterns of interaction between tourists and their hosts in Hungary. Reinforced by other, similarly split aspects of social experience in the Hungary of the post-Stalinist period of dual dependency, the way in which the Hungarian society provided room for the structural incorporation of incoming leisure migration can be described as a pattern of split adaptation and split representation.

Conversations with employees of Club Tranquil, Hungary's first and so far only tourism establishment in the "Club-Med" genre, reveal the profoundly unequal aspect of the tourist–host relationship in the hard-currency field of incoming foreign tourism. (Club Tranquil is a pseudonym. The facility is located on the southern side of a peninsula in Lake Balaton, arguably the finest waterfront real estate in Hungary. The four-star hotel village is advertised in German as an "'Island' on the Tip of the Peninsula," "the luxury resort village of the Hungarian Sea, the Balaton, in wild romantic surroundings (. . .) halfway between Vienna and Budapest."

With considerable pride for his establishment's inventiveness in providing exciting and inexpensive on-site entertainment for the guests—99% of whom are "westerners"—one of Club Tranquil's managers explained:

> Our **Abend Show** is truly unique. (. . .) You won't find it elsewhere in Eastern Europe or even in Western Europe. (. . .) The idea is that regular employees of our resort perform a stage show to the guests. This is a second, more relaxed form of establishing contact between the employee and the guest: The attendant who, during the day, hands the guests the towel at the reception desk of the swimming pool, (. . .) the waiter who serves them with the food that they had ordered, or the phone exchange operator whom they never see just hear her voice, all of these employees perform a superb program for the guests. So the next day, when they meet again in the employees' ordinary job situation, they can greet each other as good acquaintants, and the guest has a chance to say "Oh, I saw you yesterday, you were very good." Otherwise there would be little opportunity for them to have a conversation. (. . .) At the end of the show, all of the performers are introduced, and it is revealed who does what in their regular occupation for the resort. It's great fun when it is announced that the actor who impersonated Falco [a popular disco star in central Europe at the time] is in fact the head bar tender! (. . .) This creates a hilarious atmosphere. There is no cover charge for the show but at the end we engage in a little sales pitch: We carry around a small collecting-box.

This example reveals the distinctly colonial cultural and social correlates of ever-present craving for hard currency. According to Club Tranquil's CEO, most of the employees mentioned in the vignette are underpaid high-school and elementary school teachers who work for the resort during their summer holidays. In 1989, their official incomes from the resort averaged around US$125 per month, the equivalent of the mean wage in the state sector in Hungary. Under this condition, the tips collected from the guests become the most important element of income earning strategies.

With only a tiny minority of Club Tranquil's employees hired from among the population of Tranquil or its vicinity—as signaled by their special-built dorms about one kilometer from the resort—most of them are cut off from their home context. The corporate cultural management of the resort thus channels a combination of the employees' yearning for extra incomes in hard currency and the lack of contextual micro-constraints on their conduct—something that would likely prohibit these young teachers from engaging in such collective form of spectacle in their own communities—into an arrangement that provides an extra attraction for the tourists, hence improving the quality of the service provided by Club Tranquil. This example also reveals a successful effort whereby servitude-like constraints on the employees' freedom of labor—marked by the fact that they are expected to use their free time to prepare, practice, and perform a quasi-professional stage production—are translated into a market cash nexus seasoned with a dash of the exotic. The way that is achieved is through the forced redefinition of the realm of the public and the private conduct of the employees, in the service of the tourists' entertainment. This formula—the penetration by the public of the private sphere under a cash nexus—is the paradigmatic pattern of prostitution.

Finally, Club Tranquil's inventive Abend Show in effect translates the Hungarian socialist state's subsidies expended in the realm of general education and teachers' training—the main reason why Club Tranquil's employees are actually *capable* of presenting an enjoyable stage show in the first place—into hard-currency receipts for Club Tranquil, a venture jointly owned by the Hungarian state and several Austrian investors through "official" payments for the service, and "leaking" in the form of tips into the pockets of the performers-employees of the resort. In 1989, none of Club Tranquil's foreign co-owners were in the tourism business. That restricted Club Tranquil's access to West European markets as the only marketing avenue it could utilize led through the Hungarian tourism agencies. This may account for the Club's inability to break even in terms of repaying the financing spent on its construction during the early 1980s.

Vis-à-vis tourists from the other CMEA-countries, the circumstances of the Hungarian society were, on the whole, somewhat more advantageous. Due to the severe restrictions on these tourists' freedom of travel, imposed by their own states, a large part of the Hungarian tourism sector was dealing essentially with a captive audience, arriving at a decision to visit Hungary through a process of forced substitution. This was a clear prescription for improving terms of trade in these relations from the Hungarian point of view.

By the year 1989, cultural stereotypes regarding the "inferiority" of "eastern" tourists had been deeply set in Hungary. This formation was antithetical to the hegemonic discourse of the official media images of CMEA-societies. However, it rhymed in important ways with official tourism policy statements which urged, under strong influence by the economic "marketization"-reform rhetoric of the time, an increase in the share of "quality tourism," i.e., of hard-currency incomes. Attitudes among merchants in the Hungarian tourist sector reflect strong preconceived notions concerning this dimension of inequity.

A fashion clothing and travel "souvenir" boutique owner in the village of Tranquil related common "knowledge" about CMEA-tourists, using the example of her East German customers, in the following way:

The easterners don't really know how to behave. They don't even know how to say hello. They come in, we say hi, and nothing. Well, that is a strange, very strange nation, the East German nation. (. . .) They are mostly interested in the real cheap stuff: petty jewelry, a few Forints' worth of merchandise.

In contrast to westerners, the business of CMEA-tourists is of inferior value. Their presence is more of a nuisance:

Who make purchases? Well, the Germans. I mean, the **West** Germans. The others, the East Germans, and even the Russians, they come in, too, but they mostly only look at my merchandise. It's the West Germans who actually buy what they like. The Austrians also buy things but the CMEA tourists only look around.

The splitting of the Hungarian tourism sector was evident in every respect, ranging from tourism policy statements and tourism statistical data gathering, both of which consistently treated the "hard" and "soft" aspects of tourism separately, to ordinary tourism service providers whose business considerations were constantly shaped by the distinction between those "who buy" and those "who only look." (This excerpt can also be considered as a naive yet fitting critical comment on the Gaze as the focal moment of the tourist experience discussed briefly in *chapter 1*. There is no room here to elaborate on the theoretical implications.)

The only exception from the rule of relative structural disadvantages due to lack of hard currencies was marked by those tourists from the CMEA-member countries who occupied positions in their own societies that allowed them to compensate for their comparative disadvantage. This exception required the involvement of political institutions as mediating mechanisms. An important way in which home-country political leverage was transformed into tourism in Hungary was through privileged access to vacation facilities owned and subsidized by the party-state and its affiliates.

Field data collection for this study allowed a last-minute insight into the workings of this system as the manager of the Tranquil resort of the Hungarian Socialist Workers' Party agreed to give an interview approximately five months before the formal abolition of the party and the return to the state of the resort. He described the system of the allocation of rooms in the resort facility—originally built as a castle for Habsburg Archduke Joseph, confiscated by the socialist state, assigned to the care of the ruling party, and subsequently expanded by the addition of a prefab concrete building—located about three kilometers from Club Tranquil, on the same peninsular shore of Lake Balaton, as follows:

The area as a whole is five hectares. It includes a beautiful park, a beach, a small grove, and some nice walkways. We have a couple of tennis courts, a minigolf course, a volleyball court and a tiny mobile buffet in the garden. At present, we have 205 beds, 85 of them in the castle building, the rest in the new wing. (. . .) The guests come with vouchers from the party Central Committee apparatus, from the enterprises owned by the party, from the county party committee apparatuses, from among the employees of the Youth Communist League, etc. All of this is subsidized by the state budget at the rate of 50% of the full cost. Since 1970, we have received foreign vacationers through exchanges arranged through the international contacts of the party. This is based on bilateral contracts, mainly with the socialist countries, but we have also received quite a few guests from third world countries. This means that we cater for guests from about forty to sixty countries a year. (. . .) The conditions of the foreigners' holidays are exactly the same as for Hungarian guests. They receive the same service at the same prices and subsidies.

This vignette reveals a numerically quite insignificant but conceptually important way in which political power was exchanged by some citizens of CMEA-countries for good-quality tourism services in Hungary in the absence of "market monies." The main mechanism for this was the utilization of the cross-border contacts of the CMEA-countries' party-state apparatuses through bilateral barter arrangements. Summarizing the description of the international tourist linkages of the state-party, offered by the manager of the party's resort in Tranquil, such contacts can be described, in the Polányian terminology of the earlier part of this chapter, as a combination of decisional exchange and reciprocity.

The Tranquil resort of the ruling party also gave, by 1989, a clear example of the translatability of political and hard-currency-based privileges in the Hungarian context. Since the 1988 season, the Tranquil facility of the state party had combined subsidized catering for politically privileged guests with for-profit services to hard-currency tourists. Although the nearest bus stop was still called "Pártüdülő" (Party Resort), the logo of the ruling party had been removed from the outside of the gate and replaced by one announcing an inconspicuous hotel. The guard at the entrance related that his orders were to raise the electronic gate barrier for any Hungarian car with a license plate starting with an A or a B (signs of state- and party-affiliation in Hungary's old license plate system still in effect at the time), or *for any car with a west European plate*. According to the resort's manager, foreign citizens had spent 1109 guest-nights in the resort; 1057 of those were paid for in hard currencies. West Germans made up 41% of all hard-currency guest nights in July, 1989.

As a result, there were two principal ways in which the resort's services could be accessed: with state-subsidized vouchers obtained through political means, and with hard currency. Hungarian and other CMEA-politicians and their families, side-by-side with hard-currency guests, hence enjoyed the sense of seclusion provided by this superb resort facility.

As to the Austrian case, it should suffice to state here that conditions of incoming international tourism in Austria have been different in nearly all respects surveyed above. Following the repeated crises and high inflation of the immediate postwar period, the stabilization of the economy—and, hence, of the Austrian Schilling—was achieved as early as 1952 (Koren 1981:177). Subsequently, the Schilling was reattached to the new German currency, the German Mark, via a fixed exchange rate. (During the *Anschluss*, the official currency of Austria was the German imperial money, the *Reichsmark*. The Reichsmark was abandoned with the foreign occupation of Austria in 1945.) By virtue of the Austrian economy's steady, above-average growth and of its being pinned on to what was to become one of Europe's strongest currencies, the Schilling became an important hard currency itself, notwithstanding the fact that it was the legal tender of a relatively small economy.

Consequently, the financial arrangements of foreign tourism in Austria came to be much less complex conceptually than those in Hungary. First, *tourism in Austria required access to hard currencies.* This fact *ab ovo* cut off most of the potential leisure migration from the countries turned state socialist in Austria's north and east. While that certainly implied the loss of some of Austria's important traditional tourist-business linkages, the exclusion of the relatively worse-off segment of its previous tourist clientele allowed Austria to specialize in catering for an upscale demand.

The hard-currency-regime of incoming international tourism, second, prevented the splitting of Austria's tourism sector. Put differently, the "bifurcation" of the Austrian tourism sector took place outside of the country's borders, prohibiting access to Austria's tourism facilities for the citizens of the country's poorer state socialist neighbor states. These two conditions permitted the formulation of more straightforward, growth-oriented, profit-maximizing financial and development policies for tourism in Austria than in Hungary. The Stalinism versus reform-Communism debate obviously did not apply, and the "heavy-handed" approach was preempted by previous institutional arrangements. An existing, strong tourism industry including a large number of small-scale service providers, powerful political and lobbying organizations, local, regional and national chambers, etc., and decades-long market-ties to all major tourist-generating economies of central and western Europe were already well entrenched.

Third, Austria's *hard-currency-regime prevented the formation of the basic relationship of "colonial" inequality* between tourists and their hosts existing in Hungary. Although the relative income levels between the main sending countries and Austria may have been slightly disadvantageous from the Austrian point of view, the disparities have never been as grave as between hard-currency tourists and the Hungarian host society. This condition fostered, on the part of Austria, the assumption of a more equitable "bargaining" position *vis-à-vis* the dominant institutions of tourist-generating societies.

This chapter has found that the fundamental financial structure of the institutional arrangements in international leisure travel has profound political and cultural implications. Hungary's mode of insertion in the global system of touristic linkages produced the clear bifurcation of its incoming international tourism economically and politically as well as in the realm of the representations of strangers. The system of split representation which developed in Hungary implied a doubly postcolonial structure in which local actors occupied an intermediary position. They appeared as either the inferior or the superior Other *vis-à-vis* traveling strangers, depending on the political-economic regional origin of the tourist with whom the interaction took place. The process is best described as a series of stereotyped adjustments between the two systems of inequalities.

Chapter 7

Informality and Tourism Receipts in Comparative Perspective

One of the conclusions of the previous chapter's argument was that the structural conditions of the mixed-currency regime placed a large part of the tourism business outside of officially recorded channels in Hungary. This chapter, first, examines some differences in the institutional arrangements of incoming international leisure migration in the two countries by focusing on accommodation services, the single largest component of tourist spending abroad. Second, it addresses the issue of formality and informality by examining some secondary statistical material indicating the main effects of the different degrees and forms of informalization on tourism revenues. Then, it summarizes available statistical evidence on the size of international tourism receipts in the two countries.

Commercial Accommodation: Subsidized Investment and Endemic Shortages

The promotion abroad of travel to Austria began almost immediately after World War II. Despite foreign occupation, hunger, the severe destruction of the country's tourism infrastructure and high inflation, the Austrian government recognized the importance of tourism as a hard currency earner very early. The year 1947 saw the launching of the *Ausländeraktion* (approximately: Sales to Foreigners), a concerted effort between the tourism industry and the government, designed to promote, mainly to Dutch, British, and American vacationers, holidays in the few hotels of Austria that had been neither destroyed by the war nor taken over by the occupational forces. The number of foreign tourist nights arranged under this program rose from ca. 82,000 to 345,000 from 1948 to 1949 (Brusatti 1984:144). Difficulties caused by food shortages and inflation were alleviated by the introduction of a special coupon system for foreign tourists called the *Touristenkarte*. In 1949, four years after the end of the devastating war, West Germans began touring Austria in large numbers again; they have made up by far the largest group of foreign tourists in Austria ever since.

The single most important impact on Austria's tourism development can be attributed to the application of development funds—first of all the European Reconstruction Program (ERP) funds—to the reconstruction, modernization and expansion of the country's tourism infrastructure, primarily in the sphere of hotel accommodations. Between 1949 and 1955, the annual amount of capital dispensed through such subsidized investment credits into the tourism industry increased from 1.1 to 6.5% of the total ERP counterpart allocations in Austria (Brusatti 1983:151). These figures do not include such more general infrastructural investments as those expended for the reconstruction and electrification of the *Österreichische Bundesbahnen* (Austrian Railways, ÖBB), and the country's road and telecommunication systems, all of which had a direct impact on the country's ability to cater to incoming international tourism.

Due to the Soviet occupation of the northeastern part of the country up until 1955, most of the infrastructural development funds had been spent in Austria's western provinces—Vorarlberg, Tyrol, Salzburg, and Carinthia—and in the capital city, Vienna. Hence, the spatial distribution of the early allotments of development funds coincided with the distribution of demand from Austria's strongest foreign tourism markets; the areas most easily accessible from Germany and the Netherlands happened to be those most intensively developed during the first ten years after the war. With the end of the foreign occupation and the passage of the administration of the ERP funds to the national government, regional inequities were corrected. ERP funds were supplemented by such Austrian government developmental resource allocations as the *Zinsenzuschußaktion* (Interest Subsidy Program) and the *BÜRGES-Aktion* (The Small Business Credit Guarantee Program of the Federal Ministry for Commerce, Small-Scale Manufacturing and Industry, see Brusatti 1984:159). As a result, the growth in capital allocation in the tourism business was much higher than in the other branches of the economy: Between 1960 and 1970, the increase in credits extended for tourism development was 795% (Bundesleitung 1971). The tourism industry was followed by transport (584%), small scale manufacturing (257%), industry (232%), and commerce (157%) (Bundesleitung 1971).

The spatial emphasis of early development policies, favoring the western provinces, has fortunately benefitted that part of Austria whose strength lay in winter tourism. As a result, the temporal distribution of tourism in Austria became characterized by two peaks—one during the summer and another during the winter. This turned out to be a major contributor to the improved utilization of the country's touristic resources and an important way in which temporal adjustment problems in the seasonality of tourism demand, a frequent problem in single-season countries, are avoided. According to a recent study, the share of winter tourism in Austria's tourism as measured in overnight stays increased from 22 to 41% between 1955 and the "tourism year" of 1985–86 (Zimmermann 1988) so that Austria became a "winter-tourism-country" (Dorner, Glatz, and Schremmer 1986) by the early 1980s.

In Hungary, international tourism was not recognized as a significant source of revenue until the early-to-mid-1960s. Due to the country's inherited general infrastructural underdevelopment, its heavier devastation by World War II, and the Stalinist regime's developmental policies of forced industrialization which channeled most investment funds into heavy industrial production, neglected consumption, and systematically slighted the agriculture and the service branches, the country arrived into the era of its major tourism growth with a peculiarly inadequate infrastructure for international tourism.

After World War II, only a few of the most famous and largest hotels were renovated and restored as hotels in Hungary. Smaller establishments were mainly converted into housing, public buildings or vacation resorts (KSH 1989: 16). During the Stalinist period of the 1950s emphasis was placed exclusively on government-subsidized social tourism—redistributed through political channels on the workplace level and dispensed through the official trade unions—so that the share of hotels and subsidized resorts swapped proportions in twenty years: In 1937, there had been 1764 hotels and 133 resorts while, in 1957, 240 hotels and 1077 resorts were registered in Hungary (KSH 1989). The number of hotel beds in Hungary was 31.45 thousand in 1937 (KSH 1989). The Stalinist period decreased that figure by two-thirds to a minuscule 10.8 thousand in 1957 (KSH 1989) so that the number of hotel beds in Hungary had not reached that of the last prewar year until 1980. By then, of course, the country was flooded by foreign tourists. At the beginning of the 1980s, one-third of all hotel beds were located in Budapest, and the Lake Balaton area and Budapest together registered 57.8% of the country's entire commercial accommodation capacity (KSH 1990). Lake Balaton is an attraction with extremely high temporal concentration; most of its incoming tourism business takes place between mid-July and mid-August.

In 1980, Hungary registered a total of 10.45 million foreign tourist arrivals and 68.07 million foreign tourist nights. In the same year, the number of hotel beds was a mere 34,285 (KSH 1990). (This includes all hotels in the one- to five-star categories.) This implies an annual average of 304.8 foreign tourist arrivals and 1,985.4 foreign tourist nights per hotel bed. Even with the addition of all other forms of commercial accommodation—all nonsubsidized accommodations including hotels, pensions, guest houses, tourist huts, bed-and-breakfast establishments, campsites, and registered private accommodations—in Hungary, the total number of available commercial accommodations was no more than 237 thousand (KSH 1990), implying 44.09 foreign tourist arrivals and 287.2 foreign tourist nights per bed in commercial accommodation. In contrast, Austria had over six hundred thousand hotel beds alone during the same year (KSH 1990), and the total number of guest beds had reached about 1.2 million by the mid-1980s (Zimmermann 1988:155).

According to a study by the Hungarian Statistical Office, Hungary had .0044 hotel beds and altogether .0288 commercial accommodation beds per capita in 1986 (KSH 1989:19). The corresponding Austrian figure, quoted by the same study on the basis of World Tourism Organization and OECD data, was .086 and .158, respectively (KSH 1989:19). In other words, the Austrian economy had been much better equipped for the reception of a large number of tourists than Hungary. In terms of the availability of the most profitable segment of commercial tourist accommodations—hotel beds—the difference was almost twenty-fold.

These summaries suggest very forcefully that the bulk of Hungary's tourism could not possibly have been accommodated through recorded commercial channels. Table 7.1 compares total guest nights figures of registrations at commercial accommodations. During the four most recent years for which such statistics are available, only between 20.8 and 23.9% of all tourist nights were spent at commercial accommodations in Hungary. BarOn's (1989) data estimate that the total number of foreign tourist nights in Austria was around 129.5 million in 1985. An Austrian source (Fremdenverkehr in Zahlen 1991) estimates the total foreign guest nights at all commercial accommodations to be at 85.075 million nights so that the proportion of foreign tourist nights spent under

Table 7.1. Total Foreign Tourist Nights and Foreign Guest Nights at Commercial Accommodations in Hungary, 1986–89 (million nights)

	Foreign tourist nights	Of those, guest nights at commercial accommodations
1986	70.5	15.4
1987	77.6	17.5
1988	66.4	15.9
1989	83.3	17.3

Source: KSH, 1990.

commercial arrangements is 65.7%. About two-thirds of all foreign tourist nights are spent in officially recorded commercial accommodations in Austria, while only one in five takes place at recorded commercial accommodation facilities in Hungary.

Formality and Informality in Tourism Services

One-third of foreign tourist nights in Austria and ca. 80% of foreign tourist nights in Hungary are spent outside of recorded tourism accommodations. The difference can be attributed to two factors: Differences in rates of kin- or friendship-group-based reciprocal arrangements of travel, and/or disparities in the informalization of the tourist economies of the two countries. There is no *a priori* reason to assume that the proportion of those who stay with family and friends among foreign arrivals is exactly the same in the two countries. On a substantive basis, it could be argued that kin- and friendship-network-based travel is more likely in Hungary due to the fact that 5 million of the world's 15 million Hungarian speakers live outside of the borders of today's Hungary. Approximately 3 million of them live in the neighboring countries—the Romania, Czechoslovakia and Yugoslavia of the state socialist period.

It would be very difficult to attribute a discrepancy of the above magnitude solely to a higher incidence of reciprocal arrangements in Hungary's incoming tourism. The above observation about the differential rates of utilization of officially recorded commercial establishments therefore implies different rates of informalization of tourism services in the two countries.

That conclusion is perfectly consistent with previous analyses concerning the magnitude and conceptual importance of nonplanned and nonrecorded economic activities in state socialist economies. The informal sector of the state-regulated capitalist economy is defined as the sum of all economic activities outside the realm of state record keeping, regulation and taxation. Many prominent authors (Portes and Sassen-Koob 1987:31; Portes 1981, 1985; Castells and Portes 1989; Portes and Schauffler 1992) use an approach focused more sharply on regulation by defining the informal sector as "all income-earning activities that are not regulated by the state in social environments where similar activities are regulated" (Portes and Schauffler 1992:6). Regulation assumes recording and implies taxation so that the definition applied above is consistent with the structuralist approach.

Whether or not particular activities take place outside of these state controls, is only one of the two main dimensions along which state socialist economies are structured. Informality—the tendency of economic processes to take place in "hiding" from official record keeping—

occurs both in the state-owned and bureaucratically-managed segment of the state socialist economies and in small-scale private enterprise. The latter segment of state socialist economies—which is characterized by a high degree of relative independence from planning and from bureaucratic management—is called the second economy. (The idea that *informality*—economic activities outside the realm of public record keeping, regulation and scrutiny—and the *second economy* as conceptualized by conventional Hungarian economic sociology—"income earning activity outside the sale of labor to the socialist sector" (e.g., Gábor 1983, cited by Swain 1990, but see also Gábor and Galasi 1985, and Gábor 1989:597)— ought to be treated as conceptually distinct dimensions has been presented first, and in much more detail than space permits here, in Böröcz 1992c. See also Böröcz and Southworth 1995.) The following pages of this chapter seek to outline the extent and type of informality in the two countries' tourism sectors using, for lack of direct means to perform research on this particular issue, secondary research information.

It would be both naive and misleading to assume that the tourism service branch of Austria's economy is free of informal activities. The extent of informality appears to be, however, rather limited. A study aimed specifically to appraising the magnitude of personal incomes derived from hidden transactions in the Austrian economy through an econometric reanalysis of Austrian national economic statistics for 1976 (Franz 1985) has focused on two fields of informality: "moonlighting" and "off-the-record activities." The two were distinguished such that moonlighting includes all nonrecorded incomes realized by employees, on the job or elsewhere, while off-the-records activities refer to unrecorded incomes of the self-employed.

Alfred Franz's findings suggest that the two forms of informality together comprised about 3.8% of the Austrian GDP in 1976, with a little over half of the hidden incomes realized through moonlighting (1986:331). Catering to tourism is one of those areas of the Austrian economy that are particularly amenable to informality; the sum of incomes off-the-record and those from moonlighting in the "hotels and restaurants" category is estimated at 11% of all sales at such establishments (1986:333).

Specifically, "hotels, restaurants and cafés" are the most important hidden generators of incomes off-the-record (1986:331, 334–5). The self-employed in the categories of "hotels, restaurants, and cafés," "food, beverages, and tobacco," and in the "transport and communication" branches together—i.e., whose line of business has at least some touristic content—indicate an estimated total hidden income of 3800 million ATS, the equivalent of one-third of all off-the-record incomes (Franz 1985:334–5). Hidden incomes by the self-employed in Austria's tourism sector thus made up just about .5% of the Austrian GDP in 1975.

Hidden incomes of employees in the categories of "food, beverages and tobacco occupations," "waiters, cooks and related activities," and "occupations in transport and tourism industries" are estimated at 2170 million ATS, e.g., about one-sixth of the total calculated moonlighting incomes in Austria (Franz 1986:334–5). Tourism-related moonlighting thus comprises less than .3% of the Austrian GDP. Hidden incomes from tourism make up about .8% of the Austrian GDP. Given that 48,450 million ATS was recorded officially as tourism incomes from foreigners in 1975 (Fremdenverkehr in Zahlen 1989), the total amount of hidden incomes from tourism can be approximated as constituting about 12.3% of all receipts from international tourism. (The source of the tourism receipt figure does not offer tourism data on revenues from domestic tourists, while the statistical estimate of the off-the-record and moonlighting types of informality does not provide a specific figure for hidden incomes from foreigners. Thus the comparison cannot be made statistically more straightforward.)

Estimates concerning the importance of various aspects of informality in catering to foreign tourists in Hungary have been adapted from several sources. The first general-purpose social survey in Hungary, implemented in 1980, asked questions about the "second" incomes of the population. A useful study by the Economics Research Institute of the Hungarian Academy of Science assessed the differential propensities of various groups of foreign tourists to resort to informal transactions exchanging their currencies to Hungarian Forints while in Hungary. More recent studies by various Hungarian economists, judging the economic conditions, particularly the macrolevel profitability, of incoming international tourism in Hungary have also been consulted. The following pages review the relevant part of that material.

The general-purpose survey offers little by way of a lead. It does demonstrate the extreme informalization of the Hungarian economy by showing that 73.6% of all respondents admitted to drawing incomes from sources other than a "main" occupation in the first sector (Kolosi 1984: 57). The overwhelming majority of those with informal earnings are involved in subsistence and/or market agricultural production, mainly on a part time basis. However, only 2.7% of the sample reported extra incomes from tips—the indication in the survey of specifically tourism-related informality.

A working paper by the Economic Research Institute (Gazdaságkutató 1983) aims to assess the real economic processes of incoming tourism in Hungary. Its estimates are based on a survey, executed by the Hungarian Central Statistical Office, on the spending patterns of foreign tourists in Hungary and official money exchange data as recorded by the National Bank of Hungary. By contrasting the two sets of information it was possible to assess the magnitude of the differential leakages of foreign currencies.

Before summarizing the report of the Economics Research Institute, it is to be noted that the simple "black market" exchange of foreign currencies to Hungarian Forints, or *vice versa*, was not nearly the only informal arrangement of currency transactions. The exchange of foreign currencies for domestic services and merchandise also produced the same result. In cases where the ban on the exportation of cash was strictly enforced by the tourists' own state, other solutions were invented. They included, for instance, informal arrangements concerning the deposit in savings accounts in the country of origin the countervalue of services to be utilized in Hungary, with the understanding that those funds would be utilized by the Hungarian service providers if and when they should travel in the other country. This arrangement required a high degree of mutual trust among the participants and involved, typically, kin- or friendship-based ties. This example was mentioned by some informants around Lake Balaton as a way to circumvent the East German state's particularly unreasonable limitations on CMEA-exchanges of the East German Mark. (In 1988, the maximum amount of money that East German travelers were allowed to purchase officially equalled ca. 3000 Hungarian Forints, sufficient for a maximum of three days' stay on a shoestring budget at Lake Balaton.) Those Hungarian informal tourism service providers who resorted to the solution of accepting savings deposits in East Germany as payment ended up getting a very good deal due to the guaranteed exchange of all savings deposits in East Germany to West German Marks at very favorable rates as part of the German unification, a year or so later.

Another obvious way of avoiding compliance with the CMEA-states' restrictions on the exportation and importation of currencies involved the petty smuggling of commodities between different countries. In the Hungary of the 1970s and 1980s, an entire institution—called in Hungary, sarcastically, the "CMEA-markets"—emerged around such informal trade. Mainly Polish, Czechoslovak, Yugoslav and Hungarian citizens invented this form of trade and they were joined, later, by Soviets, East Germans, Romanians, and Bulgarians. What emerged was a large-scale and stable web of informal linkages across the boundaries of CMEA-states. This trade was based on three conditions: the complementary character of some aspects of the region's economies, country-by-country differences in the structure of subsidies on various groups of commodities resulting in substantial price inequalities, and the rigid, inflexible nature of "official" CMEA-trade that was unable to account for market pressures resulting from the first two conditions.

By the end of the 1980s, mainly Polish travelers—many of them guestworkers in Hungary and, thus, intimately familiar with arrangements in the domestic second economy as well as dynamics of market demand—established themselves firmly in Hungary's domestic second economy as suppliers of discount commodities ranging from children's shoes to small machine tools, from linenware to automobile parts, and from hard liquors to hard currency. In the reverse, Yugoslav citizens of Voivodina, Northern Croatia and Eastern Slovenia along with Austrians from Burgenland (that is, residents of the regions next to the Hungarian border) specialized in "private" food imports from Hungary. A similar form of regional cross-border integration emerged—under the umbrella of bilateral provisions called "small-border-traffic"—around the Hungarian-Slovakian and Hungarian-Romanian borders. During the late 1980s, the practitioners of these small-scale informal trade linkages were joined by residents of the Western Ukraine shopping for all moveable consumer items in Eastern Hungary. In a similar vein, the Lake Balaton area had become, since the mid-1970s, a relatively quiet meeting point for German families split by the "inner-German" border. Catering for such "family-reunification" holidays emerged as a distinct, stable and institutionalized branch of the second economy of the tourism services sector in Hungary.

Data adapted from the study by the Economics Research Institute, presented in Table 7.2, suggest that Hungarian rates of informality in tourism were much greater than reflected in the Kolosi-survey. According to these figures, only 27%, 33%, and 45% of the Hungarian currency spent by foreign tourists in 1980, 1981, and 1982, respectively, was obtained through official channels. Therefore, on the whole, reliance

Table 7.2. Amount of Money Spent by Foreign Tourists in Hungary 1980–82 (billion current Forints)

	1980 HUF	(%)	1981 HUF	(%)	1982 HUF	(%)
From CMEA-currencies						
Through official exchange	6.2		7.2		5.6	
Otherwise	19.5	(76)	22.5	(76)	13.5	(71)
Total	25.7		29.7		19.1	
From Yugoslav Dinar						
Through official exchange	0.3		0.7		0.6	
Otherwise	2.1	(88)	2.0	(74)	1.3	(68)
Total	2.4		2.7		1.9	
From hard currencies						
Through official exchange	3.7		6.2		9.1	
Otherwise	6.1	(62)	3.7	(37)	4.0	(31)
Total	9.8		9.9		13.1	
Altogether						
Through official exchange	10.2		14.1		15.3	
Otherwise	27.7	(73)	28.2	(67)	18.8	(55)
Total	37.9		42.3		34.1	

Source: Gazdaságkutató 1983:3.

on informality in the tourism sector was enormous. During these three years, the number of incoming foreign tourists approximated ten million, or, the size of the entire population of Hungary. *Over half of the Hungarian money spent by those tourists had not been obtained through official channels.*

Informal purchases of Forints were most prevalent among CMEA-tourists, many of whom had faced restrictions in terms of the exchange-ability of their own currencies to Forints. On the whole, between 68 and 88% of the money they spent had not passed through official money exchanges in Hungary. Due to reasons spelled out in the previous chapter, this segment of the informal money economy was characterized by the unambiguous overappreciation of the Hungarian Forint as compared to the official rates of exchange set in the bilateral CMEA-negotiations.

Yugoslav citizens occupied an intermediate position in the Hungarian system of informal currency transactions during the early 1980s. They had virtually no bureaucratic restriction on their travel, which made them similar to hard-currency tourists. However, the relative backward-ness of much of the Yugoslav economy worked to restrict their leisure travel, unless they had access to hard-currency incomes from guest labor in West Germany. However, hard-currency spendings of Yugoslav guest workers working in Germany are included in the hard- currency cell of this table. The rates of utilization of informal access to Hungarian currency by those who came with Yugoslav Dinars varied strongly during the three years included in the study. These considerations indicate that most of the undocumented exchanges of Yugoslav Dinars occurred in conjunction with informal petty trade along and through Hungary's southern border with Yugoslavia. From the point of view of the Hungarian customer, the Yugoslav Dinar was a "hard" currency. This implies that the informal transactions involving the Dinar took place at street rates below the official rate from the viewpoint of the Hungarian Forint.

Although the rates of informal exchange among hard-currency tourists had been clearly—7 to 15%—lower than among CMEA-tourists, over half of the amount of money spent by hard-currency tourists was, never-theless, obtained through informal transactions. (Up till late 1981, the Hungarian Forint had had a dual system of exchange rates *vis-à-vis* the hard currencies; rates applied in merchandise trade were significantly lower than those in tourism. The government ended its policy of, in effect, discrimination against tourism at the end of 1981 so that the 1982 figure reflects that change.) The hard-currency segment of the informal money trade in Hungary implied the clear undervaluation of the Hungarian Forint.

The tourism revenues realized in the formal tourism industry indicated a reasonably lucrative business. While, in merchandise exports, the mean annual cost of every US$ earned changed from 37.7 through 39.9 to 41.3 Forints during the three years of the study (Gazdaságkutató 1983: 25), the officially recorded tourism business of Hungary "produced" revenues at annual average rates of 20.51, 28.85, and 33.33 Hungarian Forints per US$, respectively (Gazdaságkutató 1983:25). The formal tourism industry was hence 1.84 to 1.24 times more "cost effective" in generating the average US$ in revenue than exports in tangible commodities.

This argument is reinforced and extended to the entire—formal and informal—tourism sector by Karbuczky (1986) who shows, on the basis of data for the period between 1975 and 1985, that the overall profitability of incoming foreign tourism was better than that of exports because the foreign tourists' spending "produces a net surplus in turnover tax revenues" (Karbuczky 1986:14) included in the price of consumption goods, especially luxury items like alcohol and tobacco. Vincze (1982) suggests the same conclusion. This implies that, as long as only the currency exchange portion of touristic transactions took place in the informal economy, a significant part of the profitability of incoming international tourism was preserved, due to revenues from the taxation of items purchased with the money in Hungary. Only barter and informal trade—whereby the spending of the "money" escaped the turnover tax—diminished seriously the tourism-related incomes of the national state.

The main implication of the above findings, in conjunction with the differential under- and overvaluation of the Hungarian currency in the informal currency trade of incoming international tourism, is that, on the macrolevel, the tourism of different groups of tourists produced different terms of trade. Hence, the splitting of the field of Hungary's incoming foreign tourism was reproduced in the relative terms of trade associated with groups of tourists bringing in different kinds of currency. In the case of CMEA-tourists, the combination of net tax surplus and the overappreciation of the Hungarian currency worked to reinforce each other in creating very favorable terms of trade for the tourism industry. In the case of hard-currency tourists, by contrast, the favorable Forint-costs in producing unit US$—attributable to the turnover tax structure increasing revenues from sales of consumption items—was counterbalanced by the negative effects of informal currency exchange rates.

As a further indication of the importance of informality, the study by the Economics Research Institute found that only 25 to 35% of rentals of private housing units to tourists have been recorded, regulated and taxed in Hungary (Gazdaságkutató 1983:28). As private "rooms-to-let" represented the least expensive segment of the tourism accommodation economy, and given that the proportion of hard-currency tourists was inversely related to the price-levels of accommodations—i.e., the percentage of hard-currency tourists was highest in the five-star category and declined monotonically as the level of service dropped—the least expensive, most informal segment of accommodations were utilized most often by CMEA-tourists. On the other extreme, as Páczi (1989) shows on the basis of an analysis of several Budapest hotels, the import content of accommodation services has been strongly positively correlated with the hotel's category: Five-star hotels rely most on imports both in terms of building construction and the running of the enterprise, and the proportion of imports shows a decline as the level of the hotel's service category decreases.

The above overview of the informality of the tourism business in Hungary suggests the following conclusions: First, rates of informality in Hungary's tourism sector were very high, in all likelihood nearly one order of magnitude higher than in Austria; second, the bifurcation of the Hungarian tourism sector by currency types was mirrored both in terms of the degree of informalization and the qualitative types of informal arrangements. What is most peculiar is that this combination of statistical, econometric and ethnographic materials indicates that, third, stereotypes disparaged that segment of the tourism economy—CMEA-tourism—which produced the best terms of trade, and appreciated the hard-currency segment where terms of trade were not quite as favorable. It appears that the main reason for this was that, by the time this system had emerged, the main motivation on part of the Hungarian society to cater to incoming tourists under informal arrangements was not simply an expectation of additional incomes *per se*. It was a *qualitatively more specific motivation*, mainly a yearning for *hard currency*, with little regard for the actual terms of trade or the profitability of the activity. This pent-up demand was created by the peculiar condition that a mixed-currency-regime of incoming international tourism was set up in a society where all other incomes existed exclusively in the nonhard-currency realm.

Recorded International Tourism Revenues

With these considerations in mind it is possible to examine and interpret recorded levels of tourism-related revenues in the two countries. Figure 7.1 presents international tourism receipts as recorded in the formal sectors of Austria and Hungary during the last ten years.

Both Austrian and Hungarian recorded receipts show increases over time. In fact, recorded international tourism receipts increased slightly faster in Hungary than in Austria: The eleven years included in the

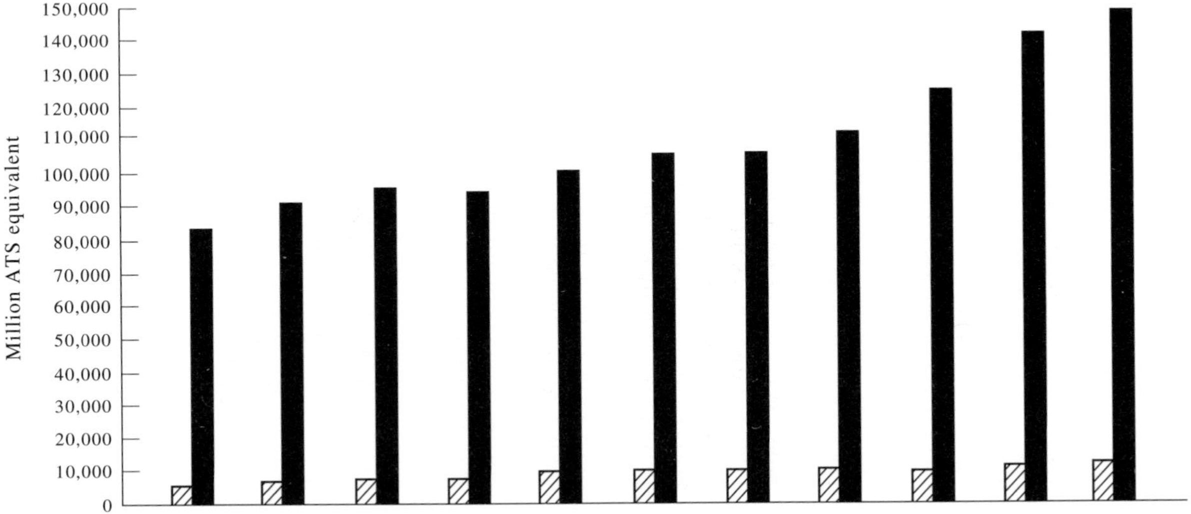

Years	1980	1981	1982	1983	1984	1985	1986	1987	1988	1989	1990
Hungary 1980–90	5875	6984	7006	7542	8787	9832	9673	9943	9530	10,654	11,367
Austria 1980–90	83,363	90,952	95,031	94,386	101,026	105,186	106,195	112,030	124,617	141,782	148,000

Source: KSH, 1990 and Tourismus in Zahlen, 1991. Hungarian figures computed at current mean annual official exchange rates in Hungary.

Figure 7.1. Recorded International Tourism Receipts in Austria and Hungary, 1980–90 (current ATS equivalent)

figure saw increases of 1.94 and 1.78 times, respectively. However, more striking is the enormous discrepancy between the two countries: Recorded international tourism receipts in Austria surpassed their Hungarian counterparts by factors of 11. to 14.2 times.

Figure 7.2 presents gross recorded tourism receipts on a per capita basis in a wider comparative perspective, using the OECD-countries as the basis of the comparison. (These are per capita data expressed in US$. That explains the discrepancy in the numerical results between the two tables.) This perspective indicates that Austria's levels represent record-high achievements; recorded levels of tourism-related receipts place most developed countries of western Europe and North America between Austria and Hungary. The main per capita tourism income receivers are the relatively small, highly developed welfare-capitalist societies of Europe: Austria, Switzerland, Denmark, and Iceland. They are followed by Spain with its approximately US$415 per capita tourism incomes, which represents a figure more than three times smaller than Austria. Its level of per capita recorded tourism-related receipts positions Hungary between Yugoslavia and Turkey. Assuming, on the basis of the middle estimate produced by the above summary of evidence concerning the size of informality in Hungary's tourism business, that two-thirds of Hungary's tourism revenues went unnoticed by official records, a correction of the Hungarian figure would increase the country's ranking by ten countries. However, that correction would also assume that informality plays no part in the tourism business of any other country on the chart. That is, of course, a completely unrealistic assumption, particularly as regards such Mediterranean destination countries as Portugal and Italy—the two countries between which Hungary's tourism receipts would fall if the correction were introduced. Even with that correction, Hungary's per capita tourism receipts would be six times less than Austria's. A similar correction for Austria, on the basis of Franz's analysis (1986) quoted above, would increase Austria's total international tourism receipts to US$1,579.80 or, to 6.8 times higher than Hungary's corrected figure.

The above comparisons of Hungary's international tourism receipts were made by converting CMEA-revenues into hard currency—ATS or US$—equivalents using the official exchange rates of the CMEA-currencies into Hungarian Forints and then, in turn, the official rates between the Forint and the relevant hard currency. Figure 7.3 specifies the proportions of Hungary's CMEA- and hard-currency receipts for eleven recent years, calculated in current Hungarian Forint equivalent. These numbers indicate a tremendous growth in the importance of hard-currency revenues for the formal sector in Hungarian tourism during the 1980s: The share of hard-currency revenues had climbed steadily from 39% in 1980 to 82% by 1990.

In January, 1991, the special arrangements provided by bilateral

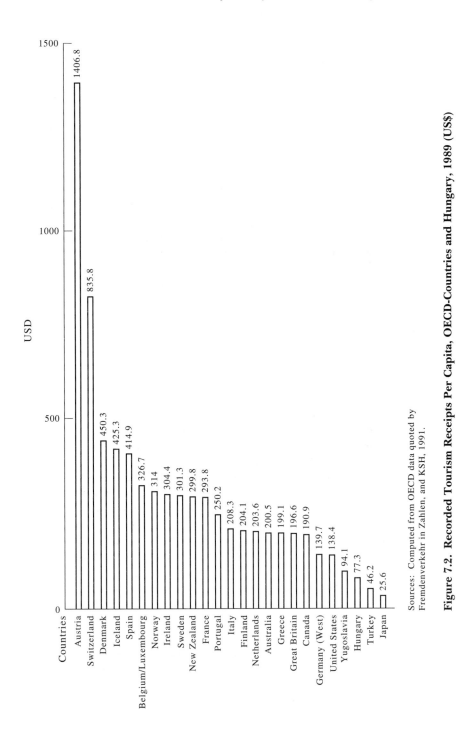

Figure 7.2. Recorded Tourism Receipts Per Capita, OECD-Countries and Hungary, 1989 (US$)

Sources: Computed from OECD data quoted by Fremdenverkehr in Zahlen, and KSH, 1991.

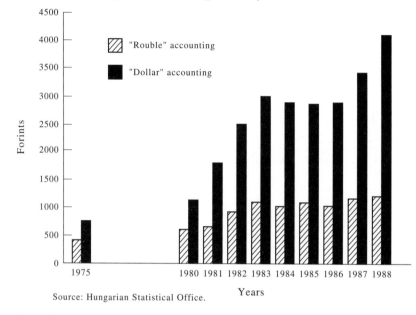

Source: Hungarian Statistical Office.

Figure 7.3. Officially Recorded Tourism Receipts in Hungary Per Arrival, by Currency Types, 1975, 1980–88 (HUF equivalent)

treaties to CMEA-currencies were annulled in Hungary. Since then, the exchange rates of none of the former CMEA-currencies have been guaranteed by the National Bank. As a result, trade in Hungary in the neighboring countries' currencies has completely shifted into the informal economy, resulting in an overappreciation of the Hungarian Forint by factors as high as 5 to 10 times.

Figure 7.4 presents the relative magnitude of Hungary's and Austria's recorded international tourism receipts as compared to export earnings. (Note that the vertical axes of the two graphs are expressed in different currencies so the absolute magnitude of the graphs are not directly comparable.) These numbers suggest that Austria's recorded tourism receipts are not only much more sizeable in absolute terms (as seen in earlier graphs), but they are also more significant in proportion to exports. International tourism as an earner of foreign currency provides a much higher proportion of Austria's national income than of Hungary's.

Figure 7.5 specifies the relationship of Hungary's recorded international tourism receipts and export earnings by currency groups, expressed in current Hungarian Forint equivalents. It indicates that, while the Soviet Rouble (SUR)-based exports of Hungary showed a decline after 1986, the magnitude of international tourism incomes in

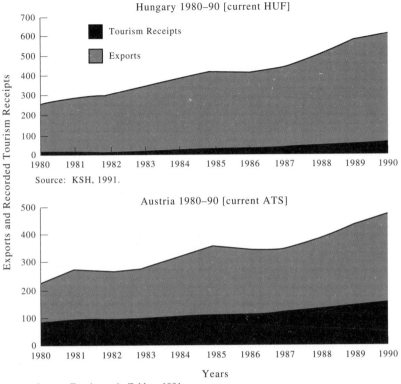

Figure 7.4. Recorded Tourism Receipts and Export Earnings, Hungary, 1980–90 (current HUF); Recorded Tourism Receipts and Export Earnings, Austria, 1980–90 (current ATS)

SUR-accounting currencies does not show such a clear descent at all. Increases in recorded hard-currency receipts from international tourism went hand-in-glove with the upswing of commodity exports in hard currencies. The magnitude of recorded nonhard-currency incomes diminishes only in relation to the steep increases in hard currency receipts.

Finally, Figure 7.6 compares the international tourism receipts in Hungary and Austria per foreign tourist arrivals, expressed in current ATS. This measure reflects accurately the differences in the amount of money spent by foreign tourists in the two countries. There are two conspicuous features revealed in this graph. First, the per capita spendings of foreign tourists have never been equal in the two countries: Hungary's figures are smaller. Second, since 1982, receipts per foreign tourist arrivals have showed consistent decline in Hungary and a steady

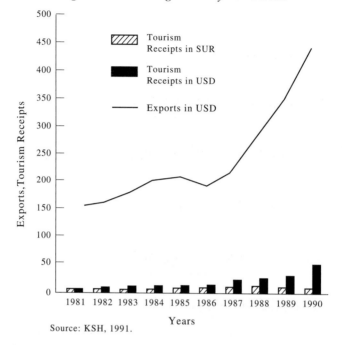

Source: KSH, 1991.

Figure 7.5. Recorded Tourism Receipts and Export Earnings in Hungary, Soft and Hard Currencies, 1981–91 (thousand million HUF)

increase in Austria. While in 1982 the Hungarian figure for recorded international tourism receipts per foreign tourist arrivals was approximately 68% of Austria's number, by 1990, Hungary's figure dwarfs to a minuscule 19% of Austria's score.

The summary comparison reveals striking differences in terms of all important aspects of recorded foreign tourism receipts in Austria and Hungary during the 1980s. Not only is the gross magnitude and the per capita extent of such revenues almost immeasurably greater for Austria, but also the relationship points in the same direction even for figures controlled for foreign tourist arrivals. The terms of trade in recorded tourism incomes have shown a particularly steep decline in Hungary, a sharp contrast to Austria's stubborn growth in that regard. As a result, Austria occupies an uncontested top position in the chart of OECD-countries in terms of its revenues from international tourism (once controlled for country size), while Hungary is found at the bottom of the same chart. It is followed only by Turkey—the only third-world country on that list—and Japan, a country known for its expensiveness, geographical distance from the main tourism-generating countries of the world, and, until recently, for its tendency of seclusion from foreign

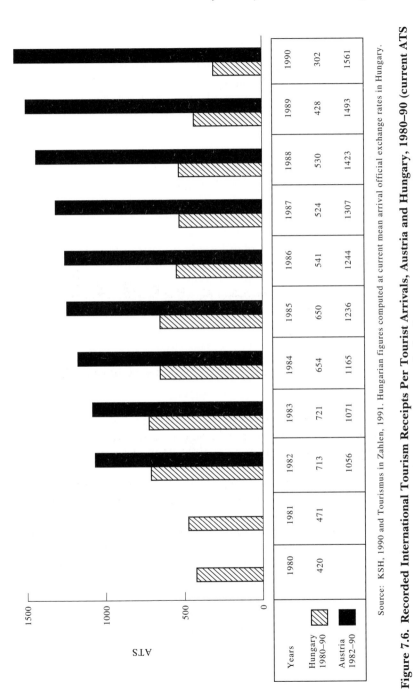

Years	1980	1981	1982	1983	1984	1985	1986	1987	1988	1989	1990
Hungary 1980–90	420	471	713	721	654	650	541	524	530	428	302
Austria 1982–90			1056	1071	1165	1236	1244	1307	1423	1493	1561

Source: KSH, 1990 and Tourismus in Zahlen, 1991. Hungarian figures computed at current mean arrival official exchange rates in Hungary.

Figure 7.6. Recorded International Tourism Receipts Per Tourist Arrivals, Austria and Hungary, 1980–90 (current ATS or equivalent)

contacts. Tourism revenues make up a very sizeable proportion of Austria's national product and, in comparison, dwindle in the case of Hungary.

The above glimpse into the social anatomy of Hungary's international tourism economy suggested that a large proportion—between 55 and 75%—of tourism revenues escaped the scope of record keeping, regulation, and taxation by the state. The main reasons for this can be summarized as follows:

1. The state has almost completely neglected the development of tourism infrastructure for the first two-to-three decades of state socialism, so that only a tiny proportion of incoming tourism demand could be satisfied in the realm of the state-owned and -managed segment of the economy which controlled the majority of capital-intensive, high-quality tourism service institutions;
2. The constitution of the pool of foreign tourists visiting Hungary was quite peculiar; it reflected the overwhelming numerical dominance of tourists with qualitatively (mainly politically) constrained and quantitatively very tight budgets. Thus a large part of the economy of Hungarian tourism was forced to cater to a low-scale tourist demand. As a result, incoming foreign tourism showed signs of endemic bifurcation in Hungary into CMEA-currency and hard-currency fragments under the mixed-currency-regime;
3. The degree of informality varied by segment, with that segment which offered higher profitability in soft currency being more informalized, so that a large proportion of the revenues so incurred escaped formal channels;
4. Finally, the involvement of a large part of the Hungarian society in catering to incoming foreign tourists was limited to the realm of informality.

The Hungarian economy as a whole underwent a tremendous process of informalization during the Kádár period between the early 1960s and the late 1980s. The initial impetus to that transformation came from the countryside, where the political compromises concerning the collectivization of the agriculture created a large number of peasant plots under private control. The vibrancy of the second economy of micro-plot farming soon spread over to other fields of the economy, and especially to incoming tourism which was gaining massive proportions at the time. As a result, the second main component of the spread of the second economy, and especially of its informal segment, was the large-scale penetration of international tourism in those areas of the country—in the capital city, in the Lake Balaton area, and on the country's borders with Austria and Yugoslavia—where there was an acute and unsatisfied touristic demand. Informal tourism business thus became an important component of the income-earning strategies of the society affected by such flows.

During the Kádár-period, the political regime's permissiveness toward clandestine, unrecorded ways of increasing personal incomes was in apparent, analytically essential contradiction to its concentrated efforts at preventing capital formation from such incomes. Hoarding and wasteful, luxury consumption were the only alternatives of dispensing with such extra incomes. The following chapter examines a consequence of these processes—the Hungarian "shopping sprees" in Vienna—by highlighting the results of a survey of Vienna's Hungarian visitors during the spring and fall of 1989.

Chapter 8 (Epilogue)

The Hungarian "Shopping Spree" in Vienna: The Underside of Austro-Hungarian Tourism

Effective January 1, 1988, the Hungarian government substantially liberalized its policies regarding the leisure travel of its citizens. Until then, Hungarians had been allowed to travel individually to the "West" only once every three years. The two exceptions to this rule were package tours organized by one of the official Hungarian travel agencies (usually an extremely overpriced alternative), and individual invitations from a friend or relative abroad who had to sponsor all travel costs. For the first time in the country's state socialist history, travel abroad was declared an unrestricted, constitutionally guaranteed civic right, so that practically anybody could have a passport which was "valid for the entire world" for five years.

However, financial constraints on tourist travel were not eased: Hungarian citizens were allowed to exchange a maximum of the equivalent of US$350 every three years for tourist travel. In addition, a "gasoline allotment" of US$150–200 was allowed, also tri-annually, which could be used to purchase foreign train, bus, boat or air tickets as well. At the same time not only trade in, but the mere possession of convertible currencies was illegal. However, the ban was never strictly enforced. Until as recently as September 1989, Hungarian banks had not been allowed to perform hard currency account transactions for Hungarian citizens without special permits, granted only to those who had legal incomes from abroad.

Yet, the mere removal of the last administrative barriers resulted in a surge of tourist departures to the "West." From 1987 to 1988, the volume of travel abroad increased greatly but not evenly: The number of total exits went up by 50% while the number of *tourist* exits remained almost constant, with a growth rate of only 3% (KSH 1989). The discrepancy indicates a large number of *excursions* (travel with no overnight stay abroad). Travel to nonsocialist destinations grew by 235% while *tourist* travel to the "West" increased much less steeply, by 72% (computed from KSH 1989). In the short run, the debureaucratization of travel to the "West" did not attract new, substantially large groups of the Hungarian society in travel abroad: The increase in travel to the "West" was paired with a slight decrease in travel to the CMEA countries. Most of the rise in travel to nonsocialist destinations was excursion travel.

As Hungary's western neighbor and one of the few "Western" countries where Hungarian tourists were not required to have an entry visa, it was in Austria that the effects of this flow were felt most directly. (At the time, the other visa-free countries for Hungarian tourists included the CMEA countries plus Finland, Sweden, and Malta.) In the course of a single year, the number of Hungarian entries into Austria increased more than *sixfold*, changing from 447 thousand in 1987 to as high as 2748 thousand in 1988 (KSH 1989). Put differently, the equivalent of 26% of Hungary's total population had visited Austria during the year 1988. This was not yet as high as the reverse flow but it was certainly approaching it: During the same two years, the number of Austrian entries into Hungary changed from 3.3 to 3.8 million—the equivalent of 44% to 51% of the Austrian population (KSH 1989).

The Survey

Between June and October, 1989, a questionnaire survey was executed with a focus on Vienna's Hungarian guests. Its purpose was to obtain a social profile of these people who had materialized so suddenly, and in such massive proportions, in Austria.

Interviewing at accommodations is methodologically very difficult; various places of accommodation are spread around a city, making the "density" of potential interviewees very low, and thus unreasonably increasing research time and costs. Besides, interviewing at lodgings may be considered to cause unnecessary inconvenience to the respondents. Low density is especially problematic in the case of travelers like Hungarians who travel on a shoestring budget and tend to economize on accommodations. The original sampling plan included the camp site at Laxenburg, along with a few youth hostels, hotels and pensions in Vienna. Experience gained during the data collection process indicated that the camp site should be kept as a location (during the summer) but the other accommodations should be dropped. Thus the sampling plan was modified. The actual sample has a reasonably even distribution among shopping places and other interviewing locations, allowing statistically meaningful split-file analyses.

The survey was a slightly modified version, translated into Hungarian and adapted by the principal researcher, of the Österreichische Gäste-befragung questionnaire, administered by the Institute for Tourism at the Vienna University of Economics. The four-page questionnaires, with 20 questions altogether, were handed out and received back by volunteer interviewers. One thousand and sixty-one valid responses to the self-administered questionnaires have been analyzed.

Socioeconomic Characteristics of Hungarians in Vienna

The social composition of Hungarians visiting Austria deviated from the country's entire population in a number of respects. The percentage of women among them was clearly lower than that in the Hungarian society: Women comprise 52% of the population of Hungary (KSH 1987), while our full sample includes only 38% women. Only 36% of those interviewed at shopping locations and only a mere 31% of those staying overnight were women. The respondents' age distribution diverged from the national figures as well: The retirement-age population was grossly underrepresented in travel to Vienna. Those between 15 and 39 years of age were overrepresented in all subsamples. Close to two-thirds of shopping tourists belonged to that age group.

Residents of the capital city, Budapest, were strongly overrepresented among Hungarian travelers in Vienna. Although Budapest is the home of only ca. 20% of the Hungarian population, the proportion of Budapesters in the full sample was 47%, and it reached 49% among excursionists. This is equivalent to saying that the residents of Budapest were about 2.5 times more likely to travel to Vienna than other Hungarians during this time. In order to facilitate the analysis of the effects of distance from Austria on travel to Austria, the geographical area of Hungary was divided into three large blocks of roughly equal territory, according to their distance from the Austrian border. These are, the western part called Transdanubia, the central area between the rivers Danube and Tisza, and eastern third including the Hungarian Plains and the mountains of the north-east.

Figure 8.1 shows the results of this comparison for those living outside the capital city. By and large, the likelihood of visiting Vienna varied inversely with geographical distance. In all groups, the percentage of those living in closest geographical proximity to Austria exceeded the figure for Hungary itself. Notice that, for shoppers, the proportion of those respondents who live in the nearby Transdanubian counties is over three times as high as expected on the basis of the figures of the Hungarian population's territorial distribution. Considering travel time and costs, it should not be surprising that those living farthest away from

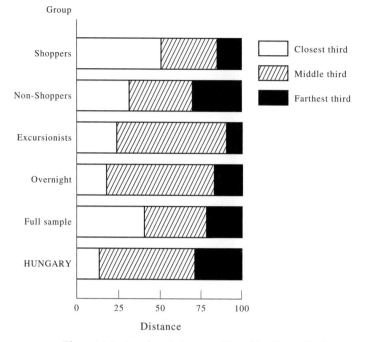

Figure 8.1. Regional Composition (% of non-Budapesters)

Austria are the least represented among "come-and-go" excursionists. The group of excursionists is mainly comprised of those coming from the central area of Hungary and those living closest to Austria.

Perhaps most distinct from the distribution of the Hungarian population as a whole, the respondents of our survey were very well educated. As Figure 8.2 suggests, taken as percentages of the respective age groups, the proportion of those with secondary education was more than three times higher, and that of those with higher education was 4 to 4.8 times higher among Vienna's Hungarian visitors than in Hungary in general.

A look at the occupational composition of the respondents, summarized in Figure 8.3, should help obtain an image on their position in the Hungarian society. Cooperative or state agricultural employees were always absent, and all groups of workers were extremely underrepresented. Intellectuals and private entrepreneurs predominated. Workers and agricultural employees together comprise about 74% of those gainfully employed in Hungary (computed from KSH 1987). In sharp contrast, their joint proportion among visitors of Vienna varied between a mere 22% and 29%, or, 2.5 to 3.4 times less. On the other hand, intellectuals, managers, private entrepreneurs etc. constitute only 26% in Hungary while they represented more than 70% of our respondents.

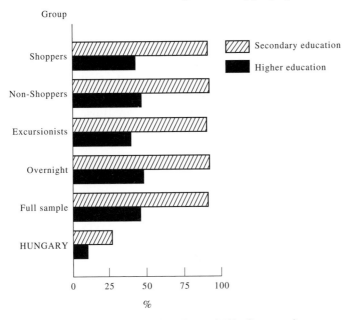

Figure 8.2. Educational Level (% of respective age group)

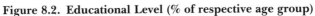
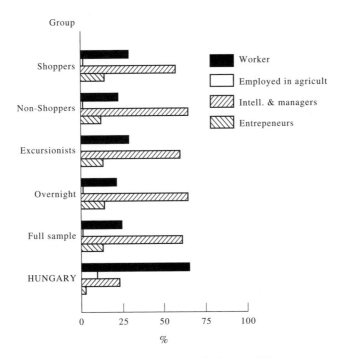

Figure 8.3. Occupational Groups (%)

The average monthly income of those interviewed was reported at HUF 10,718 per month, slightly above the national average estimated at about HUF 10,000. The most striking feature of these two figures is how little their difference actually is, considering that the average monthly income of our respondents was the equivalent of between ATS 1531 and ATS 2463 a month, way below the minimum amount of welfare aid in Austria at the time. (The "black market" rate during this period was ATS 100 = HUF 700. The official exchange rate in Hungary during this period was ATS 100 = HUF 435.) The reported level of income was so low in comparison to the price levels in Vienna's tourist service sector that it should be considered a minor miracle that our respondents were able to afford even excursions.

Figure 8.4 presents findings concerning the income distribution by groups of respondents. Those staying overnight were very much on the relatively better-off side of the distribution. The observations so far indicate that those who stayed overnight constituted a different group among the Hungarian visitors of Vienna. Their age distribution resembled more closely the Hungarian national pattern, they came more evenly from all parts of the country, not only from areas closer to the Austrian border, and they were among those better-off. It appears that

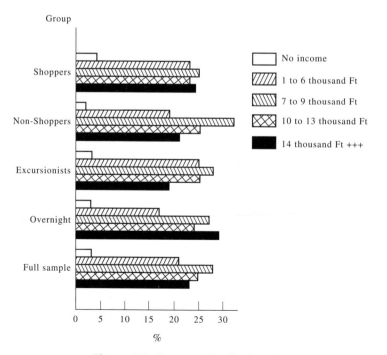

Figure 8.4. Income Distribution (%)

this, relatively small group was what could be considered *tourists* in the West European sense of the word among the Hungarian visitors of Vienna.

The Informal Component: Fieldwork Evidence

The most plausible explanation for the puzzle of the discrepancy between the Hungarian visitors' very low levels of reported income and their presence in Vienna is that what this survey captured in the subsample of those not staying overnight in Vienna (irrespective of whether they indicated "shopping" as a prime purpose of their travel or whether they were interviewed at shopping locations or elsewhere in the city) was a large number of Hungarian tourists who utilized their trip for informal trade.

During the 18 months to two years which elapsed between the initial relaxation of Hungarian travel restrictions in January, 1988, and the fieldwork for this study conducted between June, 1989, and January, 1990, the Viennese retail sector underwent a process of specialization, catering to the needs of their new Hungarian customers. The greatest interest of the Hungarian shoppers was, no doubt, in the field of consumer electronics and inexpensive electric home appliances. The most popular items sought and purchased in Vienna and taken to Hungary included color television sets, VCRs and home stereos made in the Far East, Commodore 64 computers, and a freezer-box made in Yugoslavia. What was most ironical about this last popular item was that the exact same freezer box was also sold in Hungary, not to mention that the Hungarian-made models were, according to a consensus of vendors and product-quality experts, far superior to the Yugoslavian-made item. The reason why Hungarians made these purchases in Vienna was that Viennese prices were much lower due to the overtaxation of imported household items in Hungary.

Several Viennese shopping malls began specializing in catering to Hungarians. The Austrian and Hungarian Railways jointly implemented special reduced fares for travel between Budapest and Vienna. Vienna's traffic pattern was altered in order to accommodate the sudden need of Hungarian motorists for parking space. Mariahilferstraße, one of Vienna's downtown open-air shopping streets, soon came to be considered a main area of Hungarian shoppers, and the stores on Mariahilferstraße hired Hungarian speaking shop assistants. All stores in and around the street donned large signs in Hungarian. The television and radio receivers sold in this area had been retuned for the CMEA-wavelength so that they could be used immediately in Hungary. The Viennese press rebaptized Mariahilferstraße as *Magyar*-hilferstraße. . .

Hungarians were some of the best customers any vendor could imagine. Almost none of the Hungarian shoppers appeared to be aware of, or cared to claim, the Austrian legal requirement of compulsory money-back and service guarantees for new electronic equipment. Their typical shopping style could be described as follows: The entire family leaves Hungary in a car, they drive directly to the particular store where they plan to make a purchase, they point out the merchandise they are interested in, have it packed, pay, and leave. The transaction required the presence of the entire family, including the aged and infants, because Hungarian customs regulations in effect at the time made special provisions for family members traveling together; they could add their duty-free import allowances in the case of durable consumer goods. The larger number of family members traveling together, the more expensive items could be imported free of duty. Initially, many were not even aware of the regulation which refunds the 15–32% *Mehrwertsteuer* (Value Added Tax, VAT) for merchandise purchased in Austria and exported within 30 days of purchase. The VAT-refund required filling out a small form at the store (in German of course), to be stamped upon taking the merchandise out of Austria.

Conversations with shop-keepers revealed an important and conceptually very relevant detail concerning the economic-sociological nature of this arrangement. Most shop-owners related that, to their own surprise, access to Austrian currency seemed not to be a problem for their Hungarian shoppers. Although all shop-keepers mentioned that some minuscule proportion of their trade did take place in Hungarian Forints, they insisted that Hungarians were not the people who came shopping with Hungarian money. Forints were much more likely used by Poles and Romanians in the Viennese retail stores. This is additional evidence to show how the Hungarian currency worked as a makeshift "quasi-hard" currency for citizens of the less open CMEA-countries. When asked what the shop-keepers did with the Hungarian Forints, they insisted that there was no problem in exchanging them at any of the retail banks in Vienna.

Indeed, all major consumer banks in Vienna had quoted the Hungarian Forint for several years by the time of the Hungarians' shopping spree, notwithstanding the facts that the Hungarian Forint was supposedly a "soft," CMEA-currency whose exchangeability was rather drastically limited, and that Hungarian law had, since the beginning of World War II, continuously forbidden the exportation of cash for citizens and foreigners alike, except for miniscule sums.

The jovial, winking Viennese bank employees made no secret about their bank's interest in Hungarian Forints, claiming that the Forint was one of the most sought-after currencies in their trade. As to the source of their Forint stocks, the bankers interviewed suggested that they came either from Polish travelers coming from Hungary or, in a smaller proportion, from Viennese retail shop-keepers. The demand for Hungarian cash came mainly from the Viennese lower-middle and working-class travelers who frequented the western part of Hungary and Budapest for inexpensive recreation. A weekend-trip from Vienna to Budapest by train, including two nights in registered private accommodation, meals, opera, ballet or theater performances, museums, cafés, discos, Danubian boat excursions, etc. cost at least 30–50% less than enjoying the same diversions in TwoVienna even without accounting for accommodation costs in Vienna.

The Viennese banks were exchanging the Forint at the going street rate, using the exact same bank fees as on any other currency transaction. Hence, the street rate of the Hungarian Forint throughout central Europe was *de facto* set by the major Viennese banks—the same financial institutions which had played a key role in the economic development of central Europe since the mid-nineteenth century until World War I, and the same banks which organized practically the entire series of foreign private borrowing by the Hungarian state between the early 1970s and the mid-1980s, including the construction of a new terminal for the Budapest Airport and a number of new border crossing stations on the Hungarian side of the Austro-Hungarian border, as well as a majority of Budapest's four- and five-star hotel accommodation capacity—an astounding historical continuity. During the time of this author's fieldwork in Vienna, the Yugoslav Dinar was the only other "nonhard" currency that appeared in Viennese retail banking.

After the opening-up of Czechoslovakia's borders for outgoing tourism this author witnessed in subsequent visits the arrival of another flood of foreigners in Vienna from the "east." Anticipating a consumer raid by another group of former CMEA-travelers to the pattern of the Hungarians, Viennese retail businesses expected a second windfall from the Czechs and Slovaks. That second windfall, however, never came: Czecho-Slovak citizens preferred "only to look," to borrow, again, the Hungarian shopkeeper's characterization of East German shoppers quoted earlier in this study.

Czech and Slovak visitors did not have nearly enough money to be able to afford commodity purchases in Vienna, by then one of Europe's most expensive cities. Thus their excursion-tourism was more focused on sightseeing and involved almost no shopping—an ironical, more south-central European variant on the East German citizens' famous massive stroll into West Berlin the day after the fall of the Wall. (In contrast to their West German counterparts, the Austrian authorities did not hand out bills.)

A plausible explanation for this stark difference between the Czecho-Slovak and Hungarian cases lies in the two countries' differential involvement in the informal economy of international tourism. Hungary with its much higher degree of saturation by foreign tourists, more intensive cross-border touristic linkages, and higher informal hard-currency incomes "leaking" into the hands of its citizenry, appears to have been more appropriately attuned for quick consumer gratification in Vienna.

All these considerations suggest that the Viennese "shopping spree" of Hungarians between 1988 and 1990 is to be understood in conjunction with the particular institutional arrangements, primarily the extremely high informalization, of incoming international tourism in Hungary. The "shopping spree" was mainly a consequence of the informal institutional arrangements of incoming tourism in Hungary in several, mutually interrelated ways:

1. It was the preceding twenty years' history of informality in foreign tourism in Hungary that provided, in hard currency, the financial means for Hungarians to shop in Vienna. From first-economy occupations, it would have never been possible to save enough for such trips and purchases, especially not in such massive proportions. The original incomes for these trips must have come from informal sources. As other fields of Hungary's second economy had had no hard-currency input, it could only have been the informal inflows of cash, in connection with foreign tourism in Hungary, that served as source of the currency spent in Vienna;

2. The demonstration effect of incoming foreign tourism on the Hungarian society had a tremendous role in forming, adjusting, and specifying the consumer aspirations of Hungarians. As the CMEA-based domestic retail sector was unable to satisfy such consuming desires, the logical solution was to take demand to the nearest capitalist market, i.e., to Vienna;

3. The Hungarian authorities' permissive attitude *vis-à-vis* large-scale leakages of the national currency, and all forms of petty smuggling in general, were connected with the 1980s' general sense of tolerance toward informal cross-border flows of all kinds. This sense of relaxation of restraints had largely been opened up and widened by the massive inflows of foreign tourists into the country.

4. The person-to-person micro-linkages upon which such shopping trips were built, resulting in the knowledge of exact addresses of stores and exact specifications for the commodities to be purchased, could only have developed on the basis of a preceding history of frequent travel between the two societies. This suggestion is strongly supported by the survey results: When asked "From what source of information did you learn that Vienna was worth a visit?", only about one-quarter of the respondents referred to media advertising or travel agency sources. One-third mentioned social networks explicitly, and the rest of them said "no specific information was necessary" which can only be

interpreted in the given context as a reference to social networks. Those network ties have an obvious connection to the preceding history of international tourism in the two countries.

On November 7, 1989, the last time that the anniversary of the Russian revolution of 1917 had been an official holiday in Hungary, about one million Hungarians, or 10% of the country's population, traveled to Vienna for Christmas shopping. On the way back, the traffic jam caused by the border formalities reached the Viennese suburbs, ca. 75 kilometers away. That was by far the most massive form of collective movement observed during Hungary's recent transition from state socialism.

Chapter 9

Capitalism, State Socialism, and Leisure Migration

This study plowed through a large pile of empirical materials pertaining to the relationship between inequalities and bloc-formation in the world system and international tourism. It has shown that there exists a large-scale, fundamental resemblance between configurations of the uneven development of industrial capitalism and patterns of emerging leisure migration both within the continent of Europe and in the comparative framework of Austria and Hungary. We documented that touristic representations are highly selective, and their emphases are remarkably isomorphic with the structural facts supplied by economic history. For Austria and Hungary this implies that Hungary's backwardness relative to Austria originates neither in state socialism nor in the early-twentieth-century emergence of heavy industrialization in central Europe but in the early period of the emergence of industrial capitalism under the auspices of the Habsburg empire. The uneven development of industrialization and the spread of the specific patterns of state socialism are effects which compound initial underdevelopment, rather than explaining it on their own.

Hungary has never in its recent history caught up with Austria in terms of any measure of the development of its incoming international tourism. We have also found, however, that the reproduction of disadvantages have not been mechanistic or simple at all; the degree of Hungary's backwardness in touristic terms varied tremendously, and Hungary's major setbacks in incoming international tourism have always been associated with serious disruptions of the "normal" conduct of social life due to wars, revolutions and other forms of general political violence. As a result, the ongoing pattern of Austria's relative advantages can be interpreted as interaction effects between inherited structures of relative development and a more fortunate—less violent and less disruptive—historical experience.

We examined the way in which the developmental paths of the two countries separated after World War II. Austria's statehood and economy were reconstructed in a structural cleavage between the two sociopolitical blocs which hindered temporarily the restoration of its full sovereignty, but provided important opportunities of economic, social, and political development. These included access to subsidized investment funds for reconstruction, and simultaneous, privileged access to both the capitalist and the state socialist economies as export markets.

In contrast, Hungary fell under the spell of a state socialist imperial project and was incorporated into a relationship of subordinate partnership with the Soviet Union. After the suppression of the uprising of 1956, the Hungarian society embarked upon a major "reform-communist" path of self-extrication from Stalinism. The way out of Stalinism was marked by a large-scale, wide-reaching series of political, economic, cultural, and social compromises including the gradual easing of the country's isolation from the nonstate-socialist part of the world. Incoming international tourism became an important factor in that process.

We then explored the main statistical determinants of the composition of international leisure flows to the two countries during the spectacular upswing phase of their post-World War II tourism history. A comparative statistical analysis of sending-country-specific foreign tourist arrivals and foreign tourist nights data, designed to test systematically the net effects of macrostructural predictors, has confirmed that both the socioeconomic disparities of the hierarchical structure of the world economy and the split structure of the interstate system make clearly decipherable effects on tourism with destinations in the two countries. It also demonstrated the point of vital theoretical importance that there have been very significant differences in the ways in which the two countries have been affected by such big structural conditions. As a result, the exactly parallel steepness of the two countries' tourism growth during the period between the early 1960s and the late 1980s reflected touristic structures that are substantively distinct.

On the basis of that discovery, this study analyzed some of the differences between the institutional features of tourism in the two countries, with privileged attention to the specifics of the Hungarian experience, since the Hungarian society is that part of the comparison which displayed the less studied, state socialist variant. It analyzed explicitly the qualitative differences in the monetary processes associated with international tourism, showing that the mixed-currency-regime of state socialism has created a deep crack in Hungary's international tourism sector, while the Austrian hard-currency arrangement helped preserve the unity of the economic-sociological character of incoming tourism in Austria.

We have argued that, as a result of the combination of relative under-development and state-based official attachment to the political "special money" arrangements of the CMEA-bloc, the relationship between foreign tourists and their Hungarian hosts replicated the splitting of the monetary arrangement and the division of political blocs in Hungary. As a result, both official policy considerations and social attitudes towards various groups of tourists came to be split, in a similar manner. This revealed a distinction (preference for "western" tourism) that was quite independent of the relative level of profitability associated with the tourism of various groups of foreigners (which privileged "fellow-state-socialist" tourists).

Finally, our study has shown that the qualitative differences in the external conditions and internal arrangements of international tourism have produced widely different forms and rates of informality in the two countries' tourism industries. Endemic shortages of tourism infrastructure and, for a long time, rigid economic and tourism policies of the socialist states of the region have forced most of the incoming international tourism into the rapidly expanding second economy in Hungary.

In Austria, meanwhile, conditions of incoming international tourism were more conducive to the large-scale expansion of formal small-business activity, reducing rates of informality to a fairly low level. An important aspect of informality in the Hungarian context was captured in a miniature portrait of the Hungarian visitors of Vienna during the "shopping spree" of 1988–90 which followed the complete relaxation of all restrictions on the travel abroad of Hungarian citizens by the Hungarian state. The Hungarians' intense motivation to obtain western consumer goods, the evident role of cross-border social ties in organizing these trips and structuring demand, and the level of the shoppers' spendings in hard currencies in the Austrian market where income levels were between five and twelve times higher than in Hungary, indicate that any explanation for such massive trips ought to feature informality, especially informal catering to incoming foreign tourists in Hungary, very prominently.

"Mid-Range" Implications

Tourism is not too ephemeral, mundane, or epiphenomenal for serious sociological study. It exhibits remarkable empirical regularities over time and space. Its structures reflect a strong sense of uneven development, systematically related to the macroscopic structural inequalities of industrial capitalism and of the capitalism-socialism divide.

The study of international tourism as leisure migration involves the unification of several main themes of recent macrocomparative social science and, specifically, of economic sociology. The above study of international tourism has addressed a particular form of cross-border linkages, embedded in formal and informal arrangements of weak social ties, and revealed some unintended consequences of their proliferation. This summary recaps each of those elements and examines how the above study relates to the main issues implied in them.

The concept of linkages is used in at least two, remotely related yet distinguishable ways in macrocomparative social science. Albert O. Hirschman's (1977) "generalized linkage approach" relies on a fairly restrictive conceptualization focused on economic growth. For Hirschman, "linkage effects" stand for net excess investment generated by the introduction of a particular industry or branch in the economy. In Hirschman's words, "I have defined the linkage effects of a given product line as investment-generating forces that are set in motion, through input-output relations, when productive facilities that supply inputs to that line or utilize its outputs are inadequate or nonexistent" (1977:72).

A less restrictive usage—widespread in the north American economic sociology of development—considers linkages as relatively stable, institutionalized, and patterned bundles of contacts and flows. The existence of the cross-border variant of the latter denotation—external linkages— is an elementary structural condition of external dependency. Much of the scholarly attention devoted to cross-border linkages has been focused on commodity trade, financial flow patterns and labor migrations, and is marked by a somewhat narrowly economic focus.

International leisure migration is one of the most important institutional forms of external social linkages. It is an instance which, as the above comparison of the Hungarian and Austrian cases suggests, combines aspects of commodity and money flows with human flows resulting in transient interpersonal contacts. An analysis of tourist flows thus calls for the consideration of a less "undersocialized" (Granovetter 1985) concept, that of ties through social networks.

Mark Granovetter (1973) defines the strength of an interpersonal tie as:

> a combination of the amount of time, the emotional intensity, the intimacy (mutual confiding), and the reciprocal services which characterize the tie (Granovetter 1973:1361).

The ties resulting from the penetration of a given social context by structures of international leisure migration offer a textbook example of what Granovetter characterizes as "weak ties." The main importance of conceptualizing the relative strength of ties lies in Granovetter's proposition stipulating that weak ties are more apt than strong ones to serve as bridges between separate sets of nodes so that, in situations of innovation diffusion like the abstract network-theoretical equivalent of the comparative macrosociological concept of flows discussed above:

> individuals with many weak ties are (. . .) best placed to diffuse (. . .) innovation (. . .), since some of those ties will be local bridges (Granovetter 1973:1367).

Granovetter relates this proposition to individuals and communities but there is no compelling reason for this idea to be restricted to those levels of analysis. The study of leisure migration, just like the labor migration literature, allows the examination of the formation and consequences of weak ties between societies circumscribed by state boundaries.

The cases examined in this study represent a macrostructural example whereby one set—the Hungarian society—was subjected, as outlined in *chapter 4* above, to the implementation of a major project designed to systematically cut its ties with the capitalist countries or subject them to the socialist state's control and to strengthen its relations with the societies of the state socialist bloc. Meanwhile, the other set—Austria—was detached from its previous imperial state entity, the Third Reich, and it was reconstituted in a position between the two blocs through the formula of neutrality.

The emergence of weak interpersonal ties through incoming international tourism in Austria went hand-in-glove with the reconstruction of Austria's statehood and external linkages. As a result of a number of fortunate conjunctural circumstances, the Austrian society was hence eminently well positioned to become a major vacationing destination. Consequently, the solid commercialization of its weak ties through tourism proceeded smoothly.

Hungary's extrication from its Stalinist pattern involved the emergence of a large number of weak person-to-person ties functioning as local bridges between societies positioned in different political blocs as well as connecting societies within the state socialist bloc. International tourism worked as an important and very efficient vehicle for providing institutional conditions for the emergence and solidification of such weak ties in massive proportions. The case of the most tourism-saturated state socialist society, Hungary, suggests that that change represents a major example of unintended social, political, cultural and economic consequences.

The main reasons why the political decision-makers of the Hungarian post-Stalinist state allowed for or even promoted the gradual proliferation of such weak cross-border ties, in effect abandoning the Stalinist project of totalistic state control over the boundary of the state, were as follows: First, the spirit of domestic political and economic compromises implied that the rigidity of the previous, Stalinist arrangement had to be somewhat softened in order to preserve the fundamental configuration of power and the state socialist nature of the society; second, it was expected that the partly controlled penetration of international tourism would provide serious foreign exchange earnings for the receiving state, thus helping to finance the continued reconstruction of the country's industrial base. On the basis of a casual glance at the Austrian case of the 1950s and early 1960s—the best example available for the Hungarian political strategists at the time of the mid-to-late 1960s—both of those expectations appeared to be unambiguously realistic and very promising.

In contradiction to those expectations, that series of political concessions to incoming international tourism did not result in serious increases in the state's revenues in Hungary, neither as property income to the oligopolistic owner in the economy, nor through taxation. The greater part of the foreign tourists' spendings never appeared in the official channels of money exchange, and state-owned accommodation and catering establishments only saw a miniscule proportion of the foreign tourists' spendings. The better part of tourism-related revenues were siphoned off through an intricate system of hidden, informal arrangements, quite outside the record keeping, control, or planning reach of the socialist state. Along with the concessions made in the realm of agricultural production to the peasantry, international tourism became a major driving force behind the creation of a large-scale informal economy in Hungary.

Studies of hidden economies under capitalism tend to distinguish three types of informality: (1) Informal sector of survival, characteristic of large sections of Third World societies, (2) the informal economies of sweatshop-style subcontracting arrangements, representing the major form of integration ranging from multinational corporations to vulnerable labor both in the periphery and in the advanced capitalist societies, and (3) the informality of growth through flexible specialization, a peculiarity of a handful of examples marked by a fruitful cooperation between small-scale capital, labor, and the local and/or national developmental state (see, e.g., Portes 1990).

The informality found in the state socialist societies, as revealed particularly in the tourism sector, suggests the existence of a fourth type of informality, the informality of exit. The main structural condition that determines the features of this type is the dominance of the owner-regulator state over the economy (Portes and Böröcz 1988). The political implication of the informality of exit is quite obvious in the state socialist context: It offers an avenue through which individuals and their groups are able to secure a partial sense of independence from the state which functions as the combination of an employer and a system of political control (Böröcz 1989b). As a result, the proliferation of the informality of exit brought about a second, more comprehensive, unintended consequence from the point of view of the socialist state: the gradual self-removal of the population from the control of the state. The informal

tourism sector—the cross-border version of state socialist informality—
with its complex cultural, consumptive, and political demonstration
effects, played an especially crucial role in this development.

This study also speaks to Granovetter's Polányian network analytical
thesis proposing that most behavior, and specifically economic behavior,
"is closely embedded in networks of interpersonal relations" (1985:504).
The Hungarian and Austrian experience of incoming international
leisure migration underscores the strength of that formulation in several
ways.

The examination of destination patterns has revealed that a purely
quantitative sense of monetary gain is not the main motive of international leisure migration; instead of maximizing the price differential
for the tourists' advantage, the more sought-after destinations tend to
be the relatively advanced, economically developed societies. A touristic
equivalent of the push–pull paradigm of international labor migration
research would, hence, fail miserably to explain the pattern of incoming
international leisure migration in Hungary and the massive flux of
Hungarians to Vienna described in this study.

The overview of the formal and informal institutional arrangements
of incoming international tourism business and the ideologies of
otherness surrounding leisure migration in the post-Stalinist period
indicated that the economically most profitable segment of Hungary's
tourist trade—informal services to guests from the other state socialist
societies—was the one scorned most by its beneficiaries. The preferred
segment—informal service provisions to hard-currency tourists—was
clearly less attractive in exclusively economic terms. The explanation
offered above for this phenomenon was that it was not simply economic
gain, but a qualitatively more specific form of gain—access to additional
incomes in hard currency—that was the main motivation for providing
touristic services.

This inference was reinforced by the description of the Hungarian
"shopping sprees" in Vienna which can be portrayed as the endpoint of
an informal economic circle of international tourism in Hungary. The
demand patterns of Hungarian shoppers in Vienna hardly reflected
individualistic, return-maximizing calculations of economic optimization.
Instead, they were determined by such "extra-economic" considerations
as patterns and the extent of the participants' social network
connections.

In summary, the comparison contained in this study reveals two faces
of tourism as a potent agent of social change. The Austrian case suggests
that tourism can be an important motor of economic growth, given the
existence of forces to ensure that the host society is able to achieve a
reasonable sense of parity with tourists in terms of their countries'
general levels of development. The main ways in which the Austrian

society has been able to achieve that are the restriction of access to visitors without hard currencies, and the creation and maintenance through central state support of a diffused and diversified, formal tourism industry. Under such circumstances, incoming international tourism can be recognized as a prime contributor to the widely noted, impressive improvement of Austria's position in the world economy after World War II.

In contrast, the Hungarian case suggests that incoming international leisure migration can become an avenue of partial exit from state control, slowly transforming the nature of political rule by transferring a certain economic power to the citizenry in a way that is independent of the realm of the state. Thus, the main consequence of the massive proliferation of incoming international tourism for Hungary can be located in its contribution to the individual enrichment and private autonomy of a sizeable proportion of the society, and therefore to the gradual rearrangement of the state-society relationship under state socialism.

Broader Theoretical Implications

Touristic strangeness is triply inscribed. It bears the imprint of the three contexts in which it operates: sending societies, receiving contexts, and their institutional link, the tourism industry. Leisure migration blends diverse motivations, understandings, value orientations, rates and regimes of accumulation, and mechanisms of power into a rich, thick compound. It is because of complex interplays of these elements that leisure migration offers an apparently inexhaustible variety of experience. In other words, that is why we engage in it in the first place. That same triple inscription, when manifested in different rates of the remuneration of labor, makes international leisure migration economically feasible.

Leisure migration quenches the "modern" thirst for Otherness by applying the general cultural standard of commodity fetishism through a standardized, normalized and commercialized process of playful purchase. Because of the very standardization, normalization and commercialization of experience, tourism rarely induces questioning of the status quo. Undeniable evidence of poverty, suffering, backwardness and oppression is represented as acceptable because these ills are experienced via osmosis through the only seemingly transparent walls of the environmental bubble of tourism.

The bubble acts on flows both ways: It cleanses the touristic experience from such elements of reality which might contaminate the Disney-utopia (cf., Rojek 1993b), while also purging the hosts' images of tourists of all traces of exertion. Hence, visited societies appear to tourists as sanitized, idyllic exotica, while tourists appear to hosts as a similarly sanitized and idyllic social phenomenon, a veritable leisure class. In tourism, the liminality of Strangeness is intensified by the suspension of tourists as well as hosts in this realm of the imaginary. Tourists imagine the exhibited Other's experience and hosts envisage the touristic Other's practice through a code which keeps their contact suspended between understanding and misunderstanding.

Thus we have the Janus-face of leisure migration. The structural inscription of tourism provides both the cultural and financial foundations for the process; commercial leisure travel prevents tourists and hosts from deciphering that very inscription. Leisure migration thus simultaneously employs and obscures global structures of inequality and oppression. Leisure migration is travel capitalism in this broad sense.

Appendix 1

Linguists Who Lent Support in Gathering the Material for
Chapter 2

Apridonidze, Shukia. A.S. Chikobav Institute for Linguistics, Academy of Science, Tbilisi, Georgia.

Baldunčiks, Juris. Andreja Upiša Valodas un Literatūras Institūts, Latvijas PSR Zinātņu Akadēmija, (Institute for Linguistics and Literature, Academy of Science), Riga, Latvia.

Bakhan'kov, A. E. Institut Iazykoznania im. Iakuba Kolasa AN BSSR, (Yakub Kolas Institute for Linguistics, Academy of Science), Minsk, Belorussia.

ó Baoill, Dónall P. Structural Linguistics Section, Institúid Teangeolaíochta Éireann (The Linguistics Institute of Ireland), Dublin, Ireland.

Contossopoulos, Nicolaos. Modern Greek Dictionary Center, Academy of Athens, Greece.

Crowe, Richard M. Geiriadur Prifysgol Cymru, Llyfrgell Genedlaethol Cymru (Dictionary of the Welsh Language, National Library of Wales), Aberystwyth, Wales.

de Carvalho, José Gonçalo Herculano. Departamento de Línguas e Literaturas Modernas da Universidade Autónoma de Lisboa, (Department of Modern Languages and Literatures, Autonomous University of Lisbon) Portugal.

Djahukian, G.B. and R. Mkrtchan. Institute of Linguistics, Armenian SSR Academy of Sciences, Yerevan, Armenia.

Goldenberg, Gideon. Faculty of Humanities, Hebrew and Semitic-Linguistics, The Hebrew University of Israel, Jerusalem.

Karjalainen, Irma. Kielikeskus, Tampereen Yliopisto, (Language Center, Tampere University), Finland.

Kostallari, Androkli. Instituti i Gjuhësisë dhe i Letërsisë, Akademia e Shkencave, Republika Popullore Socialiste e Shqipërisë (Institute for Linguistics and Literature, Academy of Sciences), Tirana, Albania.

Martinsson, Bodil. Svenska Akademiens Ordboksredaktion (Dictionary Publishing, Swedish Academy), Lund, Sweden.

Mitsner, Barbro Wallgren. Institutionen för nordiska språk, Göteborgs

Universitet (Institute for Northern Languages, Gothenburg University), Sweden,

Müller, Jakob. Institut za slovenski jezik Frana Ramovša, Znanstvenoraziskovalni center SAZU (Fran Ramovš Institute for the Slovene Language, Slovene Academy of Sciences) Ljubljana, Slovenia.

Rantala, Leif. Kasvatustieteiden osasto, Lapin Korkeakoulu (Center for Lapp Language) Rovaniemi, Finland.

Radoňová, Jitka. Ústav pro Jazyk Český, Československá Akademia Věd, (The Institute of Czech Language, Czecho-Slovakian Academy of Science), Praha, Czecho-Slovakia.

Rísová, Eva. Jazykovedný Ústav Ľudovíta Štúra, Slovenská Akadémia Vied, (Ľudovít Štúr Institue for the Slovak Language, Slovakian Academy of Sciences), Bratislava, Czecho-Slovakia.

Sabaliauskas, Algirda. Institute of Lithuanian Language and Literature, Academy of Sciences, Vilnius, Lithuania.

Sørensen, John Konsgard. Institut for Navneforskning, Københavns Universitets, (Linguistic Research Institute, University of Copenhagen), Denmark.

Stroop, Jan. Instituut voor Neerlandistiek, Universiteit van Amsterdam (Institute for Dutch Studies, University of Amsterdam), The Netherlands.

Vide, Carlos Martín. Departament de Filologia Romànica, Secció de Lingüística General, Facultat de Filologia, Universitat de Barcelona (Department of Romanic Philology, General Linguistics Section, Faculty of Philology, Unviersity of Barcelona), Spain.

Appendix 2

Quantitative Procedures Used in *Chapter 2*

Mental maps figures have been arrived at through the following simple procedure: First, the number of pages in each guidebook allotted to individual countries (in some cases, provinces, etc.) was counted. Second, the results were transformed into percentages of the complete volume. Those percentages are interpreted as measures of the absolute weight of attractivity and importance attached to each country. The choice of the country as the unit of analysis produces a rather crude measure of weight which is insensitive to variation within a country. This results in a set of mean values which overestimate the less attractive parts of any country at the expense of areas judged more appealing by the guidebooks' editors. However, because any appropriate measure of size for subnational, regional, etc. units (to be used, below, as a crucial control variable) is unavailable, the use of country as the unit of analysis is necessary.

The controlling procedure was the following: First, Glass and Grebenik's (1965) historical population estimates, appended when necessary by data from Freytags (1975[1914]) and Ramsay (1885), were converted into a series of single percentage distributions for the European continent as a whole for separate years with ten-year intervals between them (such as 1880, 1890, and so forth). Second, the percentages of the pages of volume allocated in the guidebooks to particular countries were divided by the percentages of population size of the given country. This procedure yielded indices in which the value of "1" marks a perfectly proportionate representation, with values less than "1" indicating underrepresentation and those above "1" suggesting overrepresentation. A similar procedure was performed by using data on the land area of the destination countries as the control variable. The resulting distribution was spread out on a wider scale but suggested the same conclusions, so its presentation was omitted here.

It is important to clarify that the use of the words underrepresentation and overrepresentation in the analysis does not imply a normative judgment concerning how extensive the representation of each of the countries should have been in these guidebooks. Rather, they refer to an implicit comparison with the relative size of those countries in terms of their population size.

The date (and often the linguistic context) of the first written record of particular lexical units, an important piece of philological information collected by linguists-historians, is often published in historical-etymological dictionaries. For this part of the study, a list of the word-equivalents of the English terms tourist, tourism and touristic was first compiled for all European languages. Then, an attempt was made to collect the dates of the first written records of the words from various dictionaries of those languages to be found in the academic libraries of Baltimore, Washington DC, Budapest, and Vienna. (The library sources consulted include Akademia Nauk 1963; Battisti and Alessio 1957; Dimitrakou 1951; Doroszewski 1967; Figuereido 1937; Gáldi 1957; Grand Larousse 1978; Grimm and Grimm 1935; Hellquist 1922; Jannarakis 1883; Knudsen et al 1957; Östergren 1964; Slovn'ik 1979; The Oxford English, 1933; Tordau et al 1983; Tsyganenko 1970; and Verhandlungen 1984 [1884].)

This effort yielded satisfactory data only for fewer than half of the words on the list. Subsequently, a number of linguistics institutes, university linguistics departments and dictionary editorial offices were asked to assist in obtaining the missing pieces of information on their particular language. Thus, the eventual completion of the list, with many items related from unpublished sources (national linguistic-historical archives, dictionary datafiles, and so forth), owes much to selfless, collegial assistance by linguist-historians in more than twenty countries all over the continent. Appendix 1 above includes the names and affiliations of those linguists from whom material has been included in the list.

A mirror translation, or calque, is a compound word translated into another language by translating each of its elements and reassembling it into a similar compound. In addition, several other languages have developed equivalents of the German *Fremdenverkehr* in the form of idiomatic expressions rather than compound words: (Catalan) *circulació d'estrangers*, (Castillan Spanish) *circulación de extranjeros*, (Romanian) *circulaţia străinilor*, (Serbo-Croatian) *promet stranaca*, (Czech) *cizinecký ruch* and *cestovní ruch*, (Slovak) *cudzinecký ruch*, (Slovene) *tujski promet*, and so forth.

In Table 2.3, the abbreviation "b/f" (before) indicates indirect inference. These are words for which the year of their first written record has not been found in etymological dictionaries. The dates indicated here mark the year of publication of the earliest mono- or bi-lingual dictionary listing these words. The abbreviation "aft" (after) refers to information from research correspondence. Wherever the table indicates the same years for denoting tourist, tourism, and touristic, it indicates that only a single time estimate was received through research correspondence, accompanied by a comment that this date refers to all three words in question.

For Map 2.3, the dates in the first column of Table 2.3 were grouped into three categories by dividing the entire time span of the data (1793 through approximately 1970) into three periods of roughly even size, minimally adjusted for the breakout of World War I: before 1854, 1854 through 1914, and after 1914. Blank areas on this map indicate missing data.

The ordinary least squares linear regression line fitted to the data in Figure 2.3 suggests an unambiguously positive relationship, with a high correlation value at $r=.737$ (from 22 datapoints).

Procedures Used in *Chapter 3*

For sets of provinces, weighted arithmetic means are used. Note that Good does not provide an estimate for Bosnia-Hercegovina which forces that province to be "missing". The horizontal axis represents per capita savings deposits (by provinces or sets of provinces) as percentages of the empire's mean value for the year 1890. It ranges from 18% (Trieste and Dalmatia) to 321% (Lower and Upper Austria). The vertical axis presents the degree of representation in guidebooks (by provinces or sets of provinces, following Good's groupings), ranging from 0 to 10.6 times, for the period of 1870 through 1908.

The computational formula of TER is as follows:
TER=100*(TA/POP) where TA is the annual number of tourist arrivals [persons/year] and POP is the size of the population during the given year [persons].

The computational formula of TN is this: TN=TA*LS where TA is the annual number of tourist arrivals [person/year] and LS is the average length of stay per tourist [nights/person].

TIR is computed by the following formula: TIR=100* ((TA*LS)/(POP*365)) where TA is the annual number of tourist arrivals [person/year], LS is the average length of stay by tourists [nights/person], POP is population size during the given year [person], and 365 is a constant [nights/year].

References

Adler, Judith
  1985 Youth on the Road: Reflections on the History of Tramping. Annals of Tourism Research 12:335–54.
Akademia Nauk SSSR
  1963 Slovar` Sovremennogo Russkogo Litaraturnogo Iazyka 15. Moskva: T. Akademia Nauk.
Akeroyd, Anne V.
  1981 Comment on Nash. Current Anthropology 22:468–9.
Allcock, John B., and Krzysztof Przedawski
  1990 Introduction. Annals of Tourism Research, Special Issue on Tourism in Centrally Planned Economies 17:1–6.
Allen, Grant
  1899 The European Tour. New York: Dodd, Mead & Co.
Anderson, Benedict
  1983 Imagined Communities: Reflections on the Origin and Spread of Nationalism. London: Verso.
Appleton's
  1870 Appleton's European Guide Book Illustrated. Including England, Scotland, and Ireland, France, Belgium, Holland, Northern and Southern Germany, Switzerland, Italy, Spain and Portugal, Russia, Denmark, Norway, and Sweden. New York: D. Appleton and Co.
Bachmann, Philipp
  1987 Tourism in Kenya: A Basic Need for Whom? Berne:Peter Lang.
Bacon, Francis
  n.d. The Essays or Counsels, Civil and Moral, of Francis Ld. Verulam Viscount of St. Albans. Mount Vernon, N.Y.: The Peter Pauper Press Reprint.
Baedeker, Karl ed.
  1883 Southern Germany and Austria, Including Hungary and Transylvania. Leipzig: Baedeker.
  1905 Austria-Hungary Including Dalmatia and Bosnia. Handbook for Travellers. Leipzig: Baedeker.
Bairoch, Paul
  1973 European Foreign Trade in the XIX Century: The Development of the Value and Volume of Exports (Preliminary Results). Journal of Economic History 2:5–36.
  1976 Europe's Gross National Product:1800–1975. Journal of Economic History 5:273–340.
  1988 Cities and Economic Development: From the Dawn of History to the Present. Translated by Christopher Braider. Chicago: The University of Chicago Press.

BarOn, Raymond
  1989 Travel and Tourism Data. A Comprehensive Research Handbook on the
    World Travel Industry. Phoenix, N.Y.: Oryx Press.
Battisti, Carlo, and Giovanni Alessio
  1957 Dizionario Etimologico Italiano. Firenze: Barbera.
Bauer, Tamás
  1978 Investment Cycles in Planned Economies. Acta Oeconomica 21(3):243–60.
Bauman, Zygmunt
  1990 Effacing the Face: On the Social Management of Moral Proximity.
    Theory, Culture & Society 7:5–38.
  1988–89 Strangers: The Social Construction of Universality and Particularity.
    Telos 78(Winter): 7–42.
Berend, Iván T.
  1986 The Crisis Zone of Europe: An Interpretation of East-Central European
    History in the First Half of the Twentieth Century. Cambridge: Cambridge
    University Press.
Berend, Iván T., and György Ránki
  1977 East-Central Europe in the 19th and 20th Centuries. Budapest: Aka-
    démiai kiadó.
  1982 The European Periphery and Industrialization 1780–1914. Translated
    By Éva Pálmai. Cambridge: Cambridge University Press and Editions De
    La Maison Des Sciences De L'homme.
  1987 Európa gazdasága A 19. században. 1780–1914. Budapest: Gondolat.
Bihari, Mihály
  1986 The Political System and the Representation of Interests. English Trans-
    lation by József Böröcz. *In* Economy and Society in Hungary, Rudolf
    Andorka and László Bertalan, eds., pp. 287–312. Budapest: Department of
    Sociology, Karl Marx University of Economics.
Binder, Johannes
  1979 Geschichte und Entwicklung der ersten Donau-Dampffschiffarts-Gesell-
    schaft 1829–1979. *In* 150 Jahre Ente DDSG, pp. 3–6. Wien: Österreichische
    Staatsdruckerei.
Black, Jeremy
  1985 The British and the Grand Tour. London: Croom Helm.
Blanchard, W. O., and S. S. Visher
  1931 Economic Geography of Europe. New York: McGraw-Hill.
Bogue, Donald J.
  1959 International Migration. *In* The Study of Population, P. M. Hauser and
    O. D. Duncan, eds., pp. 486–509. Chicago: University of Chicago Press.
Boorstin, Daniel
  1961 The Image: A Guide to Pseudo-Events in America. New York: Harper
    & Row.
Boyer, Marc
  1982 Le Tourisme. Nouvelle Edition Revue et Augmentée. Paris: Éditions du
    Seuil.
Böröcz, József
  1983 Young Foreign Tourists in Hungary. Leisure Newsletter 2(Summer):
    34–41.
  1989a Két szék között: Motívumok egy társadalomképhez XXXII(11): 72–82.
  1989b Mapping the Class Structures of State Socialism in East-Central Europe.
    Research in Social Stratification and Mobility 8:279–309.
  1990a A posztmodern társadalomtudomány: Marx—tótágast XXIII(6):38–48.

1990b Explaining Tourist Flows: Hungary as a Destination, 1960–1984. Annals of Tourism Research, Special Issue on Tourism in Centrally Planned Economies 17:19–35.

1990c A kádárizmustól a parlagi kapitalizmusig: a fejlett informalizmus építésének időszerű kérdései. Mozgó Világ 8:61–7.

1992a Dual Dependency and Property Vacuum: Social Change on the State Socialist Semiperiphery. Theory and Society 21:77–98.

1992b Informality and Second Economy in East-Central Europe. *In* Work Without Protections: Case Studies of the Informal Sector in Developing Countries, Gregory K. Schoepfle and Jorge Pérez-Lopez, eds., pp. 215–44. Washington, D.C.: U.S. Department of Labor, Bureau of International Labor Affairs.

1992c Dual Dependency and the Informalization of External Linkages: The Case of Hungary. Research in Social Movements, Conflicts and Change 14:189–209.

Böröcz, József, and Caleb Southworth
1995 Kapcsolatok és jövedelem: Magyarország, 1986–87. Szociológiai szemle, 2.

Britton, Stephen G.
1982 The Political Economy of Tourism in the Third World. Annals of Tourism Research 9:331–58.

Brown, William Adams, and Redvers Opie
1953 American Foreign Assistance. Washington, D.C.: The Brookings Institution.

Brusatti, Alois
1984 Historische Entwicklung 1884–1984. 100 Jahre Österreichischer Fremdenverkehr. Wien: Bundesministerium für Handel, Gewerbe und Industrie.

Bryden, John M.
1973 Tourism and Development. A Case Study of the Commonwealth Caribbean. Cambridge: Cambridge University Press.

Buckley, Peter J., and Stephen F. Witt
1990 Tourism in the Centrally Planned Economies of Europe. Annals of Tourism Research 17:7–18.

Budapest Statistical Office
1946 Budapest on the Threshold of the Winter 1945–46. Budapest Statistical Office.

Bundesleitung
1971 Tourism Made in Austria. Analysen, Trends, Aspekte. Wien: Bundesleitung des Österreichischen Wirschaftsbundes.

Burawoy, Michael
1976 The Functions and Reproduction of Migrant Labor: Comparative Material from Southern Africa and the United States. American Journal of Sociology 81:1050–87.

Burkart, A. J., and S. Medlik
1974 Tourism, Past, Present, and Future. London: Heinemann.

Butschek, Felix
1981 The Economic Structure. *In* Modern Austria, Kurt Steiner, ed., pp. 141–54. Palo Alto, CA: SPOSS, Inc.

Casals, Felipe García (Pavel Câmpeanu)
1980 The Syncretic Society. Translated from the French by Guy Daniels. White Plains, N.Y.: M. E. Sharpe.

Castells, Manuel, and Alejandro Portes
1989 World Underneath: The Origins, Dynamics, and Effects of the Informal

Economy. *In* The Informal Economy: Studies in Advanced and Less Developed Countries, Alejandro Portes, Manuel Castells and Lauren A. Benton, eds., pp. 11–37. Baltimore: Johns Hopkins University Press.

Câmpeanu, Pavel
1986 The Origins of Stalinism. From Leninist Revolution to Stalinist Society. Translated by Michel Vale. Armonk, N.Y.: M. E. Sharpe.
1989 The Genesis of the Stalinist Social Order. Translated by Michel Vale. Armonk, N.Y.: M. E. Sharpe.

Chase-Dunn, Christopher
1984 Transorganizational Socialism: Council for Mutual Economic Assistance and the Capitalist World-Economy. Revised version of a paper presented at the session on "Crises of Contemporary Socialism." Detroit: Annual Meetings of the American Sociological Association, August 31—September 3 1983.

Christaller, Walter
1983[1955] Beiträge zu einer Geographie des Fremdenverkehrs. *In* Geographie des Freizeit- und Fremdenverkehrs, Hofmeister, Burkhard, and Albrecht Steinecke, eds., pp. 156–69. Darmstadt: Wissenschaftliche Buchgesellschaft.
1963 Some Considerations of Tourism Location in Europe: The Peripheral Regions—Underdeveloped Countries—Recreation Areas. *In* Regional Science Association: Papers XII, pp. 95–105, Lund Congress.

Churchill, Winston S.
1953 Triumph and Tragedy. Boston: Houghton Mifflin.

Cleverdon, Robert
1979 The Economic and Social Impact of International Tourism on Developing Countries. Economist Intelligence Unit Report No. 60. London: The Economist Intelligence Unit.

Cohen, Erik
1972 Toward a Sociology of International Tourism. Social Research 164–82.
1981 Comment on Nash. Current Anthropology 22:469–70.
1982 Thai Girls and Farang Men: The Edge of Ambiguity. Annals of Tourism Research 9:403–28.
1984 The Sociology of Tourism: Approaches, Issues, and Findings. Annual Reviews of Sociology 10:373–92.

Coser, Lewis
1956 On the Function of Social Conflict. New York: The Free Press.

Crick, Malcolm
1988 Sun, Sex, Sights, Savings and Servility: Representations of International Tourism in the Social Sciences. Criticism Heresy & Interpretation 1:37–76.

Cronin, Audrey Kurth
1989 East-West Negotiations over Austria in 1949: Turning-Point in the Cold War. Journal of Contemporary History 24:125–45.

Csók Csaba
1969 Az idegenforgalom történetéből. RT-alapítás anno 1902. Idegenforgalom (9):21.

Culler, Jonathan
1981 Semiotics of Tourism. American Journal of Semiotics 1:127–40.

Czakó, Ágnes, and Endre Sik
1987 Managers' Reciprocal Transactions. In Education, Mobility and Network of Leaders in a Planned Economy, György Lengyel, ed., pp. 141–71.

Budapest: Department of Sociology, Karl Marx University of Economic Sciences.

Deák, István
1990 Beyond Nationalism. A Social and Political History of the Habsburg Officer Corps, 1848–1918. New York: Oxford University Press.

Desvignes, Lucette
1988 Le Tourisme en Bourgogne au XVIII. Siècle: Exploit Sportif ou Promenade Philosophique. *In* Voyage et Tourisme en Bourgogne à l'époque de Jefferson—Travelling through Burgundy in the Age of Jefferson, Michel Baridon, and Bernard Chevignard, eds., pp. 101–15. Éditions universitaires de Dijon.

Dimitrakou, D.
1951 Mega lexikon ellenikis glossis. Athina: Platia syntagmatos.

Dorner, Reinhard, Hans Glatz, and Christoph Schremmer
1986 Regionale Entwicklung durch Ausbau des Fremdenverkehrs? Die Fremdenverkehrsentwicklung im Spannungsfeld von wirtschaftlicher Ertragskraft und ökologischer Schönung. Kurzfassung der Studie "Eigenständige Entwicklung peripherer Regionen und umweltfreundlicher Fremdenverkehr," erstellt im Auftrag des Bundesministeriums für öffentliche Wirtschaft und Verkehr und des Bundesminiesteriums für Gesundheit und Umweltschutz, Vienna.

Doroszewski, Witold
1967 Słownik języka polskiego. Tom dziewiąty. Warszawa: PAN.

Dumazedier, Joffre
1968 Leisure. International Encyclopedia of the Social Sciences 9:248–53.

Ehrlich, Éva
1971 Economic Development and Personal Consumption Levels: An International Comparison. Acta Oeconomica 6(3):167–84.

Eisenstein, Elizabeth L.
1968 Some Conjectures about the Impact of Printing on Western Society and Thought: A Preliminary Report. Journal of Modern History 40(1):1–56.

Enloe, Cynthia
1990 Bananas Beaches & Bases. Making Feminist Sense of International Politics. Berkeley: University of California Press.

Eppel, Peter, and Heinrich Lotter
1981 Dokumentation zur österreichischen Zeitgeschichte 1955–1980. Wien: Jugend und Volk.

Evans, Peter
1979 Dependent Development: The Alliance of Multinational, State, and Local Capital in Brazil. Princeton University Press.

Farrell, Bryan H., and Robert W. McLellan, eds.
1987 Tourism and Physical Environment. Special Issue of the Annals of Tourism Research 14(1).

Feifer, Maxine
1985 Tourism in History. From Imperial Rome to the Present. New York: Stein and Day.

Figuereido, Candido de
1937 Dicionário da Língua Portuguesa, 6. edição, vol. II. Lisboa: Bertrand.

Franz, Alfred
1985 Estimates of the Hidden Economy in Austria on the Basis of Official Statistics. The Review of Income and Wealth 31(4):325–36.

Fremdenverkehr in Zahlen
1989 Fremdenverkehr in Zahlen. Österreichische und internationale Fremdenverkehrs- und Wirschaftsdaten, 24. Auflage. Wien: Bundeskammer der Gewerblichen Wirtschaft.
1991 Fremdenverkehr in Zahlen. Österreichische und internationale Fremdenverkehrs- und Wirschaftsdaten, 27. Auflage. Wien: Bundeskammer der Gewerblichen Wirtschaft.

Freytags, G.
1975 (1914) G. Freytags Karte von Oesterreich-Ungarn. Wien: Freytag-Berndt u. Artaria KG.

Gábor, István R.
1983 Második gazdaság és 'környéke'. Bulletin VI:66–166.
1989 Second Economy in State Socialism: Past Experience and Future Prospects, The Case of Hungary. European Economic Review 33:597–604.

Gábor, István R., and Péter Galasi
1985 Second Economy, State and Labour Market. *In* Labour Market and Second Economy in Hungary, Péter Galasi and György Sziráczki, eds., pp. 122–32. Frankfurt: Campus Verlag.

Galasi, Péter, and Endre Sik
1989 Invisible Incomes in Hungary. Social Justice 15(3–4):160–178.

Galasi, Péter, and György Sziráczki (eds.)
1985 Labour Market and Second Economy in Hungary. Frankfurt/Main: Campus Verlag GmBH.

Gáldi, László
1957 Szótárirodalom a felvilágosodás korában és a reformkorban. Budapest.

Gazdaságkutató
1983 Az idegenforgalom gazdaságosságának egyes kkérdéseiről. Munkaanyag. Mimeo: Gazdaságkutató Intézet.

Glass, D. V., and E. Grebenik
1965 World Population, 1800–1950. *In* The Cambridge Economic History of Europe. Volume VI. The Industrial Revolutions and After: Incomes, Population and Technological Change (I). Habakukk, H. J. and M. Postan, eds., pp. 60–138. Cambridge University Press.

Goffman, Erving
1971 Relations in Public: Microstudies of the Public Order. London: Allen Lane.

Good, David F.
1984 The Economic Rise of the Habsburg Empire, 1750–1914. Berkeley: University of California Press.

Goux, Jean-Joseph
n.d. Cash, check or charge? *In* L'argent, Martin Gorin, ed., pp. 7–23. Paris: EHESS.

Graburn, Nelson
1977 Tourism: The Sacred Journey. *In* Hosts and Guests. The Anthropology of Tourism, Valene Smith, ed., pp. 17–32. University of Pennsylvania Press.
1981 Comment on Nash. Current Anthropology 22(5)(Oct):470–1.
1982 Tourism and Prostitution. Articles Review. Annals of Tourism Research 10:437–56.

Grand Larousse
1978 Grand Larousse de la Langue Française en Sept Volumes Tome Septième, SUS-Z, et Bibliographie Historique. Paris: Librairie Larousse.

Granovetter, Mark

1973 The Strength of Weak Ties. American Journal of Sociology 78: 1360–80.

1985 Economic Action and Social Structure: The Problem of Embeddedness. American Journal of Sociology 91:481–510.

Griep, Wolfgang, and Hans-Wolf Jäger
1983 Reise und Soziale Realität am Ende des 18. Jahrhunderts. Heidelberg: Carl Winter Universitätsverlag.

Griep, Wolfgang, and Hans-Wolf Jäger
1986 Reisen im 18. Jahrhundert. Neue Untersuchungen. Heidelberg: Carl Winter Universitätsverlag.

Grieszelich, E. L.
1891 Fremdenverkehr in Wien Während der Jahre 1874 bis 1880. Wien: Statistisches Departement des Wiener Magistrates.

Grimm, Jacob, and Wilhelm
1935 Deutsches Wörterbuch. Elfter Band. 1 Abteilung. I. Teil. Leipzig: Hirzel.

Grünthal, A.
1961 Tourism in Under-Developed Countries of Africa South of the Sahara. Revue du tourisme 4.

Gulyás, József
1989 Sziget a félszigeten. Idegenforgalom 9–10.

Hall, Derek R.
1990 Stalinism and Tourism: A Study of Albania and North Korea. Annals of Tourism Research 17:36–54.
1993 Tourism in Eastern Europe. In W. Pompl and P. Lavery, eds., pp. 341–58. Tourism in Europe. Structures and Developments. Wallingford, UK: CAB International.

Hanák, Péter
1988 A kert és a műhely. Budapest: Magvető.

Harrington, David
1993 Bulgarian Tourism. A State of Uncertainty. Annals of Tourism Research 20:519–34.

Harvey, David
1989 The Condition of Postmodernity. An Enquiry into the Origins of Cultural Change. Oxford: Basil Blackwell.

Haug, C. James
1982 Leisure and Urbanism in Nineteenth-Century Nice. Lawrence: The Regents Press of Kansas.

Hegedűs, Márton
1938 A magyar idegenforgalom közgazdasági jelentősége. Budapest.

Hellquist, Elof
1922 Svensk Etymologisk Ordbok. Lund: Gleerups.

Hirschman, Albert O.
1977 A Generalized Linkage Approach to Development, with Special Reference to Staples. In Essays in Economic Development and Cultural Change in Honor of Bert F. Haselitz, Supplement, Economic Development and Cultural Change 25, Manning Nash, ed., pp. 67–98.

Hodgson, Adèle, ed.
1987 The Travel and Tourism Industry: Strategies for the Future. Oxford: Pergamon Press.

Hofmeister, Burkhard, and Albrecht Steinecke
1983 Einleitung: Zur wissenschaftsgeschichtlichen Entwicklung der Geographie des Freizeit- und Fremdenverkehrs. In Geographie des Freizeit- und

Fremdenverkehrs, Hofmeister, Burkhard, and Albrecht Steinecke, eds., pp. 1–16. Darmstadt: Wissenschaftliche Buchgesellschaft.

Høivik, Tord, and Turid Heiberg (with Vigdis Mathiesen)
  1980 Centre-Periphery Tourism and Self-Reliance. International Social Science Journal 1:69–96.

Hudman, Lloyd E.
  1979 Origin Regions of International Tourism. *In* Studies in the Geography of Tourism and Recreation. Wiener Geographische Schriften, No. 53/54, Sinnhuber, Karl A., and Felix Jülg, eds., pp. 43–9. Wien: Verlag F. Hirt.

Hungarian Institute for Economic Research
  1938 A magyar idegenforgalom alakulása 1927–1937. Budapest: Magyar Gazdaságkutató Intézet.
  1938 A Magyar Gazdaságkutató Intézet jelentése Magyarország idegenforgalmáról az 1938. évben. MS.

Huxley, Aldous
  1925 Along the Road. New York: Doran.

IBRD (International Bank for Reconstruction and Development/The World Bank)
  1985 Population Change and Economic Development. Published for the World Bank by Oxford University Press.
  1991 World Tables 1991. Baltimore: The Johns Hopkins University Press.

Idegenforgalmi, ed.
  1935 A magyar idegenforgalom évkönyve. Budapest: Az Idegenforgalmi Újságírók Szindikátusa.

Idegenforgalmi.
  1966 Idegenforgalmi adattár. Budapest.

IUOTO (International Union of Official Travel Organisations)
  1963 The United Nations Conference on International Travel and Tourism. Geneva: IUOTO.
  1976 The Impact of International Tourism on the Economic Development of the Developing Countries. Geneva: World Tourism Organization.

Jafari, Jafar
  1989 Sociocultural Dimensions of Tourism. An English Language Literature Review. *In* Tourism as a Factor of Change, Bystrzanowski, J., ed., Vienna: Vienna Centre.

Jannarakis, Antonios
  1883 Deutsch-Neugriechisches Handwörterbuch. Hannover: Hahn'sche Buchhandlung.

Jankowitsch, Peter
  1981 Foreign Policy. *In* Modern Austria, Kurt Steiner, ed., pp. 361–80. Palo Alto, Ca.: SPOSS, Inc.

Jánossy, Ferenc
  1963 A gazdasági fejlődés mérhetősége és új mérési módszere. Budapest: Közgazdasági és Jogi Könyvkiadó.

Jászi, Oszkár
  1929 The Dissolution of the Habsburg Monarchy. University of Chicago Press.

Karácsony Sándor
  n.d. A magyarság, mint idegenforgalmi probléma pp. 229–57.

Karbuczky, Imre
  1986 Kísérlet az aktív idegenforgalom hatékonysági folyamatainak és mérésének vizsgálatára 1975–1985. Budapest: Belkereskedelmi Kutatóintézet.

Keefe, Eugene K. et al
1976 Area Handbook for Austria. Washington, D.C.: U.S. Government Printing Office.
Kelly, John R.
1982 Leisure. Englewood-Cliffs, N.J.: Prentice-Hall.
Knudsen, Trygve et al
1957 Norsk Riksmålordsbok. Utgittar riksmålsvernet. Oslo: Aschenborg.
Kolosi, Tamás
1984 Státusz és réteg. Rétegződésmodell-vizsgálat III. Budapest: MSZMP KB Társadalomtudományi Intézete.
Konrád, György, and Iván Szelényi
1979[1974] The Intellectuals on the Road to Class Power. Translated from Hungarian by Andrew Arato and Richard E. Allen. New York: Harcourt Brace Jovanovich.
Koren, Stephan
1981 Monetary and Budget Policy. *In* Modern Austria, Kurt Steiner, ed., pp. 173–83. Palo Alto, Ca.: SPOSS, Inc.
Kovács, László, and Takács János
n.d. Az idegenforgalom alakulása és fejlődése Magyarországon. 1945–1965. Budapest: Országos Idegenforgalmi Hivatal-Panoráma.
Kristeva, Julia
1986 The Kristeva Reader, ed., Toril Moi. Oxford: Basil Blackwell.
1991 Strangers to Ourselves. Translated from the French by Leon S. Roudiez. New York: Columbia University Press.
KSH
1958 Feljegyzés. Magyarország 1957. évi idegenforgalma. Központi Statisztikai Hivatal, MS.
1965 Az idegenforgalom alakulása Magyarországon (1945–1965). Budapest: KSH.
1965 Külkereskedelmi évkönyv. Budapest: Központi Statisztikai Hivatal.
1970 Külkereskedelmi évkönyv. Budapest: Központi Statisztikai Hivatal.
1975 Külkereskedelmi évkönyv. Budapest: Központi Statisztikai Hivatal.
1980 Külkereskedelmi évkönyv. Budapest: Központi Statisztikai Hivatal.
1982 A lakosság idegenforgalmának társadalmi, gazdasági jellemzői. Budapest: Központi Statisztikai Hivatal.
1987 Népesség- és társadalomstatisztikai évkönyv 1986. Budapest: Központi Statisztikai Hivatal.
1989a Külkereskedelmi évkönyv. Budapest: Központi Statisztikai Hivatal.
1989b Idegenforgalmi évkönyv 1988. Budapest: Központi Statisztikai Hivatal.
1989c Magyarország idegenforgalmi szálláshelyei 1987 július 31. Budapest: Központi Statisztikai Hivatal.
1990 Idegenforgalmi évkönyv 1989. Budapest: Központi Statisztikai Hivatal.
1991 Idegenforgalmi évkönyv 1990. Budapest: Központi Statisztikai Hivatal.
Kushman, John, Alexander Groth, and Robin Childs
1980 Political Systems and International Travel. Social Science Quarterly 60:604–15.
Lanfant, Marie-Françoise, Marie-Hélene Motten, Michel Picard, Danielle Rozenberg, and Jacques de Weerdt
1978 Sociologie du Tourisme: Positions et Perspectives dans la Recherche Internationale. Paris: Centre Nationale de la Recherche Scientifique.
Larousse
1960 Larousse de poche. Dictionnaire française. New York: Simon & Schuster.

Launer, Ekkehard, and Renate Wilke-Launer (eds.)
1988 Zum Beispiel Sex Tourismus. Buchreihe Süd-Nord, Lamuv, Göttingen.
Lea, J.
1988 Tourism and Development in the Third World. London: Routlege.
Leiper, Neil
1979 The Framework of Tourism: Towards a Definition of Tourism, Tourist, and the Tourist Industry. Annals of Tourism Research 6:390–407.
1983 An Etymology of 'Tourism.' Annals of Tourism Research 10:277–81.
Lichtenberger, Elisabeth
1984 (1976) Der Massentourismus als dynamiches System: Das österreischische Beispiel. *In* Geographie des Freizeit- und Fremdenverkehrs, Burkhard Hofmeister, and Albrecht Steinecke, eds., pp. 345–72. Darmstadt: Wissenschaftliche Buchgesellschaft.
Lijphart, Arend
1975 The Comparable-Cases Strategy in Comparative Research. Comparative Political Studies 8:158–77.
MacCannell, Dean
1976 The Tourist. The New Theory of the Leisure Class. New York: Shocken Books.
Madsen Camacho, Michelle
1994 Modernization Ideology at Work: Gender and the Disciplined Body in a Mexican Tourism Zone. Paper presented at the Annual Meeting of the Society for Applied Anthropology, Cancún, Quintana Roo, México.
Mannheim, Karl
1936 (1929) Ideology and Utopia. An Introduction to the Sociology of Knowledge. Translated from the German by Louis Wirth and Edward Shils. New York: Harcourt, Brace & World.
Mansfeld, Yoel
1990 Spatial Patterns of International Tourist Flows: Towards A Theoretical Framework. Progress in Human Geography 14(3):372–90.
Markos, Béla, ed.
1942 Jelentés Budapest székesfőváros Idegenforgalmi Hivatalának huszonötesztendős munkásságáról 1916–1941. Budapest Székesfőváros Idegenforgalmi Hivatala.
Marperger, Kameralist Paul Jakob
1733 Auserlesene kleine Schriften. Leipzig und Rudolstadt. Quoted in Martens, 1986.
Marshall, George C.
1984 [1947] Secretary of State George C. Marshall's Address at the Commencement Exercises of Harvard University, Cambridge, Massachusetts, June 5, 1947. Appendix II. *In* The Marshall Plan. The Launching of the Pax Americana, Charles Mee Jr., pp. 271–3. New York: Simon and Schuster.
Martens, Wolfgang
1986 Zur Einschätzung des Reisens von Bürgersöhnen in der frühen Aufklärung (am Beispiel des Hamburger 'Patrioten' 1724–26. *In* Reisen im 18. Jahrhundert. Neue Untersuchungen, Wolfgang Griep, and Hans-Wolf Jäger, eds., pp. 34–49. Heidelberg: Carl Winter Universitätsverlag.
Mathieson, Alister, and Geoffrey Wall
1982 Tourism: Economic, Physical and Social Impacts. London: Longman.
May-Landgrebe, Silke
1987 Touristische Entwicklungsstrategien—Wege aus der Armut? Peripherie 25–26:165–80.

Mazanec, J., and H. Mikolicz
1985 Gästebefragung Österreich. GBÖ-Österreich Bericht, Summer 1985. Österreichische Gesellschaft für Angewandte Fremdenverkehrswissenschaft, Projektgruppe Wien.

Mäder, Ueli
1988 Tourism and Environment. Annals of Tourism Research 15: 274–7.

März, Edward, and Maria Szecsi
1981 Austria's Economic Development, 1945–1978. *In* Modern Austria, Kurt Steiner, ed., pp. 123–40. Palo Alto, Ca.: SPOSS, Inc.

Mead, William Edward
1972 [1914] The Grand Tour in the Eighteenth Century. New York: Benjamin Blom.

Meleghy, Tamás, Max Preglau, and Alois Tafertshofer
1985 Tourism Development and Value Change. Annals of Tourism Research 12:181–99.

Minh-ha, Trinh T.
1994 Other than myself/my other self. *In* Travellers' Tales: Narratives of home and displacement, George Robertson, Melinda Mash, Lisa Tickner, Jon Bird, Barry Curtis, and Tim Putnam, eds., pp. 9–26. London: Routledge.

Morgenroth, Wilhelm
1983[1927] Fremdenverkehr. *In* Geographie des Freizeit- und Fremdenverkehrs, Burkhard Hofmeister, and Albrecht Steinecke, eds., pp. 17–35. Darmstadt: Wissenschaftliche Buchgesellschaft.

Moscow Declaration
1943 Moscow Declaration. Department of State Bulletin IX:228.

Nash, Dennison
1977 Tourism as a Form of Imperialism. *In* Hosts and Guests. The Anthropology of Tourism, Valene Smith, ed., pp. 149–56. University of Pennsylvania Press.
1981 Tourism as an Anthropological Subject. Current Anthropology 22(5)(Oct):461–81.

Nemschak, Franz
1955 Ten Years of Austrian Economic Development, 1945–1955. Vienna, Association of Austrian Industrialists.

Oudiette, Virginie
1990 International Tourism in China. (Translated from the French by Dr John B. Allcock) Annals of Tourism Research 17:123–32.

Ouma, Joseph P. B. M
1970 Evolution of Tourism in East Africa (1900–2000). Nairobi: East African Literature Bureau.

Östergren, Olof
1964 Nusvensk Ordbok. Stockholm: Wahlström and Widström.

Österreichische Staatsdruckerei
1958 Zehn Jahre ERP in Österreich 1948/1958. Wirtschaftshilfe im Dienste der Völkerverständigung. Wien: Österreichische Staatsdruckerei.

Páczi Erzsébet
1989 A világkiállítás hatása az idegenforgalomra. Working paper. Budapest: Kopint-Datorg.

Patriarca, Silvana
1992 Numbers and the Nation: The Statistical Representation of Italy, 1820–1871. PhD-dissertation, The Johns Hopkins University, Baltimore.

1994 Statistical Nation Building and the Consolidation of Regions in Italy. Social Science History 18:359–76.

Pearce, Douglas G.
1988 Tourism Today: A Geographical Analysis. New York: Longman.

Pearlman, Michael V.
1990 Conflicts and Constraints in Bulgaria's Tourism Sector. Annals of Tourism Research 17:103–122.

Petersen, William
1978 International Migration. Annual Reviews of Sociology 4:533–75.

Phongpaichit, Pasuk
1982 From Peasant Girl to Bangkok Masseuse. Geneva: International Labour Office.

Pi-Sunyer, Oriol
1977 Through Native Eyes: Tourists and Tourism in a Catalan Maritime Community. pp. 149–56. *In* Hosts and Guests. The Anthropology of Tourism, Valene L. Smith, ed., University of Pennsylvania Press.
1981 Comment on Nash. Current Anthropology 22(5)(Oct):474–5.

Pompl, W., and P. Lavery, eds.
1993 Tourism in Europe: Structures and Developments. Wallingford, U.K.: CAB International.

Polányi, Karl
1957 The Economy as Instituted Process. *In* Trade and Market in Early Empires, Karl Polanyi, Conrad M. Arensberg, and Harry W. Pearson, eds., pp. 243–70. Glencoe, Ill: Free Press.

Portes, Alejandro
1976 The Sociology of National Development. American Journal of Sociology 82(1):55–85.
1981 Unequal Exchange and the Urban Informal Sector. *In* Labor, Class and the International System, Alejandro Portes, and John Walton, pp. 67–106. New York: Academic Press
1985 The Informal Sector: Definition, Controversy, and Relation to National Development. Review VII(1)(Summer):151–74.
1986 One Field, Many Views: Competing Theories of International Migration. *In* Pacific Bridges. The New Immigration from Asia and the Pacific Islands, James T. Fawcett, and Benjamin V. Carino, eds., pp. 53–70. New York: Center for Migration Studies.
1990 When More Can Be Less: Labor Standards, Development, and the Informal Economy. *In* Labor Standards and Development in the Global Economy. An edited collection of papers presented at the Symposium on Labor Standards and Development held in Washington, D.C., December 12–13, 1988, Stephen Herzenberg, and Jorge F. Perez-Lopez, eds., pp. 219–37. Washington, D.C.: U.S. Department of Labor.

Portes, Alejandro, and Robert L. Bach
1985 Latin Journey. Cuban and Mexican Immigrants in the United States. Berkeley: University of California Press.

Portes, Alejandro, and József Böröcz
1988 The Informal Sector under Capitalism and State Socialism: A Preliminary Comparison. Social Justice, Special Issue on the "Dynamics of the Informal Economy" 15(3–4):17–28.
1989 Contemporary Immigration: Theoretical Perspectives on Its Determinants and Modes of Incorporation. International Migration Review, Silver Issue 87:606–30.

Portes, Alejandro, and Saskia Sassen-Koob
    1987 Making It Underground: Comparative Material on the Informal Sector in Western Market Economies. American Journal of Sociology 93:30–61.
Portes, Alejandro, and Richard Schauffler
    1992 The Informal Economy in Latin America: Definition, Measurement, and Policies. Working Paper Series #5. Baltimore: Department of Sociology, Program in Comparative International Development.
Portes, Alejandro and John Walton
    1981 Labor, Class, and the International System. Chapter 2: International Migration: Conditions for the Mobilization and Use of Migrant Labor under World Capitalism. New York: Academic Press.
Pound, Norman J.
    1985 An Historical Geography of Europe. 1800–1914. Cambridge, Cambridge University Press.
Przecławski, Krzysztof
    1994 Tourism and the Contemporary World. Warsaw: University of Warsaw, Institute of Social Prevention and Readaptation, Centre for Social Problems of Education.
Przeworski, Adam
    1986 Some Problems in the Study of the Transition to Democracy. *In* Transitions from Authoritarian Rule: Comparative Perspectives, Guillermo O'Donnell, Philippe C. Schmitter, and Laurence Whitehead, eds., Baltimore: The Johns Hopkins University Press.
Przeworski, Adam, and Henry Teune
    1970 The Logic of Comparative Social Inquiry. New York: Wiley and Sons.
Ramsay, Sir Andrew C., ed.
    1885 Europe. Stanford's Compendium of Geography and Travel. Appendix II. Statistics. London: Stanford.
Rév, István
    1987 The Advantages of Being Atomized: How Hungarian Peasants Coped with Collectivization. Dissent (Summer):335–350.
Richter Sándor, and Klára Székffy
    1987 Ausztria gazdasága. Fejlődés-megtorpanás-válságjelenségek. Budapest: Közgazdasági és Jogi Könyvkiadó.
Ritter, Wigand
    1966 Fremdenverkehr in Europa. Eine wirtschafts- und sozialgeographische Untersuchung über Reisen und Urlaubsaufenthalte der Bewohner Europas. Leiden A.W. Sijthoff.
Roberts, J. M.
    1976 The Pelican History of the World. London: Penguin Books.
Robertson, Roland
    1990 Mapping the Global Condition: Globalization as the Central Concept. Theory Culture & Society 7(2–3):15–30.
Robertson, Roland, and Frank Lechner
    1985 Modernization, Globalization and the Problem of Culture in World-Systems Theory. Theory Culture & Society 2(3):103–18.
Rojek, Chris
    1993a After Popular Culture: Hyperreality and Leisure. Leisure Studies 12: 277–89.
    1993b Disney culture. Leisure Studies 12:121–35.
Said, Edward
    1978 Orientalism. New York: Vintage Books.

1990 Reflections on Exile. *In* Out There: Marginalization and Contemporary Culture, R. Fergusson et al., eds., pp. 357–8. New York: The New Museum of Contemporary Art and MIT Press.

Sampson, Anthony
1985 Empires of the Sky. The Politics, Contests and Cartels of World Airlines. New York: Random House.

Sarup, Madan
1994 Home and Identity. *In* Travellers' Tales. Narratives of Home and Displacement, George Robertson, Melinda Mash, Lisa Tickner, Jon Bird, Barry Curtis and Tim Putnam, eds., pp. 93–104. London: Routledge.

Satchel
1877 A Satchel Guide for the Vacation Tourist in Europe. A Compact Itinerary of the British Isles, Belgium and Holland, Germany and the Rhine, Switzerland, France, Austria, and Italy. New York: Hurd and Houghton.
1889 A Satchel Guide for the Vacation Tourist in Europe. A Compact Itinerary of the British Isles, Belgium and Holland, Germany and the Rhine, Switzerland, France, Austria, and Italy. New York: Hurd and Houghton.
1895 A Satchel Guide for the Vacation Tourist in Europe. A Compact Itinerary of the British Isles, Belgium and Holland, Germany and the Rhine, Switzerland, France, Austria, and Italy. New York: Hurd and Houghton.
1897 A Satchel Guide for the Vacation Tourist in Europe. A Compact Itinerary of the British Isles, Belgium and Holland, Germany and the Rhine, Switzerland, France, Austria, and Italy. New York: Houghton Mifflin Co.
1908 A Satchel Guide for the Vacation Tourist in Europe. A Compact Itinerary of the British Isles, Belgium and Holland, Germany and the Rhine, Switzerland, France, Austria, and Italy, by W. J. Rolfe, Litt. D. New York: Houghton Mifflin Co.
1912 A Satchel Guide for the Vacation Tourist in Europe. A Compact Itinerary of the British Isles, Belgium and Holland, Germany and the Rhine, Switzerland, France, Austria, and Italy, by W. J. Rolfe, Litt. D. New York:Houghton Mifflin Co.
1924 A Satchel Guide to Europe, (44th ed.) by William J. Rolfe, Litt. D., Revised and Enlarged by William D. Crockett, Ph.D. New York: Houghton Mifflin Co.
1925 A Satchel Guide to Europe, (45th ed.) by William J. Rolfe, Litt. D., Revised and Enlarged by William D. Crockett, Ph.D. New York: Houghton Mifflin Co.

Schärli, Arthur
1984 Höhepunkt des schweizerischen Tourismus in der Zeit der "Belle Epoque" unter Besonderer Berücksichtigung des Berner Oberlandes. Kulturgeschichtliche Regionalstudie. Bern: Peter Lang.

Schorske, Carl E.
1981 (1961) Fin-de-Siècle Vienna. Politics and Culture. New York: Vintage Books.

Senior, Robert
1982 The World Travel Market. New York: Facts On File Publications.

Shin, Eui Hang, and Woo Gak Lee
1983 Destinations of International Travel by the U.S. Population. International Migration 21(1):63–74.

Sigaux, G.
1966 History of Tourism. London: Leisure Arts.

Simmel, Georg
1971[1903] The Metropolis and Mental Life. *In* On Individuality and Social Forms, Donald N. Levine, ed., pp. 324–39. Chicago: The University of Chicago Press.
1971[1908] The Stranger. *In* On Individuality and Social Forms, Donald N. Levine, ed., pp. 143–49. Chicago: The University of Chicago Press.
1971[1911] The Adventurer. *In* On Individuality and Social Forms, Donald N. Levine, ed., pp. 187–98. Chicago: The University of Chicago Press.
1978[1907] The Philosophy of Money. Translated by Tom Bottomore and David Frisby from a first draft by Kaethe Mengelberg. Boston: Routlege & Kegan Paul.
1991[1895] The Alpine Journey. Theory, Culture and Society 8(3):95–98.
Sklair, Leslie
1991 Sociology of the Global System. Baltimore: The Johns Hopkins University Press.
Slovn'ik
1979 Slovn'ik ukrainskoi movi. Tom d'es'ati'. T-F. Kiev: Naukova dumka.
Snyder, David, and Edward L. Kick
1979 Structural Position in the World System and Economic Growth, 1965–1970: A Multiple-Network Analysis of Transnational Interactions. American Journal of Sociology 84(5):1096–1127.
Spannocchi, Emil
1981 Defense Policy from the Austrian Point of View. *In* Modern Austria, Kurt Steiner, ed., pp. 381–92, Palo Alto, Ca.: SPOSS, Inc.
Spivak, Gayatri Chakravorty
1988 Can the Subaltern Speak? *In* Marxism and the Interpretation of Culture. Cary Nelson and Lawrence Grossberg, eds., pp. 271–313. Urbana: University of Illinois Press.
Stafford, Jean
1985 Les Paradigmes de la Recherche en Téorologie: Etude, Analyse et Critique. Loisir et Société 8:549–60.
Steiner, Kurt, ed.
1981 Modern Austria. Palo Alto, Ca.: SPOSS, Inc.
Stewart, William E.
1983 Gesellschaftspolitische Tendenzen in der Reisebeschreibung des Ausgehenden 18. Jahrhunderts. *In* Reise und soziale Realität am Ende des 18. Jahrhuderts, Wolfgang Griep, and Hans-Wolf Jäger, eds., pp. 32–47. Heidelberg: Carl Winter Universitätsverlag.
Stokes, Gale, ed.
1991 From Stalinism to Pluralism. A Documentary History of Eastern Europe since 1945. New York: Oxford University Press.
Stoler, Ann L.
1990 Making Empire Respectable: The Politics of Race and Sexual Morality in 20th Century Colonial Cultures. American Ethnologist, 634–60.
Swain, Nigel
1990 Small Cooperatives and Economic Work Partnerships in the Computing Industries: Exceptions that Prove the Rule. *In* Market Economy and Civil Society in Hungary, C. M. Hann, ed., pp. 85–109. London: Frank Cass.
Szántó, Péter
1982 Idegenforgalom Magyarországon a XIX. század második felében. *In* A Magyar Kereskedelmi és Vendéglátóipari Múzeum Évkönyve, Budapest, Borza Tibor, ed., pp. 213–50.

Szerény
1900 Az ország és fővárosunk idegenforgalma. Budapest: Singer és Wolfner.
Szűcs, Jenő
1983 Vázlat Európa három történeti régiójáról. Budapest, Magvető.
1986 Magyarország regionális helye Európában. A középkor. *In* Európa régiói
a történelemben, Jenő Szűcs, and Péter Hanák, pp. 3–11. Budapest: Magyar
Tudományos Akadémia Történettudományi Intézet and Országos
Pedagógiai Intézet.
The Oxford English Dictionary
1933 The Oxford English Dictionary, Vol XI (T–U). Oxford: Clarendon.
Theuns, H. Leo
1984 Tourism Research Priorities: A Survey of Expert Opinions with Special
Reference to Developing Countries. Les Cahiers du Tourisme, Series C #96.
Aix-en-Provence: Centre des Hautes Etudes Touristiques.
Thomas, William Isaac and Florian Znaniecki
1958 The Polish Peasant in Europe and America. New York: Dover Publications.
Thompson, Edward P.
1967 Time, Work-Discipline, and Industrial Capitalism. Past and Present
38(Dec):56–97.
Thurot, Jean Maurice, and Gaétane Thurot
1983 The Ideology of Class and Tourism: Confronting the Discourse of Advertising. Annals of Tourism Research 10:173–89.
Tihanyi, János
1984 A magyar-német idegenforgalom történetéhez (1933–1944). Századok:
124–51.
1988a Az idegenforgalom története a két világháború között. Élet és
Tudomány 34:1046–7.
1988b Az idegenforgalom története a II. világháború után. Élet és Tudomány
34:1066–77.
Tilly, Charles
1984 Big Structures, Large Processes, Huge Comparisons. New York: Russell
Sage Foundation.
Todorov, Tzvetan
1993 On Human Diversity. Nationalism, Racism, and Exoticism in French
Thought. Trans. by Catherine Porter. Cambridge, MA: Harvard University
Press.
Tordau, Iorgu et al
1983 Dicţionarul Limbii Române. Serie Nonă, Tomul XI. Partea 3-A, Litera
T. Bucureşti: Editura Academiei Republicii Socialiste Romania.
Towner, John
1985 The Grand Tour: A Key Phase in the History of Tourism. Annals of
Tourism Research 12:297–333.
Tsyganenko, Galina Pavlovna
1970 Etimologicheskii Slovar` Russkogo Iazyka. Kiev: Radianska shkola.
Turner, Louis, and John Ash
1976 The Golden Hordes: International Tourism and the Pleasure
Periphery. New York: St. Martin's Press.
UNCTAD
1976 Handbook of International Trade and Development Statistics. New
York: United Nations.
1989 Handbook of International Trade and Development Statistics. New
York: United Nations.

United Nations
1950 Demographic Yearbook/Annuaire Démographique. New York: United Nations.
1956 Yearbook of International Trade Statistics. Geneva: United Nations.
1960 Yearbook of International Trade Statistics. Geneva: United Nations.
1962 U.N. Statistical Yearbook. New York.
1962 Yearbook of International Trade Statistics. Geneva: United Nations.
1963 U.N. Statistical Yearbook. New York.
1966 U.N. Statistical Yearbook. New York.
1967 Yearbook of International Trade Statistics. Geneva: United Nations.
1970 U.N. Statistical Yearbook. New York.
1972–73 Yearbook of International Trade Statistics. Geneva: United Nations.
1974 U.N. Statistical Yearbook. New York.
1977 Yearbook of International Trade Statistics. Geneva: United Nations.
1978 U.N. Statistical Yearbook. New York.
1981 U.N. Statistical Yearbook. New York.
1982 Transnational Corporations in International Tourism. U.N. Centre on Transnational Corporations.
1982 Yearbook of International Trade Statistics. Geneva: United Nations.
1983/4 U.N. Statistical Yearbook. New York.
1987 Yearbook of International Trade Statistics. Geneva: United Nations.
1989 Yearbook of International Trade Statistics. Geneva: United Nations.
Urry, John
1990a The Tourist Gaze. London: Sage.
1990b The 'Consumption' of Tourism. Sociology 24:23–35.
Várnegyed
1994 A VILÁGÖRÖKSÉG története. Várnegyed október 21:3.
Veblen, Thorstein
1967 The Theory of the Leisure Class. New York: The Viking Press.
Vellas, François
1985 Economie et Politique du Tourisme International. Paris: Economica.
Verhandlungen
1984[1884] Verhandlungen des am 13. und 14. April 1884 in Graz abgehaltenen Delegirtentages zur Förderung des Fremdenverkehrs in den österreischischen Alpenländern Verlag des Vereines zur Förderung des Fremdenverkehrs in Steiermark, Graz. Reprint (in facsimile) in Brusatti, Alois. in 100 Jahre Österreichischer Fremdenverkehr. Historische Entwicklung 1884–1984. Wien: Österreichische Bundesministerium für Handel, Gewerbe und Industrie.
Vincze, I.
1982 Foreign Currency Income and Profitability of Hungarian Tourism. Acta Oeconomica 29(3–4):361–70.
Waters, Somerset R.
n.d. The Big Picture: The Travel Industry World Yearbook. New York: Child and Waters.
Williams, Allan M., and Gareth Shaw
1988 Tourism and Development: Introduction. *In* Tourism and Economic Development. Western European Experiences, Allan M. Williams and Gareth Shaw, eds., pp. 1–11. London: Belhaven Press.
Williams, Anthony, and Wilbur Zelinsky
1970 On Some Patterns in International Tourist Flows. Economic Geography 46:549–67.

Wilson, John
  1980 Sociology of Leisure. Annual Review of Sociology 6:21–40.
Wood, Robert L.
  1979 Tourism and Underdevelopment in Southeast Asia. Journal of Contemporary Asia 9(3):274–87.
WTO
  1975 Tourism Compendium. Madrid: World Tourism Organization.
  1976 World Travel Statistics. Madrid: World Tourism Organization.
  1986 Economic Review of World Tourism. Madrid: World Tourism Organization.
Wu, Chung-Tong
  1982 Issues of Tourism and Socioeconomic Development. Annals of Tourism Research 9:317–30.
Zelizer, Viviana
  1990 The Social Meaning of Money: 'Special Monies.' American Journal of Sociology 95:342–77.
Zimmermann, Friedrich
  1988 Austria: Contrasting Tourist Seasons and Contrasting Regions. *In* Tourism and Economic Development: Western European Experiences, Alllen M. Williams and Gareth Shaw, eds., pp. 145–61. London: Belhaven Press.
Zolberg, Aristide
  1989 The Next Waves: Migration Theory for a Changing World. International Migration Review, Silver Issue 87:403–31.
Zolberg, Aristide, Astri Suhrke, and Sergío Aguayo
  1986 International Factors in the Formation of Refugee Movements. International Migration Review 20(2):151–69.

Author Index

Subject Index

corporate state 18
Council for Mutual Economic
  Assistance (CMEA) 90, 94, 97,
  111–12, 130, 136–150, 160–73,
  176, 182–5
currency
  soft 90, 97–98, 111, 134–51, 172,
    182–5
  hard 96, 97–98, 111, 134–51,
    161–72, 182–5, 193
  mixed, regime 133, 139–51, 153,
    188
customs 20, 33, 138, 143, 182

debt
  role of Austrian banks in
    Hungarian 97
  state 97–8
demonstration effect 140, 184, 193
dependency 196
  dual 94–9
  dimensional chains of 15
destination 30, 51, 62, 74
development
  economic 17, 59–60, 108–9,
    112–13, 127, –31, 183
  national 14–17
  uneven 2, 5, 18–21, 24, 27–32, 41,
    45–51, 61, 65, 83, 101–7,
    109–13, 130, 187, 189
  policies for tourism, in Austria 150,
    154
  policies with emphasis on heavy
    industry in Hungary 155

economy
  first 96–9
  informal 162–3, 168, 183, 192
  second 96–9, 158, 160–1, 172–3,
    184–5, 189
embeddedness
  social, of tourism 27, 190
environment 11, 13, 15
environmental bubble 51, 194–5
European Free Trade Association
  (EFTA) 93–4
European Economic Community
  (EEC) 93–4

European Reconstruction Project
  (ERP, Marshall Plan) 91,
  154
exchange
  decisional 135–9, 149
excursion 176–81, 183
exports
  invisible 13

familiarity 10
Frankfurt School 10
Fremdenverkehr 40

gender 16–17, 135
"gravity"-model of tourist flows 107,
  125, 130
Great Depression, effects on
  tourist flows 66–7, 69, 71, 73,
  80
guidebook 23–82
Guides Joanne, Les 33

historical sociology 2, 8
host 7–8, 11, 29–30, 50–1, 143–51,
  189, 193, 195
hotel 12, 145–51, 153–8, 163–6,
  183
Hungary
  Kingdom of 54, 57, 59, 72, 77
  proper 55, 80
Hungarian
  Forint 140–1, 144, 159–60, 162–4,
    166, 168, 182–3
  Question 87

idegenforgalom 41
identity 9
images 11, 48, 51, 147, 194
Imperial and Royal Danubian
  Steam Shipping Company
  (DDSG) 64
imports
  invisible 9
industrial revolution
  industrialization 27–8, 94, 108,
    139, 155, 187
informal sector 157, 192
  transactions 139, 159–60, 162–3